Healthy
Home-Style
Cooking

Meredith® Consumer Marketing
Des Moines, Iowa

Family Circle® Healthy Home-Style Cooking

Meredith® Corporation Consumer Marketing
Vice President, Consumer Marketing: David Ball
Consumer Product Marketing Director: Steve Swanson
Consumer Marketing Product Manager: Wendy Merical
Business Director: Ron Clingman
Associate Director, Production: Al Rodruck

Waterbury Publications, Inc.
Editorial Director: Lisa Kingsley
Associate Editor: Tricia Laning
Creative Director: Ken Carlson
Associate Design Director: Doug Samuelson
Production Assistant: Mindy Samuelson
Contributing Copy Editors: Terri Fredrickson, Gretchen Kauffman, Peg Smith
Contributing Indexer: Elizabeth T. Parson

Family Circle® **Magazine**
Editor in Chief: Linda Fears
Creative Director: Karmen Lizzul
Food Director: Regina Ragone, M.S., R.D.
Senior Food Editor: Julie Miltenberger
Associate Food Editor: Michael Tyrrell

Meredith Publishing Group
President: Tom Harty
Executive Vice President: Andy Sareyan
Vice President, Manufacturing: Bruce Heston

Meredith Corporation
President and Chief Executive Officer: Stephen M. Lacy

In Memoriam: E.T. Meredith III (1933–2003)

Pictured on the front cover:
Turkey and Spinach Manicotti
(recipe page 101)
Photography by Jason Donnelly

Do you crave the kind of homey cooking that soothes the soul but isn't so good for the body?

Like a bubbling casserole of macaroni and cheese? Or a juicy steak smothered in creamy mushroom sauce? Or rich and indulgent rice pudding topped with whipped cream? We all do. It's the kind of hearty, satisfying, universally loved fare that Mom or Grandma makes—the kind that just tastes like home. It's good-mood food.

Home-style cooking is synonymous with comfort and happiness, but not necessarily with healthfulness. Traditional recipes are made with ingredients that pack in unwanted calories and fat grams. But they don't have to be made that way.

Healthy Home-Style Cooking serves up more than 300 recipes for favorite family classics revamped for the way you want to eat now—lower in calories and fat, but still packed with flavor.

Although these recipes are updated for today, they're made the old-fashioned way. They start with fresh foods that naturally abound with good-for-you-ingredients but simply call for less fat than the traditional version—or they substitute a more healthful fat. They also take advantage of cooking methods and techniques that don't require large amounts of unhealthy fats and sugar.

Whether you're looking for a 30-minute weeknight dinner or want to spend a leisurely Saturday cooking or baking with friends, *Healthy Home-Style Cooking* offers a buffet of choices.

As an added help, suggested menus are scattered throughout the book to make meal planning easier and more fun. You can enjoy your favorite foods and your good health too.

Because meal planning for a busy family can be challenging, look for these helpful icons throughout the book:

 30 minutes or less: Any recipe that can be made from start to finish in 30 minutes or less.

 Kid-friendly: This symbol denotes recipes approved by kids.

contents

Mango-Strawberry Smoothies, page 28

Smart Snacks & Starters

Mediterranean Pizzettas

MAKES 24 servings **PREP** 25 minutes **BAKE** 20 minutes
OVEN 425°F

- 1 6- or 6.5-ounce package pizza crust mix
- 1 14.5-ounce can no-salt-added diced tomatoes, drained
- 3 tablespoons no-salt-added tomato paste
- 1 teaspoon dried Italian seasoning, crushed
- 2 cloves garlic, minced
- 2 cups sliced or chopped cooked chicken or turkey
- ½ cup pitted green olives and/or pitted kalamata olives, coarsely chopped
- ¼ cup sliced green onions or chopped onion
- 2 tablespoons sliced almonds and/or pine nuts
- ½ cup shredded part-skim mozzarella cheese (2 ounces)
- 1 tablespoon snipped fresh parsley

① Preheat oven to 425°F. Prepare pizza crust according to package directions. Pat dough into a greased 15 x 10 x 1-inch baking pan (crust will be thin). Bake for 5 minutes.

② In a small bowl combine tomatoes, tomato paste, Italian seasoning, and garlic; spread evenly over crust. Top with chicken, olives, onions, and almonds. Sprinkle with cheese.

③ Bake for 15 minutes or until edges of crust are golden brown. Remove from oven; sprinkle with parsley. Cut into 12 squares; cut each piece in half diagonally.

PER SERVING 71 calories; 3 g total fat (1 g sat. fat); 12 mg cholesterol; 155 mg sodium; 7 g carbohydrate; 0 g fiber; 5 g protein

Polynesian Glazed Chicken Wings

MAKES 30 appetizers **PREP** 10 minutes **BAKE** 1 hour
OVEN 400°F

- 3 pounds frozen plain chicken wing drummettes (about 30)
- ½ cup packed brown sugar
- 1 tablespoon cornstarch
- 2 teaspoons grated fresh ginger
- ¼ to ½ teaspoon crushed red pepper
- ½ cup unsweetened pineapple juice
- ½ cup reduced-sodium chicken broth or water
- ¼ cup finely chopped sweet green pepper
- 2 tablespoons reduced-sodium soy sauce
  Thinly sliced green onions (optional)

① Preheat oven to 400°F. Place frozen drummettes in a 15 x 10 x 1-inch baking pan. Bake for 50 to 60 minutes or until skins are crispy.

② Meanwhile, for glaze, in a small saucepan combine brown sugar, cornstarch, ginger, and crushed red pepper. Stir in pineapple juice, broth, sweet pepper, and soy sauce. Cook and stir on medium heat until thickened and bubbly. Cook and stir for 2 minutes more. Set aside.

③ Carefully drain off any cooking juices from baking pan. Brush drummettes with some of the glaze mixture. Bake for 10 minutes; brush with more of the glaze mixture.

④ To serve, place on a serving plate. If desired, sprinkle with green onions. Pass remaining glaze mixture.

PER APPETIZER 79 calories; 5 g total fat (1 g sat. fat); 29 mg cholesterol; 74 mg sodium; 5 g carbohydrate; 0 g fiber; 5 g protein

With a few simple tweaks, pizza and hot wings can be part of a healthy diet.

**Prosciutto-Wrapped Scallops
with Roasted Red Pepper Aïoli**

Prosciutto-Wrapped Scallops with Roasted Red Pepper Aïoli

MAKES 20 servings **PREP** 35 minutes **BROIL** 4 minutes per batch

- 10 fresh or frozen sea scallops
- 10 very thin slices prosciutto (6 to 7 ounces), halved lengthwise
- 20 medium fresh basil leaves
     Freshly ground black pepper
     Roasted Red Pepper Aïoli
     Small fresh basil leaves (optional)

① Thaw scallops, if frozen. Soak twenty 6-inch wooden skewers in enough water to cover for at least 30 minutes; drain before using.

② Meanwhile, preheat broiler. Rinse scallops; pat dry with paper towels. Cut scallops in half.

③ Lay prosciutto strips on a large cutting board. Top each prosciutto strip with a medium basil leaf; add a scallop half. Starting from a short end, roll up each prosciutto strip around scallop. Thread each appetizer onto a skewer. Sprinkle with pepper.

④ Place half of the skewers on the lightly greased unheated rack of a broiler pan. Broil 4 to 5 inches from the heat for 4 to 6 minutes or until scallops are opaque, turning once halfway through broiling. Repeat with the remaining skewers.

⑤ Serve skewers with Roasted Red Pepper Aïoli for dipping. If desired, garnish aïoli with small basil leaves.

Roasted Red Pepper Aïoli: In a blender or food processor combine ½ cup roasted sweet red peppers, drained, and 2 cloves garlic, cut up. Cover and blend or process until nearly smooth. Add ⅓ cup mayonnaise, ⅛ teaspoon salt, and dash freshly ground black pepper. Cover and blend or process until smooth. With the blender or processor running, gradually add 2 tablespoons olive oil through the opening in lid or the feed tube, blending or processing until smooth. Transfer aïoli to a small bowl. Cover and chill in the refrigerator until ready to serve.

PER SERVING 79 calories; 6 g total fat (1 g sat. fat); 6 mg cholesterol; 208 mg sodium; 1 g carbohydrate; 0 g fiber; 5 g protein

Walnut and Olive Quesadillas

MAKES 12 appetizers **PREP** 30 minutes **BAKE** 10 minutes **OVEN** 350°F

- 6 6-inch white or yellow corn tortillas
- 4 ounces part-skim mozzarella cheese, shredded (1 cup)
- 2 ounces provolone cheese, shredded (½ cup)
- ¼ cup chopped pitted ripe olives
- 3 tablespoons chopped walnuts or pine nuts, toasted
- 2 teaspoons snipped fresh oregano or ½ teaspoon dried oregano, crushed
- 1 tablespoon olive oil
- ½ cup salsa
- 1 teaspoon snipped fresh oregano or ¼ teaspoon dried oregano, crushed
     Fresh oregano sprigs (optional)

① Preheat oven to 350°F. Stack tortillas and wrap in foil. Bake about 10 minutes or until softened.

② Meanwhile, in a medium bowl combine mozzarella cheese, provolone cheese, olives, nuts, and the 2 teaspoons snipped oregano. Spread cheese mixture onto half of each tortilla. Fold tortillas in half; secure with wooden toothpicks. Brush 1 side of each quesadilla with some of the oil.

③ In an extra-large nonstick skillet or on a griddle place quesadillas, 2 or 3 at a time, oiled sides down; cook on medium heat about 4 minutes or until heated through, brushing with remaining oil and turning once. Cut each quesadilla in half.

④ Meanwhile, in a small saucepan heat salsa just until hot; stir in the 1 teaspoon snipped oregano. Transfer to a serving bowl. If desired, garnish with oregano sprigs. Serve salsa with warm quesadillas.

PER APPETIZER 98 calories; 6 g total fat (2 g sat. fat); 9 mg cholesterol; 217 mg sodium; 8 g carbohydrate; 1 g fiber; 5 g protein

{
menu

Polynesian Glazed
Chicken Wings

Lemon Avocado Dip

Spicy Tofu
Lettuce Wraps
[below]

Sweet Summertime
Tea
}

Spicy Tofu Lettuce Wraps

MAKES 8 servings **START TO FINISH** 20 minutes

- 12 ounces extra-firm tofu (fresh bean curd)
- 2 cups shredded cabbage with carrot (coleslaw mix)
- 1 8-ounce can sliced water chestnuts, drained
- ¼ cup chopped green onions (2)
- 2 tablespoons snipped fresh cilantro
- ⅓ cup Asian sweet chili sauce or stir-fry sauce
- 1 tablespoon lime juice
- 8 large leaves butterhead (Bibb or Boston) lettuce or green leaf lettuce

① Drain tofu; press out excess liquid with paper towels. In a food processor combine about half of each of the following ingredients: tofu, coleslaw mix, water chestnuts, green onions, and cilantro. Cover and process with several on/off turns until finely chopped. Transfer to a large skillet. Repeat with the remaining tofu, coleslaw mix, water chestnuts, green onions, and cilantro. Stir chili sauce and lime juice into mixture in skillet. Cook and stir over medium heat until heated through.

② If necessary, cut the center veins from lettuce leaves. Divide tofu mixture among lettuce leaves; fold or roll up. Secure with cocktail picks.

PER SERVING 88 calories; 2 g total fat (0 g sat. fat); 0 mg cholesterol; 141 mg sodium; 12 g carbohydrate; 3 g fiber; 5 g protein

Roasted Pepper Roll-Ups

MAKES 24 servings **PREP** 30 minutes **CHILL** 2 to 24 hours

- ½ of an 8-ounce package reduced-fat cream cheese (Neufchâtel), softened
- 4 ounces soft goat cheese (chèvre)
- 1 tablespoon fat-free milk
- 1 small clove garlic, minced
- ¼ teaspoon freshly ground black pepper
- ½ cup roasted sweet red peppers, drained and finely chopped
- ¼ cup snipped fresh basil
- 8 8-inch whole wheat or plain flour tortillas
- 2 cups firmly packed fresh spinach leaves

① For filling, in a medium bowl beat cream cheese with an electric mixer on medium to high for 30 seconds. Add goat cheese, milk, garlic, and black pepper; beat until smooth. Stir in red peppers and basil.

② To assemble, divide filling among tortillas, spreading evenly to within ½ inch of the edges. Arrange spinach leaves over filling to cover. Tightly roll up each tortilla into a spiral, tucking in spinach leaves as you roll. Wrap each roll in plastic wrap. Chill rolls in the refrigerator for 2 to 24 hours.

③ To serve, remove plastic wrap from rolls. Use a sharp knife to cut each rolls crosswise into 6 pieces. If desired, skewer each slice on a pick or short decorative skewer. Arrange slices on a platter.

PER SERVING (2 SLICES) 74 calories; 3 g total fat (2 g sat. fat); 6 mg cholesterol; 165 mg sodium; 9 g carbohydrate; 1 g fiber; 3 g protein

Goat cheese is a smart choice for those who are trying to eat healthfully. It's lower in both fat and calories than most cow's-milk cheeses—and because it has a distinctive flavor, just a little bit goes a long way.

Nutty Cheese-Topped Figs

Nutty Cheese-Topped Figs ③⓪

MAKES 20 bites **START TO FINISH** 15 minutes

- 10   dried Calimyrna (light) figs*
- ¼   cup light tub-style cream cheese
- 1½   teaspoons finely shredded lemon peel
- 10   Brazil nuts or toasted whole almonds, or 20 hazelnuts
- 2   teaspoons honey (optional)

① If necessary, pull on stem of each fig while holding on to the other side and gently pull to reshape. Using a sharp knife, trim off stems. Cut figs in half horizontally.

② Spoon cream cheese into a small resealable plastic bag. Snip a small hole in one corner of the bag. Pipe a small amount of cream cheese onto the center of each fig half. Sprinkle with lemon peel.

③ If using Brazil nuts or almonds, cut each nut in half crosswise. Place a nut half or whole hazelnut on top of cream cheese on each fig half. Transfer to a serving plate. If desired, drizzle with honey. Serve immediately. Or cover and chill for up to 24 hours.

*TIP: Calimyrna and Black Mission figs are the two most common varieties of dried figs you'll find at the supermarket. Calimyrna have a greenish yellow skin, a pale pink interior, and a nutty flavor. Black Mission are dark purple with a pink interior and a full, fruity flavor. If you can't find Calimyrna figs, substitute Black Mission.

PER BITE 30 calories; 2 g total fat (1 g sat. fat); 2 mg cholesterol; 15 mg sodium; 3 g carbohydrate; 1 g fiber; 1 g protein

Pepper Cheese with Apricots

MAKES 12 servings **PREP** 15 minutes **CHILL** 24 hours

- 1   16-ounce carton plain low-fat yogurt (2 hours) (without gelatin)
- ¼   cup finely snipped dried apricots
- 1   tablespoon honey
- ¼   to ½ teaspoon coarsely ground black pepper
- ½   of an 8-ounce package (½ cup) reduced-fat cream cheese (Neufchâtel), softened
- 1   tablespoon finely chopped pistachio nuts
- 48   low-fat whole grain crackers

① Line a yogurt strainer, sieve, or a small colander with three layers of 100%-cotton cheesecloth or a clean paper coffee filter. Suspend lined strainer, sieve, or colander over a bowl. In a medium bowl stir together yogurt, apricots, honey, and pepper. Spoon mixture into strainer.

② Cover with plastic wrap and chill in the refrigerator for at least 24 hours or until mixture is firm. Remove from refrigerator. Drain and discard liquid.

③ Transfer yogurt mixture to a serving bowl; stir in cream cheese. Sprinkle with nuts. Serve with crackers.

PER SERVING 123 calories; 5 g total fat (2 g sat. fat); 9 mg cholesterol; 138 mg sodium; 17 g carbohydrate; 2 g fiber; 5 g protein

For the creamiest texture and richest flavor, make the yogurt cheese with a Greek yogurt that has 2% or less fat.

Either of these fruit-centered snacks would be great as dessert at the end of a meal.

Feta-Stuffed Mini Peppers

MAKES 14 servings **PREP** 30 minutes **BAKE** 18 minutes
OVEN 375°F

- 4 ounces fresh spinach (about 3½ cups)
- 8 ounces crumbled reduced-fat feta cheese
- 28 whole miniature sweet peppers

① Preheat oven to 375°F. Thoroughly wash spinach and remove stems. Cut spinach into thin strips by gathering several spinach leaves of a similar size into a ball. Use a sharp knife to cut into shreds.

② In a large bowl combine the spinach and feta cheese. Cut a thin slice from the top or side of each of the sweet peppers. Use the handle of a spoon to scoop seeds from sweet peppers; discard.

③ Stuff sweet peppers with the feta mixture, mounding feta mixture slightly. Place stuffed sweet peppers in a 3-quart rectangular baking dish, stuffed sides up.

④ Bake for 18 to 20 minutes or until sweet peppers are slightly soft. Serve warm.

PER SERVING (2 MINI PEPPERS) 48 calories; 3 g total fat (2 g sat. fat); 14 mg cholesterol; 186 mg sodium; 2 g carbohydrate; 1 g fiber; 3 g protein

Inside-Out Tuna Salad Snack ⭐ ㉚

MAKES 4 servings **START TO FINISH** 15 minutes

- 1 3- to 3.25-ounce can chunk white tuna (water pack), drained and broken into chunks
- ½ cup seedless red grapes, halved
- ¼ cup finely chopped red onion
- 2 tablespoons light mayonnaise or salad dressing
- 2 cloves garlic, minced
- ¼ teaspoon black pepper
- ⅛ teaspoon salt
- 3 large celery stalks, ends trimmed

① In a medium bowl combine tuna, grapes, red onion, mayonnaise, garlic, pepper, and salt.

② To serve, cut each celery stalk crosswise into 4 pieces. Serve tuna mixture with celery pieces.

PER SERVING 76 calories; 3 g total fat (1 g sat. fat); 12 mg cholesterol; 237 mg sodium; 6 g carbohydrate; 1 g fiber; 6 g protein

Avocado-Pesto Stuffed Tomatoes

MAKES 30 appetizers **STAND** 30 minutes **PREP** 40 minutes

- 30 cherry tomatoes (about 1¼ pints)
- ½ of a medium avocado, seeded if necessary, peeled, and cut up
- 2 ounces cream cheese, softened
- 2 tablespoons purchased basil pesto
- 1 teaspoon lemon juice
  Snipped fresh basil (optional)

① Line a large baking sheet with paper towels; set aside. Cut a thin slice from the bottom of each tomato so it stands upright. Cut a thin slice from the top of each tomato. Carefully hollow out the cherry tomatoes with a small measuring spoon or small melon baller. Invert tomatoes onto prepared baking sheet. Let stand for 30 minutes.

② In a food processor combine avocado, cream cheese, pesto, and lemon juice. Cover and process until mixture is smooth. Spoon into a pastry bag fitted with a large plain round or open star tip.

③ Place tomatoes, open sides up, onto a serving platter. Pipe avocado mixture into the tomato shells. Serve immediately or cover loosely and chill up to 4 hours. Sprinkle with basil before serving, if desired.

PER APPETIZER 18 calories; 1 g total fat (1 g sat. fat); 2 mg cholesterol; 16 mg sodium; 1 g carbohydrate; 0 g fiber; 0 g protein

Inside-Out Tuna Salad Snack

Antipasto Kabobs

menu

Roasted Pepper
Roll-Ups

Pepper Cheese
with Apricots

Antipasto Kabobs
[below]

Nutty Cheese-
Topped Figs

Antipasto Kabobs

MAKES 6 servings **PREP** 30 minutes **MARINATE** 1 to 24 hours

1½	to 2 cups assorted fresh vegetables (such as packaged peeled fresh baby carrots, halved radishes, sweet pepper squares, whole miniature sweet peppers, or halved pattypan squash)
2	ounces part-skim mozzarella cheese, provolone cheese, or smoked Gouda cheese, cut into ½-inch pieces
2	ounces cooked smoked turkey sausage, cut into bite-size pieces
2	tablespoons basil pesto
1	tablespoon white wine vinegar
12	whole fresh basil leaves

① Place vegetables, cheese, and sausage in a resealable plastic bag set in a deep bowl. For marinade, in a small bowl combine pesto and vinegar. Pour marinade over vegetable mixture. Seal bag; turn to coat vegetable mixture. Marinate in the refrigerator for 1 to 24 hours, turning bag occasionally to coat. Drain vegetable mixture, discarding marinade.

② On twelve 4-inch-long wooden skewers alternately thread vegetables, cheese, sausage, and basil leaves.

PER SERVING (2 kabobs) 84 calories; 6 g total fat (2 g sat. fat); 13 mg cholesterol; 188 mg sodium; 3 g carbohydrate; 1 g fiber; 5 g protein

Crispy Parmesan Chips ✪ 🔟

MAKES 15 servings **PREP** 15 minutes **BAKE** 8 minutes per batch **OVEN** 350°F

30	wonton wrappers
	Nonstick cooking spray
2	tablespoons olive oil
1	clove garlic, minced
½	teaspoon dried basil, crushed
¼	cup grated Parmesan or Romano cheese

① Preheat oven to 350°F. Using a sharp knife, cut wonton wrappers diagonally in half to form 60 triangles. Coat a baking sheet with cooking spray. Arrange 20 of the triangles in a single layer on prepared baking sheet.

② In a small bowl stir together oil, garlic, and basil. Lightly brush the wonton triangles on baking sheet with some of the oil mixture; sprinkle with some of the cheese.

③ Bake about 8 minutes or until golden brown. Cool on a wire rack. Repeat with the remaining wonton triangles, oil mixture, and cheese.

PER SERVING (4 CHIPS) 69 calories; 2 g total fat (1 g sat. fat); 2 mg cholesterol; 116 mg sodium; 9 g carbohydrate; 0 g fiber; 2 g protein

Crispy Parmesan Chips

Peanut-Apple-Crunch Balls ✪

MAKES 18 balls **PREP** 20 minutes **STAND** 30 minutes

- ⅓ cup chunky peanut butter
- ¼ cup 68% vegetable oil spread
- 2 tablespoons honey
- 1 cup rice and wheat cereal flakes, crushed slightly
- 1 cup bran flakes, crushed slightly
- ⅓ cup finely snipped dried apples
- 2 tablespoons finely chopped peanuts
- ⅛ teaspoon apple pie spice
- 2 ounces white baking chocolate (with cocoa butter), chopped
- ¼ teaspoon shortening

① In a medium saucepan combine peanut butter, vegetable oil spread, and honey. Cook and stir on low heat just until melted and nearly smooth. Stir in cereals, apples, peanuts, and apple pie spice until well mixed. Remove from heat.

② Divide mixture into 18 portions. Using slightly wet hands, shape mixture into balls. Let stand on a waxed paper-lined baking sheet about 15 minutes or until firm.

③ In a small saucepan combine white chocolate and shortening; stir over low heat until melted. Drizzle balls with melted white chocolate. Let stand about 15 minutes or until white chocolate is set (if necessary, chill balls until white chocolate is firm).

PER BALL 94 calories; 6 g total fat (2 g sat. fat); 1 mg cholesterol; 76 mg sodium; 9 g carbohydrate; 1 g fiber; 2 g protein

Peanut-Apple-Crunch Balls

Mexican Spiced Popcorn ✪ ③⓪

MAKES 6 cups **START TO FINISH** 8 minutes

- ¼ teaspoon ground cumin
- ¼ teaspoon chili powder
- ⅛ to ¼ teaspoon salt
  Dash cayenne pepper
  Dash ground cinnamon
- 6 cups air-popped popcorn
- 1 to 2 tablespoons butter, melted, or nonstick cooking spray

① In a small bowl stir together cumin, chili powder, salt, cayenne pepper, and cinnamon.

② Remove uncooked kernels from popped corn. Place popped corn in a large bowl or in a large shallow baking pan. Drizzle with melted butter or lightly coat with cooking spray; toss lightly to coat. Sprinkle popcorn with seasoning mixture; stir lightly to coat.

PER CUP 31 calories; 0 g total fat; 0 mg cholesterol; 50 mg sodium; 6 g carbohydrate; 1 g fiber; 1 g protein

Bowl Game Snack Mix ③⓪

MAKES 16 servings **START TO FINISH** 15 minutes

- 10 cups air-popped popcorn
  Nonstick cooking spray
- 1 tablespoon taco seasoning mix
- 1 cup dry-roasted peanuts
- 1 cup golden raisins
- ½ cup toasted pumpkin seeds (pepitas)

① Remove uncooked kernels from popped corn. Place popped corn in a very large bowl. Lightly coat popcorn with cooking spray.

② Sprinkle popcorn with taco seasoning mix; stir lightly to coat. Stir in peanuts, raisins, and pumpkin seeds. Stir again just before serving.

PER SERVING 128 calories; 7 g total fat (1 g sat. fat); 0 mg cholesterol; 93 mg sodium; 15 g carbohydrate; 2 g fiber; 4 g protein

Black Bean Salsa

Black Bean Salsa

MAKES about 3½ cups salsa (14 servings) **PREP** 25 minutes
CHILL 4 to 24 hours

- 1 15-ounce can black beans, rinsed and drained
- 1 medium cucumber, peeled, seeded, and chopped
- 1 medium tomato, seeded and chopped
- ½ cup sliced green onions (4)
- ¼ cup lime juice
- 1 tablespoon snipped fresh cilantro
- 1 tablespoon olive oil
- ½ teaspoon ground cumin
- ⅛ teaspoon salt
- ⅛ teaspoon cayenne pepper

① In a medium bowl combine black beans, cucumber, tomato, green onions, lime juice, cilantro, oil, cumin, salt, and cayenne pepper. Cover and chill in the refrigerator for 4 to 24 hours.

PER ¼ CUP 35 calories; 1 g total fat (0 g sat. fat); 0 mg cholesterol; 98 mg sodium; 6 g carbohydrate; 2 g fiber; 2 g protein

Lemon Avocado Dip ③⓪

MAKES 8 servings **START TO FINISH** 15 minutes

- 1 ripe avocado, halved, seeded, and peeled
- 1 tablespoon lemon juice or lime juice
- ½ cup light sour cream
- 1 clove garlic, minced
- ⅛ teaspoon salt
  Lemon wedge (optional)
- 4 medium sweet red, yellow, and/or green peppers, seeded and cut into strips

① In a medium bowl use a fork to coarsely mash avocado with lemon juice. Stir in sour cream, garlic, and salt. If desired, garnish with a lemon wedge. Serve with pepper strips.

PER SERVING 72 calories; 5 g total fat (1 g sat. fat); 5 mg cholesterol; 49 mg sodium; 7 g carbohydrate; 3 g fiber; 2 g protein

Mediterranean Veggie Dip

MAKES 12 servings **PREP** 15 minutes + making yogurt cheese
CHILL up to 24 hours

  Yogurt Cheese
- ¼ cup chopped roasted sweet red pepper
- ¼ cup crumbled reduced-fat feta cheese
- 2 tablespoons thinly sliced green onion
- 2 tablespoons chopped pitted kalamata or black olives
- 2 tablespoons snipped fresh parsley
- 2 teaspoons snipped fresh oregano or ½ teaspoon dried oregano, crushed
  Assorted vegetables (such as carrot sticks, broccoli florets, cucumber spears, and/or sweet pepper strips) and/or whole grain crackers

① In a small bowl combine Yogurt Cheese, sweet pepper, feta cheese, green onion, olives, parsley, and oregano. Cover and chill up to 24 hours. Stir before serving. Serve with assorted vegetables and/or crackers.

Yogurt Cheese: Line a yogurt strainer, sieve, or a small colander with three layers of 100%-cotton cheesecloth or a clean paper coffee filter. Suspend lined strainer, sieve, or colander over a bowl. Spoon in one 16-ounce carton plain yogurt (2 cups).* Cover with plastic wrap and chill in the refrigerator for at least 24 hours. Remove from refrigerator. Drain and discard liquid. Store, covered, in refrigerator for up to 1 week.

***Tip:** Use a brand of yogurt that contains no gums, gelatin, or fillers. These ingredients may prevent the whey from separating from the curd to make cheese.

PER 2 TABLESPOONS DIP 33 calories; 1 g total fat (1 g sat. fat); 3 mg cholesterol; 82 mg sodium; 3 g carbohydrate; 0 g fiber; 3 g protein

Look for avocados that are not bruised or overly soft and that have no gouges or broken skin. Firm, ripe avocados that are ready to eat and good for slicing yield to gentle pressure when cradled in your hands. A very ripe avocado—the kind you need for mashing in Lemon Avocado Dip— feels soft (but not too soft).

Tomato-Ranch Bean Dip ③⓪

MAKES 10 servings **PREP** 15 minutes **STAND** 5 minutes

- ¼ cup dried tomatoes (not oil pack)
- 1 15-ounce can cannellini beans (white kidney beans), rinsed and drained
- ½ cup bottled reduced-calorie ranch salad dressing
- 2 cloves garlic, minced
- ½ teaspoon finely chopped canned chipotle chile pepper in adobo sauce* (optional)

  Fat-free milk (optional)
- ¼ cup snipped fresh parsley
- 5 cups assorted vegetable dippers (such as radishes, snow pea pods, celery, sweet yellow peppers, packaged peeled fresh baby carrots, and/or sliced zucchini)

① Place tomatoes in a small bowl. Add enough boiling water to cover. Let stand for 5 minutes. Drain and finely chop the tomatoes; set aside.

② In a food processor combine beans, salad dressing, garlic, and chipotle pepper (if using). Cover and process until smooth. Add milk, if needed, to thin to desired consistency. Set aside 1 teaspoon of the tomatoes and 1 teaspoon of the parsley. Stir the remaining tomatoes and the remaining parsley into bean mixture.

③ Transfer dip to a serving bowl. Top with the reserved tomatoes and parsley. Serve with vegetable dippers.

*Note: Because hot chile peppers contain volatile oils that can burn your skin and eyes, avoid direct contact with chiles as much as possible. When working with chile peppers, wear plastic or rubber gloves. If your bare hands do touch the chile peppers, wash your hands and fingernails well with soap and water when you are done.

PER SERVING 81 calories; 3 g total fat (0 g sat. fat); 3 mg cholesterol; 242 mg sodium; 12 g carbohydrate; 4 g fiber; 3 g protein

Kickoff Pepper Dip

MAKES about 2½ cups **PREP** 30 minutes **CHILL** 4 to 12 hours

- 4 large sweet red, green, yellow, or orange peppers, seeded and cut up
- 1 small onion, cut up
- ¼ cup water
- 1 8-ounce package reduced-fat cream cheese (Neufchâtel), softened
- ¼ cup low-fat mayonnaise or light salad dressing
- 2 tablespoons lemon juice
- 2 teaspoons olive oil or vegetable oil
- 1 teaspoon prepared horseradish
- ¼ teaspoon salt

  Few dashes bottled hot pepper sauce
- 3 small sweet red, yellow, orange, and/or green peppers, tops and seeds removed (optional)

  Assorted vegetable dippers (such as radishes, snow pea pods, celery, sweet yellow peppers, packaged peeled fresh baby carrots, and/or sliced zucchini) and/or breadsticks

① In a blender or large food processor combine 2 of the cut-up sweet peppers, the onion, and the water. Cover and blend or process until smooth. Add the remaining cut-up peppers; cover and blend until smooth.

② Place pureed vegetable mixture in a fine sieve; press mixture gently with the back of a wooden spoon to drain off excess liquid. Set aside.

③ In a medium bowl combine cream cheese, mayonnaise, lemon juice, oil, horseradish, salt, and hot pepper sauce. Beat with an electric mixer on medium. Beat in pureed vegetable mixture. Cover and chill in the refrigerator for 4 to 12 hours.

④ If desired, spoon dip into the 3 sweet pepper shells. Serve with assorted vegetable dippers and/or breadsticks.

PER 2 TABLESPOONS DIP 46 calories; 3 g total fat (2 g sat. fat); 9 mg cholesterol; 104 mg sodium; 3 g carbohydrate; 1 g fiber; 1 g protein

Creamy Fruit Dip

menu

Avocado-Pesto
Stuffed Tomatoes

Bowl Game Snack Mix

Rosemary
White Bean Dip
[below]

Cut-up fresh fruit

Iced tea with mint

Rosemary White Bean Dip 🔵

MAKES 1⅓ cups **START TO FINISH** 15 minutes

1	15-ounce can no-salt-added cannellini beans (white kidney beans), rinsed and drained
2	tablespoons lemon juice
2	tablespoons olive oil
1	tablespoon snipped fresh parsley
1	teaspoon snipped fresh rosemary
2	cloves garlic
⅛	teaspoon black pepper
⅓	cup chopped pitted ripe olives
	Fresh parsley sprigs (optional)
	Pita chips and/or assorted vegetable dippers

① In a food processor combine beans, lemon juice, olive oil, snipped parsley, rosemary, garlic, and pepper. Cover and process just until smooth. Stir in olives.

② To serve, transfer dip to a serving bowl. If desired, garnish with parsley sprigs. Serve with pita chips and/or vegetable dippers.

PER 2 TABLESPOONS 58 calories; 3 g total fat (0 g sat. fat); 0 mg cholesterol; 48 mg sodium; 6 g carbohydrate; 2 g fiber; 2 g protein

Creamy Fruit Dip ✪ 🔵

MAKES about 2⅓ cups **START TO FINISH** 15 minutes

1	cup sliced and peeled peaches, strawberries, mandarin oranges, and/or fresh pineapple chunks
1	8-ounce carton light sour cream
1	8-ounce package reduced-fat cream cheese (Neufchâtel)
½	teaspoon finely shredded orange peel
1	teaspoon vanilla
	Assorted fruits (such as strawberries, sliced peaches, sliced apples, and/or pineapple chunks)

① Place fruit in a blender or food processor. Cover and blend or process until almost smooth. Add sour cream, cream cheese, orange peel, and vanilla. Cover and blend or process until smooth.

② Serve dip immediately with fresh fruit. (Or cover and chill for up to 24 hours. If dip is too thick after chilling, stir in fat-free milk, 1 tablespoon at a time, to reach desired consistency.)

PER 1 TABLESPOON DIP 26 calories; 2 g total fat (1 g sat. fat); 7 mg cholesterol; 28 mg sodium; 1 g carbohydrate; 0 g fiber; 1 g protein

Apple-Cinnamon Dip: Prepare as above, except omit the 1 cup fruit and the orange peel. Add ½ cup unsweetened applesauce and ¼ to ½ teaspoon apple pie spice or ground cinnamon with the vanilla. Makes about 2 cups.

PER 1 TABLESPOON DIP 29 calories; 2 g total fat (1 g sat. fat); 8 mg cholesterol; 33 g sodium; 1 g carbohydrate; 0 g fiber; 1 g protein.

Peanut Butter Dip: Prepare as above, except omit the 1 cup fruit and the orange peel. Add ½ cup creamy peanut butter with the sour cream and 2 to 4 tablespoons of milk to reach desired consistency. Makes about 2½ cups.

PER 1 TABLESPOON DIP 42 calories; 3 g total fat (1 g sat. fat); 6 mg cholesterol; 42 g sodium; 1 g carbohydrate; 0 g fiber; 2 g protein.

Any version of this dip—the original, Apple-Cinnamon, or Peanut Butter—is great to have mixed and in the refrigerator to serve with fruit as a healthful after-school snack.

Mango-Strawberry Smoothies ✪ ⑩

MAKES 3 (8-ounce) servings **START TO FINISH** 10 minutes

- 1½ cups orange juice, chilled
- ½ of a 12.3-ounce package light silken-style tofu, chilled and drained
- 1 medium mango, pitted, peeled, and cut up (about 1 cup)
- ½ cup frozen unsweetened whole strawberries

  Fresh mango chunks, whole strawberries, and orange sections (optional)

① In a blender combine orange juice, tofu, the cut-up mango, and the ½ cup strawberries. Cover and blend until smooth. Pour into 3 glasses.

② If desired, for garnish, thread additional mango chunks, strawberries, and orange sections on 3 small skewers. Add a skewer to each serving. Serve immediately.

PER SERVING 142 calories; 1 g total fat (0 g sat. fat); 0 mg cholesterol; 52 mg sodium; 30 g carbohydrate; 2 g fiber; 5 g protein

Mango-Strawberry Smoothies

Hot Pomegranate Grog ㉚

MAKES 6 (8-ounce) servings **PREP** 15 minutes
COOK 5 minutes **COOL** 5 minutes

- 4 cups pomegranate juice
- 1 cup water
- ¾ cup orange juice
- ½ cup lemon juice
- ½ cup sugar
- 3 tablespoons rum

  Orange peel curls

① In a large saucepan combine pomegranate juice, the water, orange juice, lemon juice, and sugar. Bring mixture just to boiling. Remove from heat. Let stand for 5 minutes. Stir in rum. Serve grog in mugs. Garnish with orange peel curls.

PER SERVING 213 calories; 0 g total fat; 0 mg cholesterol; 9 mg sodium; 50 g carbohydrate; 0 g fiber; 0 g protein

Sweet Summertime Tea

MAKES 8 (8-ounce) servings **STAND** 5 minutes
PREP 15 minutes **STAND** 5 minutes **CHILL** 4 hours

- 3 cups water
- 6 black tea bags
- 4 raspberry herb tea bags or black cherry berry tea bags
- ½ cup sugar
- 5 cups cold water
- 1 cup cranberry juice

  Ice cubes

  Skewered fresh raspberries (optional)

① In a large saucepan bring the 3 cups water to boiling. Remove from heat. Add tea bags; cover and let stand for 5 minutes. Remove and discard tea bags. Stir in sugar until dissolved. Stir in cold water and cranberry juice. Transfer to a large pitcher or container. Cover and chill in the refrigerator for 4 hours or until completely chilled.

② Serve tea in glasses over ice. If desired, garnish with skewered raspberries.

PER SERVING 69 calories; 0 g total fat; 0 mg cholesterol; 8 mg sodium; 17 g carbohydrate; 0 g fiber; 0 g protein

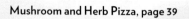
Mushroom and Herb Pizza, page 39

Better Breakfasts & Brunches

Broccoli-Soy Strata

MAKES 6 servings **PREP** 20 minutes
CHILL 8 to 24 hours **BAKE** 50 minutes
STAND 10 minutes **OVEN** 325°F

2	cups cut-up fresh broccoli or 2 cups frozen broccoli cuts, thawed
4	cups country or crusty Italian bread cut into 1-inch cubes
4	ounces process Gruyère cheese, cut up
1½	cups refrigerated or frozen egg product, thawed, or 6 eggs, lightly beaten
1½	cups light plain soymilk or fat-free milk
1	tablespoon honey mustard
½	teaspoon salt
¼	teaspoon black pepper
¼	teaspoon ground nutmeg
½	cup thinly sliced green onions (4)

① In a medium saucepan cook broccoli, covered, in a small amount of boiling salted water for 3 minutes; drain. Rinse with cold running water until cool; drain again.

② In a greased 2-quart square baking dish spread 2 cups of the bread cubes. Top with broccoli and cheese. Add the remaining 2 cups bread cubes.

③ In a medium bowl combine eggs, soymilk, mustard, salt, pepper, and nutmeg. Pour egg mixture over mixture in baking dish. Sprinkle with green onions. Cover and chill in the refrigerator for at least 8 hours or up to 24 hours.

④ Preheat oven to 325°F. Bake, uncovered, for 50 to 55 minutes or until an instant-read thermometer inserted in center registers 170°F. Let stand for 10 minutes before serving.

PER SERVING 210 calories; 7 g total fat (4 g sat. fat); 17 mg cholesterol; 581 mg sodium; 21 g carbohydrate; 2 g fiber; 15 g protein

Lox-Style Strata

MAKES 12 servings **PREP** 30 minutes
CHILL 4 to 24 hours **BAKE** 45 minutes
STAND 10 minutes **OVEN** 350°F

4	to 6 plain bagels, cut into bite-size pieces (8 cups)
1	3-ounce package thinly sliced smoked salmon (lox-style), cut into small pieces
6	ounces reduced-fat cream cheese (Neufchâtel), cut into ½-inch pieces
¼	cup finely chopped red onion
4	teaspoons dried chives, crushed
8	eggs, beaten
2	cups fat-free milk
1	cup low-fat cottage cheese
½	teaspoon dried dillweed, crushed
¼	teaspoon black pepper

① In a lightly greased 3-quart rectangular baking dish spread half of the bagel pieces. Top with salmon, cream cheese, onion, and chives. Spread remaining bagel pieces over salmon mixture.

② In a large bowl whisk together eggs, milk, cottage cheese, dillweed, and pepper. Pour evenly over layers in dish. Lightly press down layers with the back of a spoon. Cover with plastic wrap and chill for at least 4 hours or up to 24 hours.

③ Preheat oven to 350°F. Remove plastic wrap. Bake, uncovered, for 45 to 50 minutes or until set and edges are puffed and golden. Let stand for 10 minutes before serving.

PER SERVING 181 calories; 7 g total fat (3 g sat. fat); 155 mg cholesterol; 436 mg sodium; 16 g carbohydrate; 1 g fiber; 13 g protein

Stratas are the ultimate convenience food—made with fresh, natural ingredients.

Cheesy Mushroom Casserole

Tomato, Spinach, and Feta Strata

MAKES 6 servings PREP 30 minutes CHILL 4 hours
BAKE 70 minutes STAND 10 minutes OVEN 325°F

	Nonstick cooking spray
4	cups cubed whole grain bread
1	pound fresh asparagus, trimmed and cut into 1-inch pieces
1	cup chopped onion
2	cups fresh baby spinach
6	eggs
1	cup fat-free milk
⅛	teaspoon sea salt or kosher salt
⅛	teaspoon freshly ground black pepper
2	plum tomatoes, thinly sliced
½	cup reduced-fat feta cheese
¼	cup snipped fresh basil

① Coat a 2-quart rectangular baking dish with cooking spray. Arrange half of the bread cubes in the prepared baking dish.

② Cook asparagus and onion in a medium saucepan in a small amount of boiling water for 2 to 3 minutes or just until tender; stir in spinach. Immediately drain well. Spoon half of the asparagus mixture over bread in baking dish. Top with the remaining bread cubes and the remaining asparagus mixture. Set aside.

③ In a large bowl whisk together eggs, milk, salt, and pepper. Pour evenly over mixture in baking dish. With the back of a large spoon, lightly press down layers. Arrange tomato slices on top. Top with feta cheese and basil. Cover with foil; refrigerate for 4 to 24 hours.

④ Preheat oven to 325°F. Bake, covered, for 30 minutes. Uncover; bake about 40 minutes more or until center registers 180°F when tested with an instant-read thermometer (there will be some liquid left in center that will be absorbed during standing). Let stand on a wire rack for 10 minutes before serving.

PER SERVING 247 calories; 9 g total fat (3 g sat. fat); 216 mg cholesterol; 419 mg sodium; 27 g carbohydrate; 7 g fiber; 18 g protein

Cheesy Mushroom Casserole

MAKES 6 servings PREP 30 minutes BAKE 25 minutes
STAND 5 minutes OVEN 350°F

	Nonstick cooking spray
3	cups water
1	cup quick-cooking (hominy) grits
¾	cup shredded reduced-fat cheddar cheese
⅛	teaspoon salt
1	8-ounce package sliced fresh button mushrooms
1	6-ounce package sliced fresh portobello mushrooms or two 3-ounce portobello mushrooms, cleaned and sliced
¼	teaspoon black pepper
4	ounces thinly sliced prosciutto, chopped
2	cloves garlic, minced
4	egg whites, lightly beaten
2	eggs, lightly beaten
	Snipped fresh parsley (optional)

① Preheat oven to 350°F. Coat a 2-quart rectangular baking dish with cooking spray; set aside. In a large saucepan bring the water to boiling. Gradually stir in grits. Reduce heat to low. Cook, uncovered, for 5 to 7 minutes or until thick, stirring frequently. Remove from heat. Stir in ¼ cup of the cheese and the salt. Spread evenly in the prepared baking dish.

② Coat an unheated large nonstick skillet with cooking spray. Preheat skillet on medium heat. Add mushrooms and pepper. Cook about 5 minutes or until tender and any liquid is evaporated, stirring occasionally. Add prosciutto and garlic. Cook and stir for 1 minute more. Cool slightly.

③ Add egg whites and eggs to the mushroom mixture; stir to combine. Spread over grits in baking dish. Sprinkle with the remaining ½ cup cheese. Bake, uncovered, for 25 to 30 minutes or until heated through and egg mixture is set in center. Let stand for 5 minutes before serving. If desired, sprinkle with parsley.

PER SERVING 235 calories; 10 g total fat (2 g sat. fat); 81 mg cholesterol; 571 mg sodium; 23 g carbohydrate; 2 g fiber; 17 g protein

Light Colorado Quiche

MAKES 8 servings **PREP** 15 minutes **BAKE** 45 minutes
OVEN 350°F

- ½ cup fat-free milk
- 2 tablespoons all-purpose flour
- 1 cup low-fat cottage cheese
- ¾ cup refrigerated or frozen egg product, thawed
- 2 ounces reduced-fat cream cheese (Neufchâtel), cut up
- 1 cup shredded reduced-fat sharp cheddar cheese or Monterey Jack cheese (4 ounces)
- ⅛ teaspoon black pepper
  Fresh chopped tomatoes (optional)
  Snipped fresh basil or oregano (optional)

① Preheat oven to 350°F. Lightly grease a 9-inch pie plate; set aside. In a medium bowl gradually whisk milk into flour until smooth. Whisk in cottage cheese, eggs, and cream cheese (mixture will not be smooth). Stir in cheddar cheese and pepper.

② Pour mixture into prepared pie plate. Bake for 45 to 50 minutes or until puffed and golden and a knife inserted near center comes out clean. Serve immediately. If desired, garnish with tomatoes and fresh basil.

PER SERVING 107 calories; 5 g total fat (3 g sat. fat); 17 mg cholesterol; 309 mg sodium; 4 g carbohydrate; 0 g fiber; 11 g protein

Light Colorado Quiche

Mexican-Style Scrambled Eggs ●⓪

MAKES 4 servings **START TO FINISH** 30 minutes **OVEN** 350°F

- 1 cup water
- ¼ cup thinly sliced green onions (2)
- ¼ cup chopped sweet red or green pepper
- 1 8-ounce carton refrigerated or frozen egg product, thawed
- ¼ cup fat-free milk
- ⅛ teaspoon black pepper
- 4 7-inch whole wheat flour tortillas
- 1 teaspoon butter or margarine
- ½ cup shredded reduced-fat cheddar cheese (2 ounces)
- ⅓ cup salsa

① Preheat oven to 350°F. In a small saucepan combine the water, green onions, and sweet pepper. Bring to boiling; reduce heat. Simmer, uncovered, for 5 to 7 minutes or until vegetables are tender. Drain well. In a medium bowl stir together eggs, milk, and black pepper. Stir in cooked vegetables.

② Stack tortillas; wrap in foil. Bake about 10 minutes or until warm. (Or just before serving, cover and microwave tortillas on high about 1 minute.)

③ Meanwhile, in a large skillet melt butter on medium heat. Pour in egg mixture. Cook, without stirring, until mixture begins to set on bottom and around edges. With a spatula or large spoon, lift and fold partially cooked eggs so uncooked portion flows underneath. Sprinkle with cheese. Continue cooking for 2 to 3 minutes or until eggs are cooked through but still glossy and moist.

④ Immediately spoon egg mixture down the center of each warm tortilla. Fold tortilla in half or roll up. Top with salsa.

PER SERVING 183 calories; 6 g total fat (3 g sat. fat); 13 mg cholesterol; 381 mg sodium; 19 g carbohydrate; 1 g fiber; 12 g protein

With so many salsas on the market, you can experiment with the kinds you like. These Mexican-Style Scrambled Eggs are delicious with a roasted salsa verde or chipotle salsa as well as the more traditional tomato-based type.

Mexican-Style Scrambled Eggs

Omelet de Provence

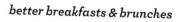

Omelet de Provence ③⓪

MAKES 2 servings **START TO FINISH** 30 minutes

Nonstick cooking spray

2 cups sliced fresh mushrooms

3 tablespoons sliced green onions

1 clove garlic, minced

1 cup refrigerated or frozen egg product, thawed, or 4 eggs, lightly beaten

¼ teaspoon herbes de Provence or dried thyme or basil, crushed

⅛ teaspoon salt

Dash black pepper

1 teaspoon olive oil

¼ cup shredded part-skim mozzarella cheese (1 ounce)

1 medium plum tomato, chopped

1 tablespoon finely shredded Asiago or Parmesan cheese

Fresh basil or parsley leaves (optional)

① Lightly coat an unheated small nonstick skillet with flared sides with cooking spray. Preheat skillet on medium heat. Add mushrooms, green onions, and garlic; cook and stir until mushrooms are tender. Using a slotted spoon, remove mushroom mixture from skillet; set aside. If necessary, drain skillet; carefully wipe out skillet with paper towels.

② In a medium bowl combine eggs, herbes de Provence, salt, and pepper.

③ Add ½ teaspoon of the oil to the skillet; heat skillet on medium heat. Pour half of the egg mixture into skillet. Using a wooden or plastic spatula, immediately begin stirring the eggs gently but continuously until mixture resembles small pieces of cooked egg surrounded by liquid egg. Stop stirring. Cook 30 to 60 seconds more or until egg mixture is set but still glossy and moist.

④ Sprinkle with 2 tablespoons of the mozzarella cheese. Top with half of the mushroom mixture. Continue cooking just until cheese begins to melt. Using the spatula, lift and fold an edge of the omelet partially over filling. Remove from skillet; cover and keep warm.

⑤ Repeat with the remaining oil, egg mixture, mozzarella cheese, and mushroom mixture. Top omelets with tomato, Asiago cheese, and, if desired, fresh basil.

PER SERVING 168 calories; 6 g total fat (3 g sat. fat); 13 mg cholesterol; 512 mg sodium; 10 g carbohydrate; 2 g fiber; 20 g protein

Mushroom and Herb Pizza

MAKES 8 servings **PREP** 40 minutes **BAKE** 12 minutes **OVEN** 425°F

1 16-ounce loaf frozen honey-wheat bread dough, thawed

6 eggs

⅓ cup fat-free milk

Nonstick cooking spray

1 tablespoon olive oil

3 cups sliced fresh mushrooms (8 ounces) (such as stemmed shiitake, cremini, and/or button)

⅓ cup snipped fresh basil and/or parsley or 2 teaspoons dried Italian seasoning, crushed

1 tablespoon snipped fresh oregano (optional)

3 cloves garlic, minced

¼ teaspoon salt

1 cup shredded part-skim mozzarella cheese (4 ounces)

¼ cup finely shredded Parmesan cheese

Freshly ground black pepper (optional)

① Preheat oven to 425°F. Lightly grease a 15 x 10 x 1-inch baking pan; set aside. On a lightly floured surface, roll bread dough to a 15 x 10-inch rectangle. Transfer dough to prepared baking pan. Press into prepared pan, building up edges slightly. Prick dough generously with a fork. Let dough stand for 5 minutes. Bake about 10 minutes or until lightly browned. Let cool for 5 minutes.

② In a bowl whisk together eggs and milk. Coat an unheated large nonstick skillet with cooking spray. Preheat over medium heat. Pour in egg mixture. Cook, without stirring, until mixture begins to set on the bottom and around edges. With a spatula, lift and fold the partially cooked egg mixture so the uncooked portion flows underneath. Continue cooking over medium heat for 2 minutes or until egg mixture is cooked through but is still glossy and moist. Transfer to a bowl; set aside.

③ In the same skillet heat oil over medium heat. Add mushrooms, basil, oregano (if using), garlic, and salt; cook for 5 to 7 minutes or just until mushrooms are tender. Fold cooked eggs into mushroom mixture.

④ Sprinkle mozzarella cheese over partially baked crust. Top evenly with egg mixture and Parmesan cheese.

⑤ Bake for 12 to 15 minutes or until edges are golden brown and pizza is heated through. If desired, sprinkle with pepper before serving.

PER SERVING 274 calories; 11 g total fat (3 g sat. fat); 170 mg cholesterol; 575 mg sodium; 30 g carbohydrate; 3 g fiber; 17 g protein

Bacon 'n' Egg Pockets ✪ ③⓪

MAKES 4 servings **START TO FINISH** 15 minutes

- 4 egg whites
- 2 eggs
- 3 ounces Canadian bacon, chopped
- 3 tablespoons water
- 2 tablespoons sliced green onion (1) (optional)
- ⅛ teaspoon salt

  Nonstick cooking spray
- 2 large whole wheat pita bread rounds, halved crosswise
- ½ cup shredded reduced-fat cheddar cheese (2 ounces) (optional)

① In a medium bowl combine egg whites, eggs, Canadian bacon, the water, green onion (if desired), and salt. Beat with a wire whisk or rotary beater until well mixed.

② Lightly coat an unheated large nonstick skillet with cooking spray. Preheat on medium heat. Add egg mixture to skillet. Cook, without stirring, until mixture begins to set on the bottom and around the edges. With a spatula or large spoon, lift and fold the partially cooked eggs so the uncooked portion flows underneath. Continue cooking about 2 minutes or until egg mixture is cooked through but is still glossy and moist. Immediately remove from heat.

③ Fill pita bread halves with egg mixture. If desired, sprinkle with cheese.

PER SERVING 162 calories; 4 g total fat (1 g sat. fat); 118 mg cholesterol; 616 mg sodium; 18 g carbohydrate; 2 g fiber; 13 g protein

Poblano-Tofu Scramble

Poblano-Tofu Scramble

MAKES 4 servings **PREP** 25 minutes **COOK** 10 minutes

- 1 16- to 18-ounce package extra-firm tub-style tofu (fresh bean curd)
- 1 tablespoon olive oil
- 1 or 2 fresh poblano chile(s), seeded and chopped* (½ to 1 cup total)
- ½ cup chopped onion
- 2 cloves garlic, minced
- 1 teaspoon chili powder
- ½ teaspoon ground cumin
- ½ teaspoon dried oregano, crushed
- ¼ teaspoon salt
- 1 tablespoon lime juice
- 2 plum tomatoes, seeded and chopped (about 1 cup)

  Fresh cilantro sprigs (optional)

① Drain tofu; cut tofu in half and pat dry each half with paper towels. Crumble tofu into a medium bowl. Set aside.

② In a large nonstick skillet heat oil on medium-high heat. Add chile, onion, and garlic; cook and stir for 4 minutes. Add chili powder, cumin, oregano, and salt. Cook and stir for 30 seconds more.

③ Add crumbled tofu to chile mixture. Reduce heat. Cook for 5 minutes, gently stirring occasionally. Just before serving, drizzle with lime juice and fold in tomatoes. If desired, garnish with cilantro.

*Tip: Because chiles contain volatile oils that can burn your skin and eyes, avoid direct contact with them as much as possible. When working with chiles, wear plastic or rubber gloves. If your bare hands do touch the peppers, wash your hands and fingernails well with soap and warm water.

PER SERVING 182 calories; 10 g total fat (1 g sat. fat); 0 mg cholesterol; 158 mg sodium; 11 g carbohydrate; 3 g fiber; 13 g protein

Tofu is a nutritional bonanza—it's high in protein and calcium and low in fat. It's also a cholesterol-free food. Savory Poblano-Tofu Scramble makes a terrific supper as well as a hearty breakfast.

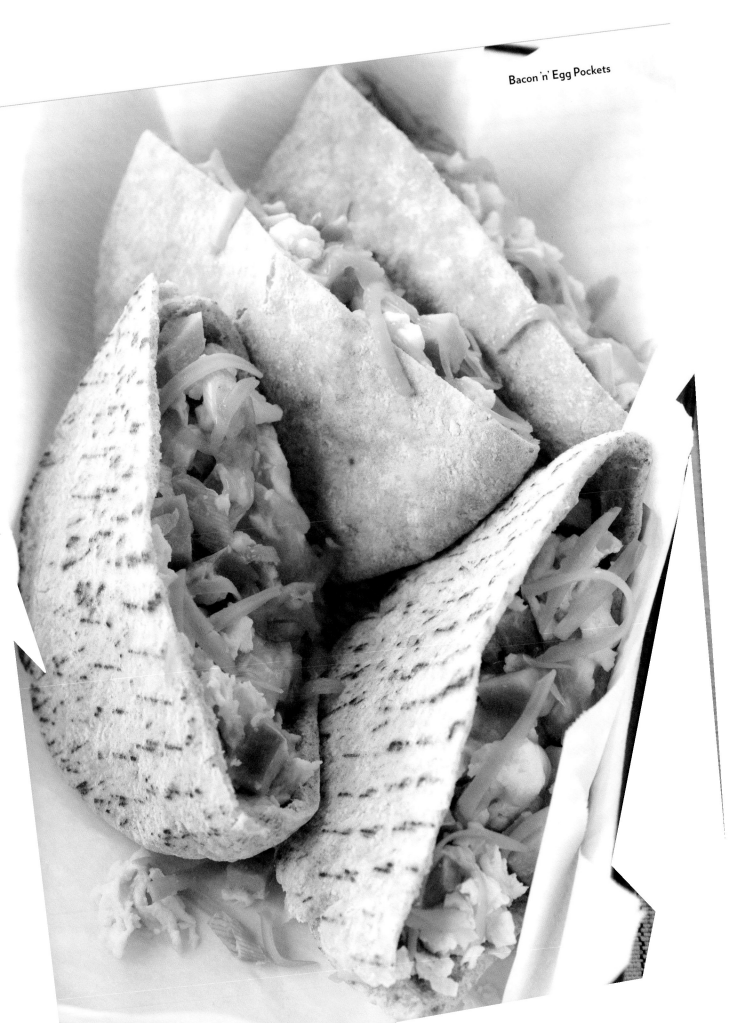

Super Breakfast Burritos

Super Breakfast Burritos ③⓪

MAKES 6 burritos **START TO FINISH** 30 minutes

- 2 teaspoons olive oil
- 2 medium fresh poblano chile peppers, seeded and chopped*
- ¾ cup canned black beans, rinsed and drained
- ¾ cup frozen corn, thawed
- ⅓ cup purchased tomato salsa or green salsa
- ½ teaspoon ground cumin
- ½ teaspoon chili powder
- 6 eggs
  - Dash salt
  - Dash black pepper
- 6 8-inch whole grain tortillas, warmed according to package directions
- 3 ounces queso fresco or reduced-fat Monterey Jack cheese, shredded (¾ cup)
- ¼ cup snipped fresh cilantro
- ½ cup purchased tomato salsa or green salsa (optional)

① In a large skillet heat 1 teaspoon olive oil on medium heat. Add chile peppers; cook about 3 minutes or just until tender, stirring occasionally. Stir in beans, corn, ⅓ cup salsa, cumin, and chili powder. Cook and stir 2 minutes or until heated through. Remove vegetable mixture from skillet.

② In a bowl whisk together eggs, salt, and black pepper. In the same skillet heat the remaining 1 teaspoon oil on medium heat. Pour in egg mixture. Cook, without stirring, until mixture begins to set on the bottom and around edges. With a spatula, lift and fold the partially cooked eggs so the uncooked portion flows underneath. Continue cooking on medium heat for 2 minutes or until egg mixture is cooked through but is still glossy and moist. Remove from heat. Fold in vegetable mixture.

③ Spoon about ⅔ cup egg mixture down the center of each tortilla. Top with cheese and cilantro. Fold sides of tortillas up over filling. Roll up tortillas starting at one end. Cut in half. If desired, serve with ½ cup salsa.

***Tip:** Because chile peppers contain volatile oils that can burn your skin and eyes, avoid direct contact with them as much as possible. When working with chile peppers, wear plastic or rubber gloves. If your bare hands do touch the peppers, wash your hands and fingernails well with soap and warm water.

PER BURRITO 297 calories; 12 g total fat (4 g sat. fat); 216 mg cholesterol; 602 mg sodium; 29 g carbohydrate; 12 g fiber; 20 g protein

Fennel and Asparagus Pie

MAKES 6 servings **PREP** 30 minutes **BAKE** 42 minutes
STAND 10 minutes **OVEN** 425°F/375°F

- ½ of a 15-ounce package (1 crust) rolled refrigerated unbaked piecrust
- 1 medium fennel bulb
- 1 pound fresh asparagus, trimmed and cut into 1-inch pieces
- ½ cup chopped onion
- ¾ cup fat-free milk
- 2 tablespoons all-purpose flour
- 3 eggs
- 1 tablespoon snipped fresh basil or 1 teaspoon dried basil, crushed
- ½ teaspoon salt
- ⅛ teaspoon black pepper
- 1 cup shredded part-skim mozzarella cheese (4 ounces)
  - Fresh basil leaves (optional)

① Preheat oven to 425°F. Let piecrust stand at room temperature according to package directions. Line a 9-inch pie plate with piecrust. Crimp edge as desired. Line unpricked pastry with a double thickness of foil. Bake for 8 minutes. Remove foil. Bake for 4 to 5 minutes more or until pastry is set and dry. Remove from oven. Reduce oven temperature to 375°F.

② Meanwhile, trim top off fennel bulb, reserving some of the feathery leaves for garnish. Trim fennel bulb and thinly slice. In a covered medium saucepan, cook fennel, asparagus, and onion in a small amount of boiling water for 4 to 6 minutes or just until vegetables are tender.

③ In a medium bowl whisk together milk and flour until smooth. Add eggs, snipped or dried basil, salt, and pepper, whisking until combined.

④ Spoon fennel mixture into baked piecrust. Sprinkle with cheese. Slowly pour egg mixture over all.

⑤ Bake, uncovered, for 30 to 35 minutes or until egg mixture is set in center. If necessary, to prevent overbrowning, cover edge of pie with foil for the last 5 to 10 minutes of baking. Let stand for 10 minutes before serving. Top with reserved fennel leaves and, if desired, fresh basil leaves.

PER SERVING 290 calories; 15 g total fat (6 g sat. fat); 122 mg cholesterol; 524 mg sodium; 28 g carbohydrate; 3 g fiber; 12 g protein

Farmer's Casserole ✪

MAKES 6 servings **PREP** 25 minutes **BAKE** 40 minutes **STAND** 5 minutes **OVEN** 350°F

Nonstick cooking spray

- 3 cups frozen shredded hash brown potatoes
- ¾ cup shredded Monterey Jack cheese with jalapeño or shredded cheddar cheese (3 ounces)
- 1 cup diced cooked ham or Canadian bacon
- ¼ cup sliced green onions (2)
- 1 cup refrigerated or frozen egg product, thawed, or 4 eggs, lightly beaten
- 1½ cups fat-free milk or one 12-ounce can evaporated fat-free milk
- ⅛ teaspoon black pepper

① Preheat oven to 350°F. Coat a 2-quart square baking dish with cooking spray. Arrange potatoes evenly in bottom of baking dish. Sprinkle with cheese, ham, and green onions.

② In a medium bowl combine eggs, milk, and pepper. Pour egg mixture over potato mixture in baking dish.

③ Bake, uncovered, for 40 to 45 minutes or until a knife inserted near center comes out clean. Let stand 5 minutes before serving.

Farmer's Casserole for 12: Prepare as directed, except double all ingredients and use a 3-quart rectangular baking dish. Bake, uncovered, for 45 to 55 minutes or until a knife inserted near the center comes out clean. Let stand 5 minutes before serving. Makes 12 servings.

Make-Ahead Directions: Prepare as directed through Step 2. Cover and chill in the refrigerator for up to 24 hours. To serve, preheat oven to 350°F. Bake, uncovered, for 50 to 55 minutes or until a knife inserted near the center comes out clean. Let stand 5 minutes before serving.

PER SERVING 208 calories; 6 g total fat (3 g sat. fat); 27 mg cholesterol; 610 mg sodium; 23 g carbohydrate; 2 g fiber; 17 g protein

For Puffed Oven-Baked Pancakes with the lightest texture and most volume, let the egg sit at room temperature for 30 minutes before using.

Puffed Oven-Baked Pancakes ③⓪

MAKES 2 servings **PREP** 10 minutes **BAKE** 15 minutes **OVEN** 400°F

Nonstick cooking spray

- 1 egg, lightly beaten
- 3 tablespoons all-purpose flour
- 3 tablespoons fat-free milk
  Dash salt
- 2 tablespoons orange marmalade
- ⅔ cup sliced fresh fruit (such as strawberries, peeled kiwifruit, nectarines, pears, and/or peeled peaches)

① Preheat oven to 400°F. Lightly coat two 4½-inch individual pie plates, 10-ounce custard cups, or 10-ounce au gratin dishes with cooking spray; set aside.

② In a small bowl combine egg, flour, milk, and salt. With a wire whisk or rotary beater beat until smooth. Immediately pour batter into prepared pie plates. Bake for 15 to 20 minutes or until pancakes are puffed and well browned.

③ Meanwhile, place orange marmalade in a small microwave-safe dish. Microwave, uncovered, on high about 30 seconds or until melted.

④ To serve, top puffed pancakes with fruit; spoon melted marmalade over fruit. Serve warm.

PER SERVING 162 calories; 3 g total fat (1 g sat. fat); 106 mg cholesterol; 131 mg sodium; 30 g carbohydrate; 2 g fiber; 6 g protein

Puffed Oven-Baked Pancakes

Farmer's Casserole

Streusel-Crunch French Toast

Streusel-Crunch French Toast ✪

MAKES 6 servings **PREP** 20 minutes
CHILL 2 to 24 hours **BAKE** 30 minutes **OVEN** 375°F

	Nonstick cooking spray
3	eggs
1	cup evaporated fat-free milk
3	tablespoons sugar
2	teaspoons vanilla
1	teaspoon ground cinnamon
¼	teaspoon ground nutmeg
6	1-inch-thick slices crusty whole wheat country-style bread
⅔	cup crushed shredded wheat biscuits
1	tablespoon butter, melted
2	cups sliced fresh strawberries

① Lightly coat a 3-quart rectangular baking dish with cooking spray; set aside. In a medium bowl lightly beat eggs with a rotary beater or wire whisk. Beat in evaporated milk, 1 tablespoon of the sugar, the vanilla, ½ teaspoon of the cinnamon, and the nutmeg. Arrange bread slices in a single layer in prepared baking dish. Pour egg mixture evenly over bread. Cover and chill in the refrigerator for at least 2 hours or up to 24 hours, turning bread slices once with a wide spatula.

② Preheat oven to 375°F. In a small bowl combine the remaining 2 tablespoons sugar and the remaining ½ teaspoon cinnamon; set aside. In another small bowl combine shredded wheat, butter, and 2 teaspoons of the cinnamon-sugar mixture. Sprinkle evenly over bread slices in dish. Bake, uncovered, about 30 minutes or until lightly browned.

③ Meanwhile, in a small bowl combine the strawberries and the remaining cinnamon-sugar mixture. Serve with French toast.

PER SERVING 231 calories; 6 g total fat (2 g sat. fat); 113 mg cholesterol; 255 mg sodium; 34 g carbohydrate; 4 g fiber; 12 g protein

Streusel-Crunch French Toast is baked, not fried, which cuts down on fat and calories. It's also made with whole wheat country-style bread—for an extra dose of fiber.

Overnight Waffles

MAKES 20 (4-inch) waffles **PREP** 10 minutes
CHILL overnight **BAKE** per waffle baker directions

2¼	cups all-purpose flour
2	tablespoons sugar
1	package active dry yeast
½	teaspoon salt
1⅔	cups fat-free milk
2	eggs
⅓	cup canola oil
1	teaspoon vanilla
1¼	cups low-sugar raspberry preserves (optional)
5	cups fresh raspberries (optional)

① In a large bowl stir together flour, sugar, yeast, and salt; add milk, eggs, oil, and vanilla. Beat with an electric mixer until thoroughly combined. Cover batter loosely and chill overnight or up to 24 hours.

② Stir batter. Pour about ¾ cup batter onto grids of a preheated, lightly greased waffle baker. Close lid quickly; do not open until done. Bake according to manufacturer's directions. When done, use a fork to lift waffle off grid. Repeat with remaining batter. Serve warm. Discard any remaining batter.

③ If desired, cut waffles into strips and serve with preserves and fresh raspberries.

PER WAFFLE 104 calories; 4 g total fat (0 g sat. fat); 22 mg cholesterol; 74 mg sodium; 13 g carbohydrate; 0 g fiber; 3 g protein

Overnight Cornmeal Waffles: Prepare as above, except reduce flour to 1½ cups and add ¾ cup cornmeal.

Overnight Waffles

Rhubarb-Banana Muffins ✪

MAKES 24 muffins **PREP** 25 minutes **BAKE** 18 minutes
COOL 5 minutes **OVEN** 400°F

- ½ cup granulated sugar
- 2 tablespoons butter, softened
- 2¾ cups all-purpose flour
- 2 teaspoons baking powder
- 2 teaspoons ground cinnamon
- ½ teaspoon baking soda
- ½ teaspoon salt
- ½ cup refrigerated or frozen egg product, thawed, or 2 eggs, lightly beaten
- 1 cup mashed bananas (3 large)
- ¾ cup packed brown sugar
- ½ cup canola oil
- 1½ cups frozen chopped rhubarb, thawed and drained

① Preheat oven to 400°F. Lightly grease twenty-four 2½-inch muffin cups or line with paper bake cups. In a small bowl combine granulated sugar and butter. Using your fingers, combine until crumbly; set aside.

② In large bowl combine flour, baking powder, cinnamon, baking soda, and salt. Make a well in the center of flour mixture; set aside.

③ In a medium bowl combine eggs, bananas, brown sugar, and oil. Add egg mixture all at once to flour mixture, stirring just until moistened (batter should be lumpy). Fold in rhubarb.

④ Spoon batter into prepared muffin cups, filling each about two-thirds full. Sprinkle with granulated sugar mixture.

⑤ Bake about 18 minutes or until wooden toothpick inserted in centers comes out clean. Cool in muffin cups on a wire rack for 5 minutes. Remove from muffin cups; serve warm.

PER MUFFIN 154 calories; 6 g total fat (1 g sat. fat); 3 mg cholesterol; 113 mg sodium; 24 g carbohydrate; 1 g fiber; 2 g protein

Adding pureed fruit—such as applesauce or mashed banana—to baked goods makes them extra moist and tender without the addition of lots of butter or oil.

Apple-Pumpkin Muffins

MAKES 12 muffins **PREP** 25 minutes **BAKE** 25 minutes
COOL 5 minutes **OVEN** 375°F

- Nonstick cooking spray
- 1¼ cups all-purpose flour
- ½ cup whole wheat flour
- 3 tablespoons toasted wheat germ
- 2 teaspoons pumpkin pie spice or apple pie spice
- 1½ teaspoons baking powder
- ½ teaspoon salt
- ¼ teaspoon baking soda
- ½ cup refrigerated or frozen egg product, thawed, or 2 eggs, slightly beaten
- 1 cup canned pumpkin
- ¾ cup buttermilk or sour milk*
- ⅓ cup unsweetened applesauce
- ¼ cup packed brown sugar
- 2 tablespoons cooking oil

① Preheat oven to 375°F. Lightly coat twelve 2½-inch muffin cups with nonstick cooking spray; set aside. In a large bowl stir together all-purpose flour, whole wheat flour, wheat germ, pumpkin pie spice, baking powder, salt, and baking soda; set aside.

② In a medium bowl combine egg, pumpkin, buttermilk, applesauce, brown sugar, and oil; add pumpkin mixture all at once to flour mixture. Stir just until moistened.

③ Divide batter evenly among prepared muffin cups, filling each about two-thirds full. Bake about 25 minutes or until golden brown and a toothpick inserted near centers comes out clean.

④ Cool in muffin cups on a wire rack for 5 minutes. Remove from muffin cups; serve warm.

*Tip: To make ¾ cup sour milk, place 2¼ teaspoons lemon juice or vinegar in a glass measuring cup. Add enough milk to equal ¾ cup total liquid; stir. Let mixture stand for 5 minutes before using.

PER MUFFIN 127 calories; 3 g total fat (1 g sat. fat); 1 mg cholesterol; 192 mg sodium; 22 g carbohydrate; 2 g fiber; 4 g protein

Pineapple-Glazed Banana-Blueberry Muffins

Pineapple-Glazed Banana-Blueberry Muffins ✪

MAKES 12 muffins **PREP** 20 minutes **BAKE** 15 minutes
COOL 5 minutes **OVEN** 400°F

1¾   cups all-purpose flour
⅓   cup packed brown sugar
2   teaspoons baking powder
½   teaspoon ground cinnamon
¼   teaspoon salt
¾   cup mashed ripe banana
½   cup milk
¼   cup butter, melted
1   egg, lightly beaten
1   teaspoon vanilla
¾   cup fresh or frozen blueberries
¼   cup pineapple jam
    Pineapple jam (optional)

① Preheat oven to 400°F. Grease twelve 2½-inch muffin cups; set aside.

② In a large bowl combine flour, brown sugar, baking powder, cinnamon, and salt. Make a well in center of flour mixture; set aside.

③ In a medium bowl combine banana, milk, butter, egg, and vanilla. Add banana mixture all at once to flour mixture. Stir just until moistened (batter should be lumpy). Fold in blueberries.

④ Spoon batter into prepared muffin cups, filling each about three-fourths full. Spoon 1 teaspoon pineapple jam into batter in each muffin cup.

⑤ Bake for 15 to 20 minutes or until golden and a wooden toothpick inserted in centers comes out clean. Cool in muffin cups on wire racks for 5 minutes. Remove from muffin cups; serve warm. If desired, pass additional pineapple jam.

PER MUFFIN 174 calories; 5 g total fat (2 g sat. fat); 29 mg cholesterol; 133 mg sodium; 30 g carbohydrate; 2 g fiber; 3 g protein

Lemon Bread

MAKES 1 loaf (16 slices) **PREP** 30 minutes **BAKE** 45 minutes
COOL 10 minutes **STAND** overnight **OVEN** 350°F

1¾   cups all-purpose flour
¾   cup sugar
2   teaspoons baking powder
¼   teaspoon salt
¼   cup refrigerated or frozen egg product, thawed, or 1 lightly beaten egg
1   cup fat-free milk
¼   cup cooking oil or melted butter
2   teaspoons finely shredded lemon peel
1   tablespoon lemon juice
½   cup chopped toasted almonds or walnuts
2   tablespoons lemon juice (optional)
1   tablespoon sugar (optional)

① Preheat oven to 350°F. Grease the bottom and ½ inch up sides of an 8 x 4 x 2-inch loaf pan; set aside. In a medium bowl stir together flour, the ¾ cup sugar, the baking powder, and salt. Make a well in center of flour mixture; set aside.

② In another medium bowl combine the egg, milk, oil, lemon peel, and the 1 tablespoon lemon juice. Add egg mixture all at once to flour mixture. Stir just until moistened (batter should be lumpy). Fold in nuts. Spoon batter into prepared pan.

③ Bake for 45 to 55 minutes or until a wooden toothpick inserted near center comes out clean. If desired, stir together the 2 tablespoons lemon juice and the 1 tablespoon sugar. While bread is still in the pan, brush lemon-sugar mixture over the top of the loaf. Cool in pan on a wire rack for 10 minutes. Remove from pan. Cool completely on a wire rack. Wrap and store overnight before serving.

PER SLICE 140 calories; 5 g total fat (1 g sat. fat); 0 mg cholesterol; 80 mg sodium; 21 g carbohydrate; 1 g fiber; 3 g protein

Lemon-Poppy Seed Bread: Prepare as above, except substitute 1 tablespoon poppy seeds for the almonds or walnuts.

Zucchini Chip Bread

MAKES 2 loaves (24 servings) **PREP** 30 minutes
BAKE 55 minutes **COOL** 10 minutes
STAND overnight **OVEN** 350°F

- 3 cups all-purpose flour*
- ¾ cup sugar
- 1 teaspoon baking soda
- 1 teaspoon ground nutmeg
- ½ teaspoon salt
- ½ teaspoon ground cinnamon
- ¼ teaspoon baking power
- ¾ cup refrigerated or frozen egg product, thawed
- ½ cup unsweetened applesauce
- ½ cup cooking oil
- 1 tablespoon finely shredded orange peel
- 2 teaspoons vanilla
- 2 cups shredded zucchini
- 1 cup chopped walnuts, toasted
- 1 cup semisweet chocolate pieces

① Preheat oven to 350°F. Grease bottom and ½ inch up the sides of two 8 x 4 x 2-inch loaf pans. Set aside.

② In a large bowl combine flour, sugar, baking soda, nutmeg, salt, cinnamon, and baking powder. In a small bowl combine egg product, applesauce, oil, orange peel, and vanilla; add to flour mixture. Stir until just moistened. Fold in zucchini, walnuts, and chocolate pieces.

③ Divide mixture evenly between prepared pans. Bake about 55 minutes or until a toothpick inserted near centers comes out clean. Cool in pans on wire rack 10 minutes. Remove bread from pans and cool completely on rack. For easier slicing, wrap and store overnight.

*Note: You can substitute 1½ cups whole wheat pastry flour for 1½ cups of the all-purpose flour.

PER SLICE 197 calories; 10 g total fat (2 g sat. fat); 0 mg cholesterol; 120 mg sodium; 25 g carbohydrate; 1 g fiber; 4 g protein

Blueberry Buckwheat Pancakes ⭐ ㉚

MAKES 12 pancakes **START TO FINISH** 30 minutes

- ½ cup buckwheat flour
- ½ cup whole wheat flour
- 1 tablespoon sugar
- ½ teaspoon baking powder
- ¼ teaspoon baking soda
- ¼ teaspoon salt
- 1¼ cups buttermilk or sour milk*
- ¼ cup refrigerated or frozen egg product, thawed, or 1 egg, lightly beaten
- 1 tablespoon vegetable oil
- ¼ teaspoon vanilla
- ¾ cup fresh or frozen blueberries
- Blueberries
- Maple syrup (optional)

① In a medium bowl stir together buckwheat flour, whole wheat flour, sugar, baking powder, baking soda, and salt. Make a well in center of flour mixture; set aside. In a small bowl combine buttermilk, egg product, oil, and vanilla. Add buttermilk mixture all at once to flour mixture. Stir just until combined but still slightly lumpy. Stir in blueberries.

② Heat a lightly greased griddle or heavy skillet on medium heat until a few drops of water sprinkled on griddle dance across the surface. For each pancake, pour a scant ¼ cup batter onto hot griddle. Spread batter into a circle about 4 inches in diameter.

③ Cook on medium heat for 2 to 4 minutes or until pancakes are browned, turning to cook second sides when pancake surfaces are bubbly and edges are slightly dry. Serve immediately or keep warm in a loosely covered ovenproof dish in a 300°F oven. Serve with blueberries and, if desired, maple syrup.

*Tip: To make 1¼ cups sour milk, place 4 teaspoons lemon juice or vinegar in a 2-cup glass measuring cup. Add enough fat-free milk to equal 1¼ cups liquid; stir. Let stand for 5 minutes before using.

PER PANCAKE 66 calories; 2 g total fat (0 g sat. fat); 1 mg cholesterol; 122 mg sodium; 11 g carbohydrate; 1 g fiber; 3 g protein

Honey-Orange Granola

Fruit and Caramel Oatmeal 🕤

MAKES 2 servings **START TO FINISH** 10 minutes

- 2   1-ounce envelopes instant oatmeal (plain)
- 1   cup fresh fruit, such as blueberries, raspberries, sliced banana, sliced strawberries, and/or sliced peaches
- 2   tablespoons chopped pecans, toasted
- 2   teaspoons sugar-free caramel-flavor ice cream topping

    Fat-free milk (optional)

① In 2 microwave-safe bowls prepare oatmeal according to package directions. Top each serving with fresh fruit and pecans. Drizzle with ice cream topping. If desired, heat in microwave on high for 30 seconds. If desired, serve with milk.

PER SERVING 211 calories; 7 g total fat (1 g sat. fat); 0 mg cholesterol; 83 mg sodium; 35 g carbohydrate; 6 g fiber; 5 g protein

Just a drizzle of sugar-free caramel ice cream topping turns a bowl of plain oatmeal into a special treat.

Fruit and Caramel Oatmeal

Honey-Orange Granola ✪

MAKES 12 (⅓-cup) servings **PREP** 15 minutes
BAKE 30 minutes **OVEN** 325°F

    Nonstick cooking spray
- 2½   cups regular rolled oats
- 1   cup wheat flakes
- ⅓   cup Grape Nuts® or whole bran cereal
- ⅓   cup sliced almonds or pecan pieces
- ⅓   cup orange juice
- 2   tablespoons honey
- ¼   teaspoon ground allspice
- ¼   teaspoon ground cinnamon

    Low-fat yogurt, fat-free milk, and/or fresh fruit

① Preheat oven to 325°F. Coat a 15 x 10 x 1-inch baking pan with cooking spray; set aside. In a large bowl stir together oats, wheat flakes, Grape Nuts, and nuts. In a small saucepan stir together orange juice, honey, allspice, and cinnamon. Cook and stir just until boiling. Remove from heat. Pour over oat mixture, tossing just until coated.

② Spread oat mixture evenly in prepared pan. Bake, uncovered, for 30 to 35 minutes or until oats are lightly browned, stirring twice. Remove from oven. Immediately turn out onto a large piece of foil; cool completely. Serve with yogurt, milk, and/or fresh fruit.

Make-Ahead Directions: Prepare as directed. Store in an airtight container in the refrigerator for up to 2 weeks or in the freezer for up to 3 months.

PER SERVING 136 calories; 3 g total fat (0 g sat. fat); 0 mg cholesterol; 39 mg sodium; 23 g carbohydrate; 3 g fiber; 4 g protein

Prepared granolas may be high in fiber and protein—but they're also high in fat and sugar. Making your own granola allows you to have the great taste and crunch of this classic breakfast cereal without the not-so-good-for-you elements that come in the commercial stuff.

Peanut Butter Breakfast Bars ✿

MAKES 16 servings **PREP** 20 minutes **BAKE** 28 minutes
OVEN 325°F

	Nonstick cooking spray
4	cups sweetened oat cereal flakes with raisins
¾	cup quick-cooking rolled oats
½	cup all-purpose flour
½	cup snipped dried apples
2	eggs, lightly beaten
½	cup honey
½	cup chunky peanut butter
⅓	cup butter, melted

① Preheat oven to 325°F. Line a 9 x 9 x 2-inch baking pan with foil. Lightly coat foil with cooking spray; set aside. In a large bowl combine cereal flakes, oats, flour, and apples. Set aside.

② In a small bowl stir together eggs, honey, peanut butter, and butter. Pour over cereal mixture. Mix well. Transfer mixture to prepared pan. Using the back of a large spoon, press mixture firmly into pan.

③ Bake for 28 to 30 minutes or until edges are browned. Cool completely in pan on a wire rack. Cut into bars. Wrap bars individually in plastic wrap. Store in the refrigerator for up to 3 days.*

*Tip: For longer storage, place individually wrapped bars in a freezer container or freezer bag; seal, label, and freeze for up to 3 months. To serve, thaw in refrigerator overnight.

PER SERVING 208 calories; 9 g total fat (3 g sat. fat); 37 mg cholesterol; 131 mg sodium; 29 g carbohydrate; 2 g fiber; 5 g protein

These grab-and-go breakfast bars are made with all-natural ingredients—just oat cereal, rolled oats, dried apples, eggs, honey, peanut butter, and butter. They are a great start to a busy day or a midmorning pick-me-up in place of something from the vending machine.

Morning Parfait ❸⓪

MAKES 4 servings **START TO FINISH** 20 minutes

¼	cup raisins
1	teaspoon finely shredded orange peel (set aside)
2	tablespoons orange juice
1	teaspoon vanilla
½	of an 8-ounce package reduced-fat cream cheese (Neufchâtel), softened
1	tablespoon sugar
2	cups fresh raspberries, blueberries, sliced strawberries, and/or cut-up peaches
½	cup low-fat granola
	Honey (optional)
	Shredded orange peel (optional)

① In a small microwave-safe bowl combine raisins and orange juice. Cover and microwave on high for 30 to 45 seconds; let stand for 1 minute to plump raisins. Stir in vanilla; set aside.

② In a medium bowl combine cream cheese and sugar; beat with an electric mixer on low to medium until smooth. Stir in raisin mixture and the 1 teaspoon orange peel.

③ In 4 parfait glasses layer half of the cream cheese mixture, half of the fruit, and half of the granola. Repeat layers. If desired, drizzle with honey. If desired, garnish with additional orange peel.

PER SERVING 209 calories; 8 g total fat (4 g sat. fat); 22 mg cholesterol; 149 mg sodium; 32 g carbohydrate; 4 g fiber; 5 g protein

Morning Parfait

Apples and Granola Breakfast Crisp

menu

Omelet de Provence

Apples and Granola
Breakfast Crisp
[below]

Rhubarb-Banana
Muffins

Cranberry-Ginger Tea

Apples and Granola Breakfast Crisp

MAKES 4 (½-cup) servings **PREP** 15 minutes
COOK 10 minutes **STAND** 10 minutes

1 tablespoon butter

2 medium apples (such as Rome or Pink Lady), peeled if desired, cored, and quartered

1 tablespoon packed brown sugar

½ teaspoon grated fresh ginger or ¼ teaspoon ground ginger

Dash ground cardamom or ground cinnamon

1 6-ounce container fat-free plain Greek yogurt or fat-free plain yogurt

1 teaspoon finely shredded lemon peel

4 teaspoons honey

¼ cup low-fat granola

① In a medium skillet heat butter on medium heat. Add apples and cook about 5 minutes or until apples are golden brown, turning occasionally. Reduce heat to medium-low. Stir in brown sugar, ginger, and cardamom. Cook and stir for 5 minutes or until apples are nearly tender. Remove skillet from heat. Cover and let stand for 10 minutes until apples are tender.

② Meanwhile, combine yogurt with lemon peel. Divide cooked apples among 4 individual serving bowls. Top with Greek yogurt. Drizzle with honey. Sprinkle with granola.

PER SERVING 145 calories; 3 g total fat (2 g sat. fat); 8 mg cholesterol; 56 mg sodium; 26 g carbohydrate; 2 g fiber; 5 g protein

Tropical Ambrosia Salad ㉚

MAKES 10 servings **START TO FINISH** 20 minutes

1 24-ounce jar refrigerated mango slices, drained and coarsely chopped

1 24-ounce jar refrigerated grapefruit sections, drained

1 20-ounce can pineapple chunks (juice pack), drained

Sour Cream-Orange Dressing

½ cup large flaked coconut or dried coconut chips, toasted*

1 to 2 tablespoons pomegranate seeds (optional)

① In a large bowl stir together mango, grapefruit, and pineapple. Add dressing, stirring gently to coat. Sprinkle with coconut and pomegranate seeds (if using). Serve immediately.

Sour Cream-Orange Dressing: In a small bowl stir together ½ cup light sour cream; 2 tablespoons frozen orange juice concentrate, thawed; and 1 tablespoon packed brown sugar.**

PER SERVING 158 calories; 3 g total fat (2 g sat. fat); 3 mg cholesterol; 40 mg sodium; 33 g carbohydrate; 1 g fiber; 2 g protein

***Tip:** To toast coconut, spread in a single layer in a shallow baking pan. Bake in a 350°F oven for 5 to 10 minutes or until golden brown, stirring once or twice. Watch carefully so coconut does not burn.

****Sugar Substitute:** Choose from Sweet'N Low Brown or Sugar Twin Granulated Brown. Follow package directions to use product amount equivalent to 1 tablespoon brown sugar.

PER SERVING WITH SUBSTITUTE: same as above, except 153 calories, 32 g carbohydrate, 18 g sugar

This classic fruit salad gets a fresh and healthful update. In place of the standard mini marshmallows is a sprinkling of antioxidant-rich pomegranate seeds.

Fruit Bowl Salad with Honey-Mint Dressing 30

MAKES 9 (1-cup) servings **START TO FINISH** 25 minutes

- 2 tablespoons snipped fresh mint
- 2 tablespoons lime juice
- 2 tablespoons orange juice
- 2 tablespoons honey
- 1 small cantaloupe
- 1½ cups strawberries, hulled and halved or quartered
- ¾ cup red seedless grapes
- 4 kiwifruits, peeled and cut into ½-inch pieces

① For the dressing, in a large bowl whisk together mint, lime juice, orange juice, and honey. Set aside.

② Cut cantaloupe in half and remove the seeds. Use a melon baller to scoop out fruit. Add melon balls, strawberries, grapes, and kiwifruits to dressing in bowl; toss lightly to coat. Serve immediately or cover and chill up to 3 hours.

PER SERVING 68 calories; 0 g total fat; 0 mg cholesterol; 9 mg sodium; 17 g carbohydrate; 2 g fiber; 1 g protein

Fresh Figs with Yogurt and Honey

MAKES 2 servings **PREP** 15 minutes **CHILL** 8 hours

- 1 cup plain low-fat yogurt
- ½ teaspoon vanilla
- 2 fresh figs, cut up, or apricots, pitted and cut up
- 1 tablespoon coarsely chopped walnuts, toasted
- 2 teaspoons honey
  Finely shredded lemon peel (optional)

① Line a strainer with 100%-cotton cheesecloth or a paper coffee filter; place over a large mug. Spoon yogurt into lined strainer. Cover; chill in the refrigerator for at least 8 hours or up to 24 hours. (Yogurt will thicken to form a soft cheese.)

② Discard liquid in mug. In a small bowl gently stir together the thickened yogurt and vanilla; fold in figs. Spoon into 2 small dessert dishes. Sprinkle with walnuts; drizzle with honey. If desired, sprinkle with lemon peel.

PER SERVING 157 calories; 4 g total fat (1 g sat. fat); 7 mg cholesterol; 80 mg sodium; 24 g carbohydrate; 2 g fiber; 7 g protein

Watermelon Lemonade ✪

MAKES 8 (10-ounce) servings **PREP** 30 minutes **COOL** 20 minutes **CHILL** 4 hours

- 5 large lemons
- 3 cups water
- 1 cup sugar
- 8 cups seeded and cubed watermelon (about 5 pounds with rind)
  Kiwi Cubes and/or Watermelon Cubes or ice cubes
  Lemon twists (optional)

① With a vegetable peeler, remove peel from lemons in strips; set aside. Juice lemons (you should have about 1½ cups juice).

② For lemon syrup, in a medium saucepan heat and stir the lemon strips, water, and sugar on medium heat until the sugar dissolves. Remove from heat; let stand at room temperature for 20 minutes. Stir in lemon juice. Pour lemon syrup into a 1-gallon jar or pitcher.

③ In a food processor or blender puree 4 cups of the watermelon until very smooth. Strain through a coarse sieve set over a large bowl, pressing pulp to release juice. Repeat with the remaining 4 cups watermelon (you should have about 10 cups juice total). Add watermelon juice to the lemon syrup. Cover; chill in the refrigerator for at least 4 hours or up to 8 hours. Strain mixture through a colander; discard lemon strips. If desired, cover and chill in the refrigerator for up to 24 hours more.

④ To serve, fill eight 12-ounce glasses with Kiwi Cubes and/or Watermelon Cubes. Pour the Watermelon Lemonade over the ice. If you like, garnish each glass with a lemon twist.

PER SERVING 155 calories; 0 g total fat; 0 mg cholesterol; 5 mg sodium; 41 g carbohydrate; 1 g fiber; 1 g protein

Kiwi Cubes: Peel 4 kiwifruits and cut into 8 pieces each. Fill compartments of 2 ice cube trays with cut fruit. Add cold water; freeze until firm.

Watermelon Cubes: Cut 1-inch cubes from watermelon flesh. Place cubes in a single layer in a 15 x 10 x 1-inch baking pan. Freeze 1 to 2 hours or until firm. If storing longer than 4 hours, transfer to a freezer bag or container; seal, label, and freeze until served.

Deep-Dark Hot Cocoa

Apple Cider Punch ③⓪

MAKES about 15 (6-ounce) servings
START TO FINISH 5 minutes

- 6 cups apple cider, chilled
- 2 cups orange juice, cranberry-raspberry juice, or orange-mango juice, chilled
- ½ cup lemon juice
- 1 750-ml bottle sparkling white grape juice or sparkling wine, chilled

① In a punch bowl or large pitcher combine apple cider, orange juice, and lemon juice. Slowly add grape juice. Serve immediately.

PER SERVING 99 calories; 0 g total fat; 0 mg cholesterol; 20 mg sodium; 25 g carbohydrate; 0 g fiber; 0 g protein

Here's a sparkling punch for a special brunch. If there are children present, you can serve two versions—one with sparkling white grape juice and one with sparkling white wine.

Apple Cider Punch

Cranberry-Ginger Tea ③⓪

MAKES 4 (8-ounce) servings **START TO FINISH** 15 minutes

- 4 cups water
- 4 bags red rooibos tea, white tea, or green tea
- 2 thin slices fresh ginger
- ½ cup canned whole cranberry sauce

① In medium saucepan bring water just to boiling. Remove from heat; add tea bags and ginger. Let stand for 3 to 5 minutes. Meanwhile, place cranberry sauce in blender; cover and blend until almost smooth.

② Remove and discard tea bags and ginger from water. Stir blended cranberry mixture into tea mixture until well mixed. Serve immediately. Or cover and chill in the refrigerator to serve cold; stir before serving.

PER SERVING 55 calories; 0 g total fat; 0 mg cholesterol; 17 mg sodium; 14 g carbohydrate; 0 g fiber; 0 g protein

Deep-Dark Hot Cocoa ✪ ③⓪

MAKES 4 (8-ounce) servings **START TO FINISH** 10 minutes

- ½ cup unsweetened cocoa powder
- ¼ cup bittersweet chocolate pieces
- 4 cups fat-free milk
- 1 tablespoon honey or sugar

① In a medium saucepan stir together cocoa powder and chocolate pieces. Whisk in milk and honey. Heat on medium heat just until boiling, whisking constantly.

PER SERVING 176 calories; 5 g total fat (3 g sat. fat); 5 mg cholesterol; 106 mg sodium; 28 g carbohydrate; 4 g fiber; 11 g protein

This lightly sweetened, lightened-up cocoa is for true fans of dark chocolate. Based on bittersweet chocolate, it also contains unsweetened cocoa powder and just a touch of honey or sugar.

Mustard Crisp Chicken , page 93

Pleasing Poultry

Baked Herbed Chicken ✪

MAKES 4 servings **PREP** 20 minutes **BAKE** 25 minutes
OVEN 375°F

- 4   skinless, boneless chicken breast halves (1 to 1¼ pounds total)
       Salt
       Coarse black pepper
- ½   of an 8-ounce package cream cheese, softened
- ¼   cup finely chopped sweet red or green pepper
- ½   teaspoon snipped fresh rosemary or tarragon or ¼ teaspoon dried rosemary or tarragon, crushed
- 1   tablespoon olive oil
- 1   tablespoon snipped fresh chives

① Preheat oven to 375°F. Place each chicken breast half between 2 pieces of plastic wrap. Using the flat side of a meat mallet, pound chicken lightly until about ⅛ inch thick. Remove plastic wrap.

② Sprinkle chicken with salt and black pepper. Top each chicken piece with 2 tablespoons of the cream cheese and 1 tablespoon of the sweet pepper. Sprinkle with rosemary. Fold in sides; roll up from bottom, pressing edges to seal. If necessary, secure with wooden toothpicks.

③ In a large skillet cook chicken rolls in hot oil on medium-high heat about 4 minutes or until light brown on all sides. Transfer to a 2-quart square baking dish. Sprinkle with additional black pepper.

④ Bake for 25 to 30 minutes or until chicken is no longer pink. Sprinkle with chives.

PER SERVING 292 calories; 15 g total fat (7 g sat. fat); 113 mg cholesterol; 307 mg sodium; 1 g carbohydrate; 0 g fiber; 35 g protein

Roasted vegetables are a delicious and nutritious side dish for either of these chicken dishes. Try either baby carrots or Brussels sprouts that have been trimmed and halved. Toss the vegetables in olive oil, salt, and freshly ground black pepper. Spread in a single layer on a rimmed baking sheet and roast in a 450°F oven until slightly charred and caramelized. Yum!

menu

Caesar-Style Salad with Crispy Parmesan Rounds

Wild rice pilaf

Chicken Breasts with Lemon and Herbs [below]

Fruit sorbet

Chicken Breasts with Lemon and Herbs ㉚

MAKES 4 servings **START TO FINISH** 30 minutes

- ⅓   cup snipped fresh parsley
- 1   tablespoon snipped fresh oregano
- 1   tablespoon finely shredded lemon peel
- 3   cloves garlic, minced
- 4   skinless, boneless chicken breast halves (1 to 1¼ pounds total)
       Salt
       Black pepper
- 2   tablespoons butter
- ¼   cup reduced-sodium chicken broth

① In a small bowl stir together parsley, oregano, lemon peel, and garlic. Set aside. Sprinkle chicken with salt and pepper.

② In a large skillet cook chicken in hot butter on medium-high heat about 6 minutes or until brown, turning once. Remove skillet from heat. Transfer chicken to a plate. Stir half of the herb mixture into drippings in skillet; add broth. Return to heat.

③ Bring to boiling, stirring to scrape up crusty browned bits. Return chicken to skillet; reduce heat. Simmer, covered, about 8 minutes or until chicken is no longer pink (170°F). Serve chicken with broth mixture. Sprinkle with the remaining herb mixture.

PER SERVING 213 calories; 7 g total fat (4 g sat. fat); 97 mg cholesterol; 154 mg sodium; 1 g carbohydrate; 0 g fiber; 33 g protein

Mediterranean Stuffed Chicken

Mediterranean Chicken and Polenta ③⓪

MAKES 4 servings **PREP** 15 minutes **BAKE** 10 minutes
OVEN 375°F

- ½ of a 6.5-ounce jar oil-packed dried tomatoes with Italian herbs
- 4 skinless, boneless chicken breast halves (1 to 1¼ pounds total)
  Salt
  Black pepper
- 1 cup assorted olives, pitted
- ½ cup dry white wine or reduced-sodium chicken broth
- 4 small bay leaves (optional)
- 3 cups water
- 1 cup yellow cornmeal
- 1 cup cold water
- 1 teaspoon salt

① Preheat oven to 375°F. Drain dried tomatoes, reserving oil. Sprinkle chicken with salt and pepper. In a large oven-going skillet heat the reserved oil on medium-high heat. Add chicken; cook about 6 minutes or until brown, turning once. Remove skillet from heat.

② Add dried tomatoes, olives, wine, and, if desired, bay leaves to chicken in skillet. Transfer to oven. Bake for 10 to 15 minutes or until chicken is no longer pink (170°F).

③ Meanwhile, for polenta, in a large saucepan bring the 3 cups water to boiling. In a medium bowl combine cornmeal, the 1 cup cold water, and the 1 teaspoon salt; gradually stir into boiling water. Cook until mixture is thick and bubbly, stirring frequently and adjusting heat as needed to maintain a slow boil. Remove and discard bay leaves. Serve chicken with polenta and olive mixture.

PER SERVING 370 calories; 8 g total fat (1 g sat. fat); 66 mg cholesterol; 575 mg sodium; 46 g carbohydrate; 3 g fiber; 30 g protein

Mediterranean Stuffed Chicken ③⓪

MAKES 4 servings **PREP** 20 minutes **COOK** 12 minutes

- 4 skinless, boneless chicken breast halves (1 to 1½ pounds total)
- ¼ cup crumbled reduced-fat feta cheese (1 ounce)
- ¼ cup finely chopped marinated artichoke hearts
- 2 tablespoons finely chopped roasted sweet red pepper
- 2 tablespoons thinly sliced green onion (1)
- 2 teaspoons snipped fresh oregano or ½ teaspoon dried oregano, crushed
- ⅛ teaspoon black pepper
  Nonstick cooking spray

① Using a sharp knife, cut a pocket into each chicken breast half by cutting horizontally through the thickest portion to, but not through, the opposite side. Set aside.

② In a small bowl combine cheese, artichoke hearts, roasted sweet pepper, green onion, and oregano. Spoon mixture evenly into pockets in chicken. If necessary, secure openings with wooden toothpicks. Sprinkle chicken with black pepper.

③ Coat a large nonstick skillet with cooking spray; heat skillet on medium heat. Add chicken; cook for 12 to 14 minutes or until no longer pink (170°F), turning once.

Grilling Directions: For a charcoal grill, grill chicken on the rack of an uncovered grill directly over medium coals for 12 to 15 minutes or until no longer pink (170°F), turning once halfway through grilling. (For a gas grill, preheat grill. Reduce heat to medium. Place chicken on grill rack over heat. Cover and grill as above.)

PER SERVING 171 calories; 5 g total fat (2 g sat. fat); 68 mg cholesterol; 226 mg sodium; 2 g carbohydrate; 0 g fiber; 28 g protein

Chicken infused with Mediterranean flavors—wine, olives, and cheese—is always a hit.

Tomato-Apricot Chicken ③⓪

MAKES 4 servings **START TO FINISH** 25 minutes

- 4 skinless, boneless chicken breast halves (1 to 1¼ pounds total)
  Salt
  Black pepper
- 1 tablespoon olive oil
- 1 clove garlic, sliced
- 1 28-ounce can diced tomatoes, undrained
- ½ cup snipped dried apricots
- ⅓ cup golden raisins

① Sprinkle chicken with salt and pepper. In a very large skillet cook chicken in hot oil on medium-high heat for 8 minutes, turning once. Add garlic; cook and stir for 1 minute more.

② Add tomatoes, apricots, and raisins. Bring to boiling; reduce heat. Simmer, covered, for 3 to 5 minutes or until chicken is no longer pink (170°F). Cook, uncovered, until tomato mixture is desired consistency. Season to taste with additional salt and pepper.

PER SERVING 314 calories; 5 g total fat (1 g sat. fat); 82 mg cholesterol; 636 mg sodium; 34 g carbohydrate; 6 g fiber; 36 g protein

Tomato-Apricot Chicken

Mushroom and Chicken Stroganoff ③⓪

MAKES 6 servings **START TO FINISH** 25 minutes

- 1 8-ounce carton light sour cream
- 2 tablespoons all-purpose flour
- 1 tablespoon Worcestershire-style marinade for chicken
- ½ teaspoon dried thyme, crushed
- ½ teaspoon instant chicken bouillon granules
- ¼ teaspoon black pepper
- ½ cup water
- 1 8-ounce package fresh mushrooms, sliced
- ½ cup chopped onion (1 medium)
- 2 cloves garlic, minced
- 1 tablespoon canola oil or olive oil
- 2½ cups coarsely shredded cooked chicken
- 3 cups hot cooked wide noodles
- ½ cup chopped tomato (1 medium)

① In a small bowl combine ⅔ cup of the sour cream, the flour, Worcestershire-style marinade, thyme, bouillon granules, and pepper. Gradually stir in the water until combined. Set aside.

② In a very large skillet cook mushrooms, onion, and garlic in hot oil on medium-high heat until tender, stirring occasionally. Stir in chicken.

③ Add sour cream mixture to chicken mixture; cook and stir until thickened and bubbly. Reduce heat; cook and stir for 2 minutes more.

④ Serve chicken mixture over hot cooked noodles. Top with the remaining sour cream and tomato.

PER SERVING 322 calories; 12 g total fat (4 g sat. fat); 88 mg cholesterol; 191 mg sodium; 29 g carbohydrate; 2 g fiber; 24 g protein

Light sour cream and chicken instead of beef make this creamy classic weigh in at just 322 calories and 12 grams of fat per serving. A chopped tomato topping adds a fresh touch.

Mushroom and Chicken Stroganoff

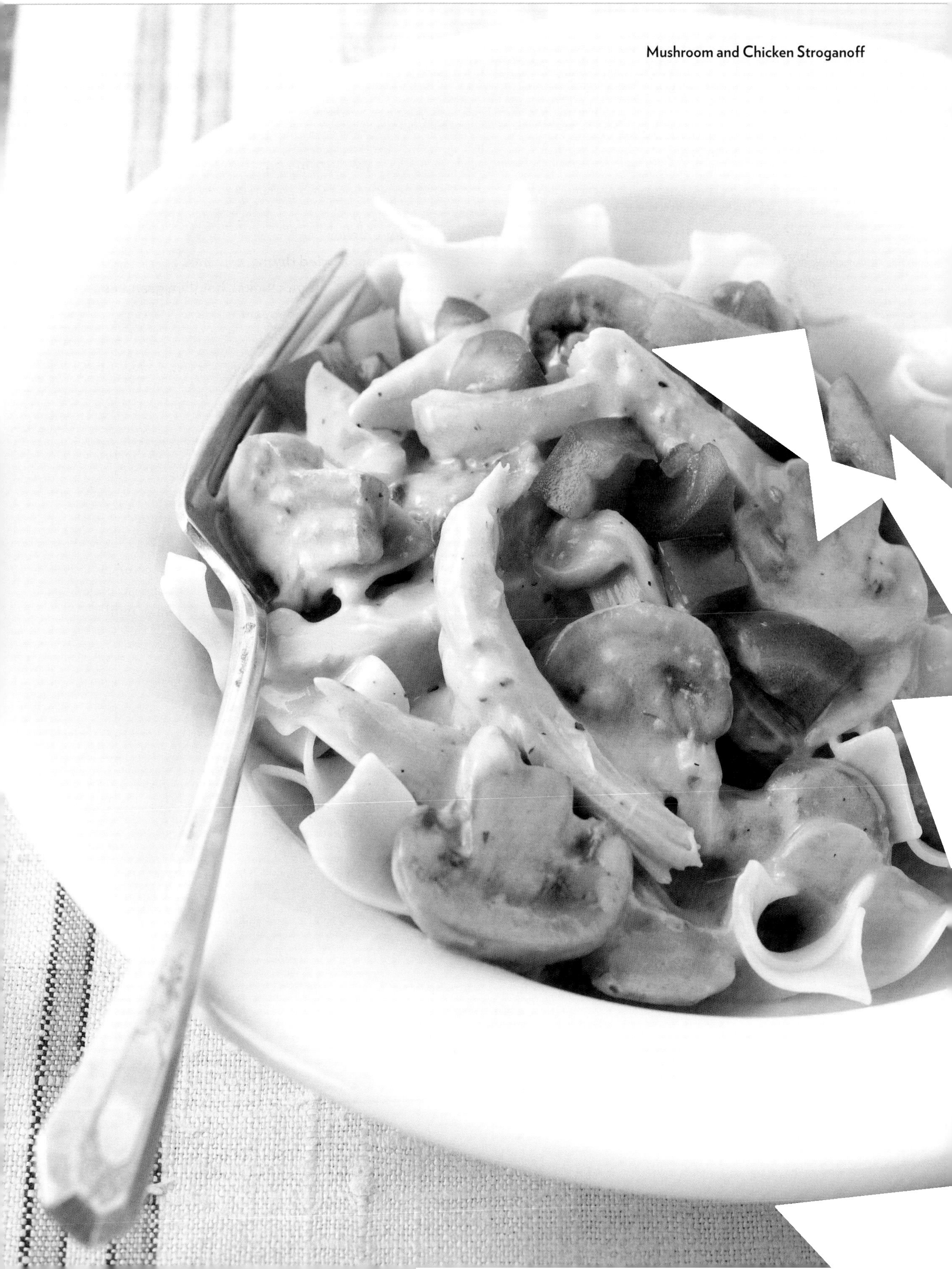

Poblano Chicken Bundles

Poblano Chicken Bundles

MAKES 4 servings **PREP** 30 minutes **COOK** 20 minutes

- 4   6-ounce skinless, boneless chicken breast halves
- 2   tablespoons snipped fresh cilantro
- 12   2½ x ½-inch strips fresh poblano chile (1 large) or 3 large fresh jalapeños, quartered and seeded*
- 4   2½ x ½-inch sticks reduced-fat Monterey Jack cheese (1½ to 2 ounces total)
- ⅓   cup yellow cornmeal
- 1   teaspoon chili powder
- ¼   teaspoon salt
- 1   egg white, lightly beaten
- 1   tablespoon water
- 1   tablespoon canola oil or olive oil
- ½   cup pico de gallo or salsa (optional)

  Snipped fresh cilantro (optional)

① Place each chicken breast half between 2 pieces of plastic wrap. Using the flat side of a meat mallet, pound chicken lightly until about ⅛ inch thick. Remove plastic wrap.

② Divide the 2 tablespoons cilantro evenly among chicken pieces. Place 3 chile pieces and 1 cheese stick across the center of each chicken piece. Fold in sides; roll up from bottom. Secure with wooden toothpicks.

③ In a shallow dish combine cornmeal, chili powder, and salt. In another shallow dish combine egg white and the water. Dip chicken bundles into egg white mixture, then into cornmeal mixture, turning to coat.

④ In a large nonstick skillet heat oil on medium heat. Add chicken bundles. Cook about 10 minutes or until brown on all sides. Reduce heat to medium-low. Cook, covered, for 10 to 12 minutes more or until chicken is no longer pink, turning once. If desired, serve with pico de gallo and sprinkle with additional cilantro.

*Tip: Because chiles contain volatile oils that can burn your skin and eyes, avoid direct contact with them as much as possible. When working with chiles, wear plastic or rubber gloves. If your bare hands do touch the peppers, wash your hands and fingernails well with soap and warm water.

PER SERVING 301 calories; 8 g total fat (2 g sat. fat); 106 mg cholesterol; 350 mg sodium; 11 g carbohydrate; 1 g fiber; 44 g protein

Chicken Kabobs with Peach Salsa

MAKES 2 servings **PREP** 20 minutes
MARINATE 2 to 4 hours **GRILL** 6 minutes

- 3   tablespoons rice vinegar
- 1   tablespoon reduced-sodium soy sauce
- 1   teaspoon packed brown sugar
- 1   teaspoon grated fresh ginger
- 8   ounces skinless, boneless chicken breast halves, cut lengthwise into 1-inch strips
- ½   of a medium peach, chopped
- 2   tablespoons chopped sweet red pepper
- 2   teaspoons finely chopped red onion
- 2   teaspoons snipped fresh cilantro
- ½   teaspoon lime juice
- ¼   teaspoon finely chopped, seeded fresh jalapeño*

① In a resealable plastic bag set in a deep bowl combine vinegar, soy sauce, brown sugar, and ginger. Add chicken strips. Seal bag; turn to coat chicken. Marinate in the refrigerator for 2 to 4 hours, turning bag occasionally.

② Drain chicken, discarding marinade. Thread chicken onto two 10- to 12-inch metal skewers, leaving ¼ inch between pieces. For a charcoal grill, grill chicken skewers on the rack of an uncovered grill directly over medium coals for 6 to 8 minutes or until chicken is no longer pink, turning occasionally to brown evenly. (For a gas grill, preheat grill. Reduce heat to medium. Place chicken skewers on grill rack over heat. Cover and grill as above.)

③ Meanwhile, for peach salsa, in a small bowl combine peach, sweet pepper, onion, cilantro, lime juice, and jalapeño. Serve chicken skewers with peach salsa.

*Tip: Because chiles contain volatile oils that can burn your skin and eyes, avoid direct contact with them as much as possible. When working with chiles, wear plastic or rubber gloves. If your bare hands do touch the peppers, wash your hands and fingernails well with soap and warm water.

PER SERVING 171 calories; 1 g total fat (0 g sat. fat); 66 mg cholesterol; 326 mg sodium; 9 g carbohydrate; 1 g fiber; 27 g protein

Apricot Chicken Kabobs 30

MAKES 4 servings **PREP** 20 minutes **GRILL** 8 minutes

- 1 pound skinless, boneless chicken breast halves, cut into 1-inch pieces
- 1½ teaspoons Jamaican jerk seasoning
- 1 cup fresh sugar snap pea pods or snow pea pods, strings and tips removed
- 1 cup fresh or canned pineapple chunks
- 1 medium sweet red pepper, seeded and cut into 1-inch pieces
- ¼ cup apricot spreadable fruit

① Sprinkle chicken with about half of the jerk seasoning; toss gently to coat. Cut any large pea pods in half crosswise.

② On 10- to 12-inch skewers,* alternately thread chicken, pea pods, pineapple, and sweet pepper, leaving ¼ inch between pieces.

③ For sauce, in a small saucepan combine the remaining jerk seasoning and spreadable fruit. Heat and stir just until spreadable fruit is melted; set aside.

④ For a charcoal grill, grill chicken skewers on the rack of an uncovered grill directly over medium coals for 8 to 10 minutes or until chicken is no longer pink and vegetables are crisp-tender, turning once halfway through grilling and brushing occasionally with sauce during the last 3 minutes of grilling. (For a gas grill, preheat grill. Reduce heat to medium. Place chicken skewers on grill rack over heat. Cover and grill as above.)

*Tip: If using wooden skewers, soak in water for at least 30 minutes; drain before using.

PER SERVING 199 calories; 2 g total fat (0 g sat. fat); 66 mg cholesterol; 173 mg sodium; 20 g carbohydrate; 2 g fiber; 27 g protein

Balsamic-Glazed Chicken Tenders 30

MAKES 4 servings **START TO FINISH** 25 minutes

- 1 small orange
- ⅔ cup cinnamon applesauce
- ¼ cup balsamic vinegar
- ½ teaspoon salt
- ½ teaspoon ground cardamom or ¼ teaspoon ground nutmeg
- ½ teaspoon black pepper
- 1 pound chicken breast tenderloins
  Salt
  Black pepper
- 2 teaspoons vegetable oil
  Fresh thyme sprigs (optional)

① Finely shred peel from orange; set aside. Squeeze juice from orange. In a medium saucepan combine orange juice, applesauce, vinegar, the ½ teaspoon salt, cardamom, and the ½ teaspoon pepper. Bring to boiling; reduce heat. Simmer, uncovered, for 10 minutes, stirring occasionally. Remove from heat; cover and keep warm.

② Sprinkle chicken lightly with additional salt and pepper. In a very large nonstick skillet heat oil on medium-high heat. Add chicken; cook about 4 minutes or until golden brown on bottom. Turn chicken and add ½ cup of the applesauce mixture. Cook for 2 to 3 minutes more or until chicken is no longer pink (170°F).

③ To serve, top chicken mixture with orange peel and, if desired, thyme sprigs. Pass the remaining applesauce mixture.

PER SERVING 208 calories; 4 g total fat (1 g sat. fat); 66 mg cholesterol; 207 mg sodium; 15 g carbohydrate; 1 g fiber; 27 g protein

Mild tasting chicken transforms into something interesting with just a few simple ingredients.

Apricot Chicken Kabobs

Chicken and Dumplings

Chicken and Dumplings ✪

MAKES 4 servings **PREP** 25 minutes **COOK** 45 minutes

- 4 bone-in chicken breast halves or thighs (about 1½ pounds total), skinned
- 2½ cups water
- 1 medium onion, sliced and separated into rings
- 1 teaspoon instant chicken bouillon granules
- 1 teaspoon snipped fresh thyme or ¼ teaspoon dried thyme, crushed
- ¼ teaspoon black pepper
- 2 cups sliced carrots (4 medium)
- 1 medium fennel bulb, trimmed and cut into bite-size strips (1½ cups)
- ¼ cup cold water
- 2 tablespoons cornstarch
  Dumplings
  Fresh herb sprigs (optional)

① In a large saucepan combine chicken, the 2½ cups water, onion, bouillon granules, dried thyme (if using), and pepper. Bring to boiling; reduce heat. Simmer, covered, for 25 minutes. Stir in carrots and fennel. Return to boiling; reduce heat. Simmer, covered, for 10 minutes more.

② Remove chicken from saucepan; set aside. Skim fat from broth. In a small bowl stir together the ¼ cup cold water and cornstarch; stir into broth in saucepan. Cook and stir until thickened and bubbly. Return chicken to saucepan; stir in fresh thyme (if using).

③ Drop Dumplings batter from a tablespoon into 8 mounds onto the hot chicken mixture. Simmer, covered, about 10 minutes or until a wooden toothpick inserted into a dumpling comes out clean. If desired, garnish with herb sprigs.

Dumplings: In a small bowl stir together 1 cup all-purpose flour, 1½ teaspoons baking powder, ⅛ teaspoon salt, and ⅛ teaspoon coarse black pepper. In another small bowl combine 1 lightly beaten egg, ¼ cup fat-free milk, and 1 tablespoon vegetable oil. Pour into flour mixture; stir with a fork until combined.

PER SERVING 327 calories; 6 g total fat (1 g sat. fat); 110 mg cholesterol; 558 mg sodium; 37 g carbohydrate; 12 g fiber; 29 g protein

Jerk Chicken and Slaw ㉚

MAKES 4 servings **START TO FINISH** 30 minutes

- 3 heads baby bok choy, trimmed and thinly sliced
- 2 cups shredded red cabbage
- ½ of a fresh pineapple, peeled, cored, and chopped
- 2 tablespoons cider vinegar
- 4 teaspoons packed brown sugar
- 2 teaspoons all-purpose flour
- 2 teaspoons Jamaican jerk seasoning
- 4 skinless, boneless chicken breast halves (1 to 1¼ pounds total)
  Nonstick cooking spray

① For pineapple slaw, in a very large bowl combine bok choy, cabbage, and pineapple. In a small bowl combine vinegar and 2 teaspoons of the brown sugar. Drizzle over bok choy mixture; toss gently to coat. Set aside.

② In a resealable plastic bag combine the remaining 2 teaspoons brown sugar, the flour, and jerk seasoning. Add chicken, one piece at a time, shaking to coat.

③ Lightly coat a grill pan or a very large heavy skillet with cooking spray; heat pan on medium heat. Add chicken; cook for 8 to 10 minutes or until no longer pink (170°F), turning once. Slice chicken. Serve chicken with pineapple slaw.

PER SERVING 205 calories; 2 g total fat (0 g sat. fat); 66 mg cholesterol; 318 mg sodium; 19 g carbohydrate; 3 g fiber; 29 g protein

Jerk Chicken and Slaw

Chicken and Black Bean Wraps ③⓪

MAKES 4 servings **START TO FINISH** 25 minutes

- ½   cup Black Bean-Smoked Chile Dip
- 4   7- to 8-inch whole wheat flour tortillas
- 2⅓ cups chopped cooked chicken breast or turkey breast (about 12 ounces)
- 4   cups shredded or torn romaine lettuce or whole fresh baby spinach leaves
- 1   cup coarsely snipped fresh cilantro
- ¼   cup salsa

① Spread Black Bean-Smoked Chile Dip on one side of tortillas. Top with chicken; add lettuce, cilantro, and salsa. Roll up tortillas. If desired, secure with toothpicks.

Black Bean-Smoked Chile Dip: In a small saucepan heat 1 tablespoon canola oil on medium heat. Add ¾ cup finely chopped onion, 1 teaspoon ground coriander, and 1 teaspoon ground cumin. Cook, covered, about 10 minutes or until onion is very tender, stirring occasionally. Remove from heat; stir in ¼ cup snipped fresh cilantro. Transfer onion mixture to a blender or food processor. Add one 15-ounce can black beans, rinsed and drained; ½ cup water; 1 tablespoon lime juice; 1 teaspoon finely chopped chipotle chile in adobo sauce; and ⅛ teaspoon salt. Cover and blend or process until nearly smooth. If desired, cover and chill for up to 3 days before using. Makes 1⅔ cups.

PER SERVING 324 calories; 8 g total fat (2 g sat. fat); 72 mg cholesterol; 600 mg sodium; 24 g carbohydrate; 14 g fiber; 38 g protein

Chicken and Black Bean Wraps

menu

Green Bean Salad

Crusty bread

Lemon-Thyme Roasted Chicken with Fingerlings [below]

Frozen vanilla yogurt

Lemon-Thyme Roasted Chicken with Fingerlings ③⓪

MAKES 4 servings **START TO FINISH** 30 minutes

- 4   teaspoons canola oil or olive oil
- 1   teaspoon dried thyme, crushed
- ½   teaspoon kosher salt or ¼ teaspoon regular salt
- ¼   teaspoon black pepper
- 1   pound fingerling potatoes, halved lengthwise, or tiny new red or white potatoes, halved
- 4   skinless, boneless chicken breast halves (1 to 1¼ pounds total)
- 2   cloves garlic, minced
- 1   lemon, thinly sliced
      Thyme leaves (optional)

① In a very large skillet heat 2 teaspoons of the oil on medium heat. Stir in ½ teaspoon of the thyme, the salt, and pepper. Add potatoes; toss gently to coat. Cook, covered, for 12 minutes, stirring twice.

② Stir potatoes; push to one side of skillet. Add the remaining 2 teaspoons oil. Arrange chicken on opposite side of skillet. Cook, uncovered, for 5 minutes.

③ Turn chicken. Top with garlic and the remaining ½ teaspoon thyme. Arrange lemon slices on chicken. Cook, covered, for 7 to 10 minutes more or until chicken is no longer pink (170°F) and potatoes are tender. If desired, sprinkle with thyme leaves.

PER SERVING 255 calories; 6 g total fat (1 g sat. fat); 66 mg cholesterol; 307 mg sodium; 21 g carbohydrate; 3 g fiber; 29 g protein

Mediterranean Chicken Panini

Mediterranean Chicken Panini ③⓪

MAKES 4 servings **START TO FINISH** 30 minutes

Nonstick cooking spray

2 skinless, boneless chicken breast halves (about 8 ounces total)

Dried Tomato-Pepper Spread

4 miniature squares whole wheat bagel bread or multigrain ciabatta rolls, split

1 small zucchini

① Lightly coat a panini griddle, covered indoor electric grill, or large nonstick skillet with cooking spray; heat on medium heat or heat according to the manufacturer's directions. Add chicken. If using griddle or grill, close lid and grill for 6 to 7 minutes or until chicken is no longer pink (170°F). (If using skillet, cook chicken for 10 to 12 minutes or until no longer pink [170°F], turning once.) Cool chicken slightly; cut each piece in half horizontally, then cut crosswise into 2-inch slices.

② To assemble, spread Dried Tomato-Pepper Spread on cut sides of bread squares. Place chicken on bottoms of bread squares. Using a vegetable peeler, cut very thin lengthwise strips from zucchini. Place zucchini on chicken. Add bread tops, spread sides down. Press lightly. Lightly coat the top and bottom of each sandwich with cooking spray.

③ Place sandwiches on griddle, grill, or skillet, in batches if necessary. If using griddle or grill, close lid and grill for 2 to 3 minutes or until bread is toasted. (If using skillet, place a heavy saucepan or skillet on top of sandwiches. Cook for 1 to 2 minutes or until bottoms are toasted. Carefully remove saucepan or top skillet; it may be hot. Turn sandwiches; top again with the saucepan or skillet. Cook for 1 to 2 minutes more or until bread is toasted.)

Dried Tomato-Pepper Spread: In a small bowl combine ¼ cup dried tomatoes (not oil-packed) and 2 tablespoons boiling water. Cover and let stand for 5 minutes. Transfer undrained tomatoes to a food processor. Add ¼ cup roasted sweet red pepper; 1 tablespoon balsamic vinegar; ½ teaspoon snipped fresh oregano or ¼ teaspoon dried oregano, crushed; 1 clove garlic, minced; and dash black pepper. Cover and process until smooth. Makes ⅓ cup.

PER SERVING 238 calories; 2 g total fat (0 g sat. fat); 354 mg sodium; 35 g carbohydrate; 5 g fiber; 21 g protein

Chicken Salad Sandwiches ③⓪

MAKES 4 servings **START TO FINISH** 25 minutes

1 cup chopped cooked chicken breast (5 ounces)

⅓ cup chopped apple or finely chopped celery

1 hard-cooked egg, chopped

2 tablespoons plain low-fat yogurt

2 tablespoons light mayonnaise or salad dressing

⅛ teaspoon salt

⅛ teaspoon black pepper

8 slices whole wheat bread

4 leaf lettuce or romaine lettuce leaves

1 medium tomato, thinly sliced

½ of a small cucumber, thinly sliced (about ¾ cup)

① In a medium bowl stir together chicken, apple, and hard-cooked egg. Stir in yogurt, mayonnaise, salt, and pepper.*

② To assemble, line 4 of the bread slices with lettuce; top with tomato. Add cucumber, chicken mixture, and the remaining 4 bread slices. Cut each sandwich in half.

***Tip:** If desired, cover and chill the chicken mixture for up to 4 hours before using.

PER SERVING 248 calories; 7 g total fat (2 g sat. fat); 86 mg cholesterol; 447 mg sodium; 28 g carbohydrate; 5 g fiber; 18 g protein

Chicken Salad Sandwiches

Curried Chicken-Mango Wraps

MAKES 6 servings **MARINATE** 30 minutes **PREP** 25 minutes

12	ounces skinless, boneless chicken breast halves, cut into ¼-inch slices
1	tablespoon curry powder
1	teaspoon ground coriander
¼	teaspoon salt
¼	teaspoon black pepper
2	cups shredded romaine lettuce
1	cup watercress, tough stems removed
2	tablespoons lemon juice
2	teaspoons olive oil
1	tablespoon olive oil
1	cup thinly sliced red onion
1	cup chopped mango
6	7- to 8-inch whole wheat flour tortillas

① In a medium bowl combine chicken, curry powder, coriander, salt, and pepper. Cover and marinate in the refrigerator for 30 minutes.

② In a medium bowl combine lettuce and watercress. Drizzle with lemon juice and the 2 teaspoons oil; toss gently to coat.

③ In a large skillet heat the 1 tablespoon oil on medium heat. Add chicken and red onion; cook and stir for 4 to 6 minutes or until chicken is no longer pink. Add mango; cook and stir until heated through.

④ To assemble, divide lettuce mixture and chicken mixture among tortillas. Roll up tortillas.

PER SERVING 260 calories; 8 g total fat (2 g sat. fat); 33 mg cholesterol; 459 mg sodium; 23 g carbohydrate; 12 g fiber; 22 g protein

Curried Chicken-Mango Wraps

Chicken, Spinach, and Pear Pitas ③⓪

MAKES 6 servings **START TO FINISH** 30 minutes

12	ounces skinless, boneless chicken breast halves
1	tablespoon balsamic vinegar
3	large whole wheat pita bread rounds, halved crosswise
¼	cup light mayonnaise or salad dressing
1	ounce soft goat cheese (chèvre)
1	tablespoon fat-free milk
1	teaspoon balsamic vinegar
2	tablespoons thinly sliced green onion (1)
1½	cups fresh spinach leaves
1	small pear or apple, thinly sliced

① Brush both sides of chicken with some of the 1 tablespoon vinegar. For a charcoal grill, grill chicken on the rack of an uncovered grill directly over medium coals for 12 to 15 minutes or until no longer pink (170°F), turning once and brushing with the remainder of the 1 tablespoon vinegar halfway through grilling. (For a gas grill, preheat grill. Reduce heat to medium. Place chicken on grill rack over heat. Cover and grill as above.) Cut chicken into ½-inch slices.

② Meanwhile, wrap pita bread in foil. While chicken is grilling, add pita packet to grill. Grill about 8 minutes or until bread is warm, turning once halfway through grilling.

③ For sauce, in a small bowl use a fork to stir together mayonnaise, goat cheese, milk, and the 1 teaspoon vinegar. Stir in green onion.

④ To assemble, arrange spinach, pear, and chicken in pita bread halves. Spoon about 1 tablespoon of the sauce into each pita half.

PER SERVING 216 calories; 6 g total fat (2 g sat. fat); 39 mg cholesterol; 293 mg sodium; 24 g carbohydrate; 3 g fiber; 18 g protein

Broiling Directions: Preheat broiler. Brush chicken with vinegar as directed. Place chicken on the unheated rack of a broiler pan. Broil 4 to 5 inches from the heat for 12 to 15 minutes or until no longer pink (170°F), turning once and brushing with the remainder of the 1 tablespoon vinegar halfway through broiling. Heat pita bread according to package directions. Continue as directed.

Chicken, Spinach, and Pear Pitas

Italian Panko Fried Chicken

Chicken Tacos ⭐ 🕥

MAKES 6 servings **START TO FINISH** 30 minutes

Nonstick cooking spray
1 cup chopped onion (1 large)
1 clove garlic, minced
2 cups chopped cooked chicken (10 ounces)
1 8-ounce can tomato sauce
1 4-ounce can diced green chiles, drained
½ teaspoon chili powder (optional)
¼ teaspoon ground cumin (optional)
12 taco shells or 6- to 8-inch corn or flour tortillas, warmed*
2 cups shredded lettuce
½ cup chopped, seeded tomato (1 medium)
½ cup finely shredded reduced-fat cheddar cheese and/or Monterey Jack cheese (2 ounces)

① Coat a large skillet with cooking spray; heat skillet on medium heat. Add onion and garlic; cook about 5 minutes or until onion is tender, stirring occasionally.

② Stir in chicken, tomato sauce, green chiles, and, if desired, chili powder and cumin. Cook and stir until heated through.

③ Divide chicken mixture among taco shells or tortillas. Top with lettuce, tomato, and cheese. If using, roll up tortillas.

*Tip: To warm tortillas, stack and wrap the tortillas tightly in foil. Bake in a 350°F oven about 10 minutes or until heated through.

PER SERVING 279 calories; 12 g total fat (3 g sat. fat); 48 mg cholesterol; 434 mg sodium; 23 g carbohydrate; 3 g fiber; 19 g protein

Italian Panko Fried Chicken

MAKES 4 servings **PREP** 15 minutes **BAKE** 25 minutes **OVEN** 450°F

Nonstick cooking spray
3 egg whites
1 tablespoon Dijon mustard
1 cup seasoned panko (Japanese-style bread crumbs) or 1 cup plain panko mixed with 1 teaspoon dried Italian seasoning, crushed
¼ cup grated reduced-fat Parmesan cheese
½ cup all-purpose flour
4 skinless, boneless chicken breast halves (about 1½ pounds total)
¾ cup marinara sauce, heated

① Preheat oven to 450°F. Place a wire rack on a baking sheet and coat with cooking spray.

② In a shallow dish whisk together egg whites and mustard. In a second shallow dish stir together panko and cheese. Place flour in a third shallow dish. Dip chicken into flour, turning to coat evenly and shaking off excess flour. Dip chicken into egg mixture, then into panko mixture, turning to coat. Place on the prepared rack.

③ Bake for 15 minutes; turn chicken over. Bake about 10 minutes more or until chicken is no longer pink (170°F). If desired, set oven temperature to broil; broil chicken about 1 minute or until coating is light brown. Serve chicken with warm marinara sauce.

PER SERVING 392 calories; 7 g total fat (1 g sat. fat); 106 mg cholesterol; 937 mg sodium; 31 g carbohydrate; 2 g fiber; 49 g protein

Crisp, juicy, oven-fried chicken is good for body and soul.

Crisp Chicken Parmesan

MAKES 4 servings **PREP** 25 minutes **BAKE** 15 minutes
OVEN 425°F

Olive oil nonstick cooking spray

¼ cup refrigerated or frozen egg product, thawed, or 2 egg whites, lightly beaten

1 tablespoon water

1 clove garlic, minced

1 cup bran cereal flakes, crushed (about ½ cup crushed)

¼ cup grated Parmesan cheese

1 teaspoon dried Italian seasoning, crushed

1 pound chicken breast tenderloins

4 ounces dried multigrain or whole grain spaghetti

1 cup eggplant peeled (if desired) and cut into 1-inch pieces

1½ cups light tomato-basil pasta sauce

1 cup torn fresh spinach leaves

½ cup chopped plum tomatoes

Fresh basil leaves (optional)

① Preheat oven to 425°F. Line a 15 x 10 x 1-inch baking pan with foil; lightly coat foil with cooking spray. Set pan aside. In a shallow dish combine egg, the water, and garlic. In another shallow dish combine crushed bran flakes, cheese, and Italian seasoning.

② Dip chicken into egg mixture, turning to coat evenly and allowing excess to drip off. Dip chicken into bran mixture, turning to coat. Place chicken in the prepared baking pan. Coat tops of chicken pieces with cooking spray. Bake for 15 to 20 minutes or until chicken is no longer pink (170°F).

③ Meanwhile, cook spaghetti according to package directions; drain. Return to hot pan; cover and keep warm. For sauce, coat a medium saucepan with cooking spray; heat saucepan on medium heat. Add eggplant; cook about 5 minutes or until tender, stirring occasionally. Add pasta sauce; heat through. Stir in spinach and tomatoes.

④ To serve, divide hot cooked spaghetti among 4 dinner plates. Top with sauce and chicken. If desired, garnish with basil.

PER SERVING 336 calories; 4 g total fat (1 g sat. fat); 70 mg cholesterol; 532 mg sodium; 38 g carbohydrate; 6 g fiber; 38 g protein

Chicken Taco Casserole ✪

MAKES 6 servings **PREP** 25 minutes **BAKE** 30 minutes
STAND 5 minutes **OVEN** 350°F

12 ounces packaged chicken breast stir-fry strips

2 cloves garlic, minced

1 teaspoon chili powder

Nonstick cooking spray

2 teaspoons canola oil

¾ cup chopped sweet red or green pepper (1 medium)

1 medium onion, halved and thinly sliced

1 10-ounce package frozen chopped spinach, thawed and squeezed dry

1½ cups salsa

4 6-inch corn tortillas, coarsely torn

¾ cup shredded reduced-fat Monterey Jack cheese (3 ounces)

½ cup cherry tomatoes, chopped (optional)

½ of an avocado, seeded, peeled, and chopped (optional)

Fresh cilantro leaves (optional)

① Preheat oven to 350°F. In a medium bowl toss together chicken, garlic, and chili powder. Coat a large nonstick skillet with cooking spray; heat skillet on medium-high heat. Add chicken. Cook and stir for 4 to 6 minutes or until chicken is no longer pink. Remove chicken from skillet; set aside.

② Pour oil into skillet. Add sweet pepper and onion. Cook on medium heat about 5 minutes or until tender, stirring occasionally. Stir in spinach.

③ Coat a 2-quart square baking dish with cooking spray. Spread about ½ cup of the salsa in the prepared baking dish. Top with half of the tortillas, half of the chicken mixture, and half of the spinach mixture. Pour half of the remaining salsa over spinach mixture and top with half of the cheese. Repeat layers once, except do not top with the remaining cheese.

④ Bake, covered, for 30 to 35 minutes or until heated through. Sprinkle with the remaining cheese. Let stand for 5 minutes before serving. If desired, garnish with tomatoes, avocado, and cilantro.

PER SERVING 196 calories; 6 g total fat (2 g sat. fat); 43 mg cholesterol; 544 mg sodium; 15 g carbohydrate; 4 g fiber; 20 g protein

Poached Chicken Salad

Mexican Chicken Salad ③⓪

MAKES 4 servings **START TO FINISH** 30 minutes

- 4 skinless, boneless chicken breast halves (1 to 1¼ pounds total)
- 1 teaspoon ground ancho chile or chili powder
- ½ teaspoon dried oregano, crushed
- ½ teaspoon dried thyme, crushed
- ⅛ teaspoon salt
- ⅛ teaspoon black pepper
- 2 tablespoons orange juice
- 1 tablespoon olive oil
- 1 tablespoon white wine vinegar
- 1 teaspoon honey
- 4 cups shredded romaine lettuce
- 2 oranges, peeled and sectioned
- 1 avocado, seeded, peeled, and sliced
- ¼ cup crumbled queso fresco or shredded reduced-fat Monterey Jack cheese (1 ounce)

① Preheat broiler. Place each chicken breast half between 2 pieces of plastic wrap. Using the flat side of a meat mallet, pound chicken lightly until about ½ inch thick. Remove plastic wrap.

② In a small bowl stir together ground chile, oregano, thyme, salt, and black pepper. Sprinkle mixture evenly over chicken; rub in with your fingers.

③ Place chicken on the unheated rack of a broiler pan. Broil 4 to 5 inches from the heat for 6 to 8 minutes or until chicken is no longer pink (170°F), turning once halfway through broiling. Slice chicken.

④ Meanwhile, in a medium bowl whisk together orange juice, oil, vinegar, and honey. Add lettuce; toss gently to coat.

⑤ To serve, divide lettuce mixture among 4 dinner plates. Top with chicken, oranges, and avocado. Sprinkle with cheese.

PER SERVING 306 calories; 13 g total fat (3 g sat. fat); 68 mg cholesterol; 153 mg sodium; 18 g carbohydrate; 7 g fiber; 30 g protein

Poached Chicken Salad ③⓪

MAKES 4 servings **START TO FINISH** 30 minutes

- 1 lemon
- 1 pound skinless, boneless chicken breast halves, cut into 2-inch pieces
- 1 cup chicken broth
- 4 cloves garlic, minced
- 1 teaspoon dried oregano, crushed
- 1 seedless cucumber
- 1 5-ounce container honey-flavored Greek yogurt
- 4 tomatoes, sliced
   Salt
   Black pepper
   Fresh oregano sprigs (optional)

① Finely shred peel from lemon; squeeze juice from lemon. In a medium saucepan combine lemon peel, lemon juice, chicken, broth, garlic, and dried oregano. Bring to boiling on medium-high heat; reduce heat. Simmer, covered, about 10 minutes or until chicken is no longer pink (170°F). Drain, reserving ⅓ cup of the cooking liquid.

② Meanwhile, chop half of the cucumber; slice the remaining cucumber. For dressing, in a medium bowl whisk together yogurt and the reserved cooking liquid. Remove half of the dressing; set aside. Add chicken and chopped cucumber to the remaining dressing; toss gently to coat.

③ To assemble, layer tomatoes and sliced cucumber on 4 dinner plates. Top with chicken mixture. Drizzle with some of the reserved dressing. Season to taste with salt and pepper. If desired, garnish with fresh oregano. Pass the remaining reserved dressing.

PER SERVING 196 calories; 3 g total fat (1 g sat. fat); 68 mg cholesterol; 480 mg sodium; 13 g carbohydrate; 3 g fiber; 32 g protein

Because poaching is a cooking method that requires no fat—just liquid such as broth, water, or wine—dishes cooked this way are usually lean. Poached Chicken Salad, for example, has just 3 grams of fat and 196 calories per serving—certainly healthful enough that you can also enjoy a little bread with dinner.

Chicken, Pear, and Parmesan Salad ㉚

MAKES 4 servings   **START TO FINISH** 25 minutes

- 2   tablespoons cider vinegar or white wine vinegar
- 2   tablespoons olive oil or canola oil
- 1   tablespoon honey
- ¼   teaspoon salt
- ¼   teaspoon black pepper
- 5   cups torn fresh spinach leaves
- 2   cups shredded or chopped cooked chicken breast (10 ounces)
- 2   pears cored and thinly sliced
- ½   of a small red onion, thinly sliced
- ¼   cup dried cranberries or raisins
- ¼   cup shaved Parmesan cheese (1 ounce)

① For dressing, in a small screw-top jar combine vinegar, oil, honey, salt, and pepper. Cover and shake well.

② In a large salad bowl combine spinach, chicken, pears, onion, and cranberries. Shake dressing. Drizzle dressing over spinach mixture; toss gently to coat. Top with cheese.

PER SERVING 306 calories; 11 g total fat (3 g sat. fat); 64 mg cholesterol; 343 mg sodium; 26 g carbohydrate; 4 g fiber; 26 g protein

Chicken and Portobellos with Mustard Cream

Chicken and Portobellos with Mustard Cream

MAKES 6 servings   **PREP** 15 minutes
COOK 5 to 6 hours (low) or 2½ to 3 hours (high)

- 3   fresh portobello mushroom caps, sliced
- 2   cloves garlic, minced
- 3½ to 4 pounds meaty chicken pieces (breast halves, thighs, and drumsticks), skinned
- 2   teaspoons dried rosemary, crushed
- ½   teaspoon salt
- ¼   teaspoon black pepper
- ¼   cup reduced-sodium chicken broth
- ¼   cup dry white wine
- 2   cups shredded romaine lettuce
- ½   cup light sour cream
- 1   tablespoon country Dijon mustard
     Fresh rosemary sprigs (optional)

① In a 4- to 5-quart slow cooker combine mushrooms and garlic. Sprinkle chicken with dried rosemary, salt, and pepper. Place chicken in cooker. Pour broth and wine over chicken.

② Cover and cook on low-heat setting for 5 to 6 hours or on high-heat setting for 2½ to 3 hours.

③ Using a slotted spoon, remove chicken and mushrooms from cooker; discard cooking liquid. Using 2 forks, pull chicken apart into shreds. Line a serving platter with lettuce; top with shredded chicken and mushrooms.

④ For mustard cream, in a small bowl combine sour cream and mustard. Serve chicken and mushrooms with mustard cream. If desired, garnish with fresh rosemary.

PER SERVING 209 calories; 7 g total fat (2 g sat. fat); 96 mg cholesterol; 393 mg sodium; 4 g carbohydrate; 1 g fiber; 31 g protein

If you don't like the stems on spinach leaves and don't want to spend the time destemming them, buy baby spinach. The stems are so tender—if they're present at all—they're not the least bit bothersome.

Mustard Crisp Chicken

Mustard Crisp Chicken

MAKES 6 servings **PREP** 20 minutes
MARINATE 2 to 24 hours **BAKE** 40 minutes
OVEN 375°F

- ¼   cup Dijon mustard
- 2   tablespoons water
- 2   teaspoons snipped fresh thyme or ¾ teaspoon dried thyme, crushed
- 1   clove garlic, minced
- ¼   teaspoon paprika
- ¼   teaspoon black pepper
- ¾   cup fine dry bread crumbs
- 2½ to 2¾ pounds meaty chicken pieces (breast halves, thighs, and drumsticks), skinned
- 2   tablespoons butter, melted

① Line a 15 x 10 x 1-inch baking pan with foil; set aside. In a medium bowl combine mustard, the water, thyme, garlic, paprika, and pepper. Place bread crumbs in a shallow dish.

② Dip chicken into mustard mixture, turning to coat evenly and allowing excess to drip off. Dip chicken into bread crumbs, turning to coat.

③ Arrange chicken in the prepared baking pan so the pieces do not touch. Cover tightly with plastic wrap. Marinate in the refrigerator for 2 to 24 hours.

④ Preheat oven to 375°F. Drizzle chicken with melted butter. Bake for 40 to 50 minutes or until chicken is no longer pink (170°F for breasts; 180°F for thighs and drumsticks) and coating is golden brown. Do not turn during baking.

PER SERVING 258 calories; 11 g total fat (4 g sat. fat); 87 mg cholesterol; 387 mg sodium; 10 g carbohydrate; 1 g fiber; 27 g protein

Mustard Crisp Chicken is an ideal dish for casual entertaining or to take to a potluck. Make it up to 24 hours ahead, to marinate in the refrigerator—then just bake it until hot and crispy.

Kalamata Lemon Chicken

MAKES 4 servings **PREP** 15 minutes **BAKE** 35 minutes
OVEN 400°F

- 1   to 1¼ pounds skinless, boneless chicken thighs
- 1   tablespoon olive oil
- 1   14-ounce can reduced-sodium chicken broth
- ⅔   cup dried orzo pasta (rosamarina)
- ½   cup pitted kalamata olives
- ½   of a lemon, cut into wedges or chunks
- 1   tablespoon lemon juice
- 1   teaspoon dried Greek seasoning
- ¼   teaspoon black pepper
     Reduced-sodium chicken broth, heated (optional)
     Snipped fresh oregano (optional)

① Preheat oven to 400°F. In a 4-quart oven-going Dutch oven cook chicken in hot oil on medium-high heat about 5 minutes or until brown on all sides. Drain off fat. Stir in the can of broth, pasta, olives, lemon wedges, lemon juice, Greek seasoning, and pepper. Transfer to oven.

② Bake, covered, about 35 minutes or until chicken is no longer pink (180°F). Ladle into shallow bowls. If desired, serve with additional broth and garnish with oregano.

PER SERVING 304 calories; 10 g total fat (2 g sat. fat); 94 mg cholesterol; 523 mg sodium; 25 g carbohydrate; 2 g fiber; 27 g protein

Kalamata Lemon Chicken

Golden Grilled Chicken Thighs with Apricots

MAKES 4 servings **PREP** 25 minutes
MARINATE 2 to 4 hours **GRILL** 12 minutes

1	pound skinless, boneless chicken thighs
	Salt
	Black pepper
½	cup apricot nectar
6	tablespoons apricot preserves
¼	cup snipped fresh mint
1	tablespoon olive oil
1	tablespoon sherry vinegar
1	clove garlic, minced
½	teaspoon curry powder
4	medium apricots, halved
¼	cup chopped green onions (2)
¼	cup chopped pistachio nuts
1	tablespoon Dijon mustard
1	teaspoon olive oil
½	teaspoon mustard seeds
¼	teaspoon salt

① Sprinkle chicken with salt and pepper. Place chicken in a large resealable plastic bag set in a shallow dish. For marinade, in a small bowl combine ¼ cup of the nectar, 2 tablespoons of the preserves, half of the mint, the 1 tablespoon oil, vinegar, garlic, and curry powder. Pour marinade over chicken. Seal bag; turn to coat chicken. Marinate in the refrigerator for 2 to 4 hours.

② Drain chicken, discarding marinade. For a charcoal grill, grill chicken on the rack of an uncovered grill directly over medium coals for 12 to 15 minutes or until chicken is no longer pink (180°F), turning once halfway through grilling. (For a gas grill, preheat grill. Reduce heat to medium. Place chicken on grill rack over heat. Cover and grill as above.) While chicken is grilling, add apricots, cut sides down, to grill. Grill about 5 minutes or until lightly browned.

③ For sauce, in a bowl combine the remaining ¼ cup nectar, the remaining 4 tablespoons preserves, the remaining mint, green onions, 3 tablespoons of the pistachios, the mustard, the 1 teaspoon oil, mustard seeds, and the ¼ teaspoon salt.

④ Serve chicken with apricots and sauce. Sprinkle with the remaining 1 tablespoon pistachios.

PER SERVING 348 calories; 13 g total fat (2 g sat. fat); 94 mg cholesterol; 504 mg sodium; 33 g carbohydrate; 2 g fiber; 25 g protein

Chicken with Broccoli and Garlic

MAKES 4 servings **START TO FINISH** 35 minutes

¼	cup all-purpose flour
¼	teaspoon salt
¼	teaspoon black pepper
4	skinless, boneless chicken thighs (about 12 ounces)
1	tablespoon olive oil
1	bulb garlic, separated into cloves, peeled, and sliced (about ¼ cup)
1	cup reduced-sodium chicken broth
3	tablespoons white wine vinegar
2	tablespoons honey
1	16-ounce package shredded broccoli (broccoli slaw mix)
2	tablespoons coarsely chopped pecans

① In a large resealable plastic bag combine flour, salt, and pepper. Add chicken; seal bag. Shake to coat.

② In a large skillet heat oil on medium heat. Add chicken and cook for 10 to 12 minutes or until chicken is tender and no longer pink (180°F), turning once. Transfer chicken to a plate; cover and keep warm.

③ Add garlic to skillet. Cook and stir for 1 minute. Add broth, vinegar, and honey. Bring to boiling; reduce heat. Simmer, uncovered, for 5 minutes. Stir in shredded broccoli. Return to boiling; reduce heat. Cover and simmer for 8 to 10 minutes more or until broccoli is crisp-tender. Stir in pecans. Serve the broccoli mixture with the chicken.

PER SERVING 270 calories; 10 g total fat (2 g sat. fat); 68 mg cholesterol; 392 mg sodium; 24 g carbohydrate; 3 g fiber; 23 g protein

To efficiently and speedily peel garlic cloves: Place a single clove on a cutting board, then place the broad side of a chef's knife on the clove. Using your fist, rap firmly the knife blade. The peel should split, allowing it to be easily removed.

Cajun Turkey Sandwiches

menu

Italian-Style
Vegetables

Sliced cantaloupe

Italian Turkey
Sandwiches
[below]

Whole Wheat Carrot-
Raisin Cookies

Italian Turkey Sandwiches ✪ ③⓪

MAKES 4 servings **START TO FINISH** 20 minutes

2 turkey breast tenderloins (about 1 pound total)
⅓ cup fine dry bread crumbs
2 teaspoons dried Italian seasoning, crushed
2 teaspoons olive oil
3 tablespoons light mayonnaise or salad dressing
2 tablespoons snipped fresh basil
8 ½-inch slices Italian bread, toasted
   Fresh basil leaves (optional)
1 cup roasted sweet red and/or yellow pepper
   cut into thin strips

① Split turkey tenderloins in half horizontally. In a resealable plastic bag combine bread crumbs and Italian seasoning. Add turkey pieces, 1 at a time, shaking to coat.

② In a very large nonstick skillet heat oil on medium heat. Add turkey; cook about 10 minutes or until no longer pink (170°F), turning once. In a small bowl stir together mayonnaise and the snipped basil.

③ To assemble, spread mayonnaise mixture on 1 side of bread slices. Layer 4 of the bread slices with basil leaves (if using) and turkey; top with roasted sweet pepper. Add the remaining 4 bread slices, spread sides down.

PER SERVING 384 calories; 9 g total fat (2 g sat. fat); 74 mg cholesterol; 522 mg sodium; 39 g carbohydrate; 3 g fiber; 35 g protein

Cajun Turkey Sandwiches ③⓪

MAKES 4 servings **START TO FINISH** 20 minutes

⅓ cup light mayonnaise or salad dressing
1 teaspoon purchased salt-free Cajun seasoning
   or Homemade Salt-Free Cajun Seasoning
1 clove garlic, minced
8 very thin slices firm-texture whole wheat
   bread, toasted if desired
1 cup fresh spinach leaves
8 ounces sliced, lower-sodium cooked turkey
   breast
4 tomato slices
1 small sweet green pepper or fresh poblano
   chile,* seeded and sliced

① In a small bowl stir together mayonnaise, Cajun seasoning, and garlic. Spread mixture on one side of bread slices.

② Top 4 of the bread slices with spinach. Layer with turkey, tomato, and sweet pepper. Top with the remaining 4 bread slices, spread sides down. Cut each sandwich in half.

Homemade Salt-Free Cajun Seasoning: In a small bowl stir together ¼ teaspoon white pepper, ¼ teaspoon garlic powder, ¼ teaspoon onion powder, ¼ teaspoon paprika, ¼ teaspoon black pepper, and ⅛ to ¼ teaspoon cayenne pepper.

*Tip: Because chiles contain volatile oils that can burn your skin and eyes, avoid direct contact with them as much as possible. When working with chiles, wear plastic or rubber gloves. If your bare hands do touch the peppers, wash your hands and fingernails well with soap and warm water.

PER SERVING 210 calories; 9 g total fat (1 g sat. fat); 37 mg cholesterol; 635 mg sodium; 19 g carbohydrate; 3 g fiber; 16 g protein

A slice of juicy, sweet cantaloupe is a nice accompaniment to any style of turkey sandwich—Italian, Cajun, or otherwise.

Citrus Turkey Spinach Salad 🕒

MAKES 4 servings **START TO FINISH** 25 minutes

- 8   cups fresh baby spinach or torn fresh spinach leaves
- 8   ounces cooked turkey, cut up
- 2   pink grapefruit, peeled and sectioned
- 2   oranges, peeled and sectioned
    Orange-Poppy Seed Dressing
- 2   tablespoons sliced almonds, toasted (optional)

① In a large bowl combine spinach, turkey, grapefruit sections, and orange sections.

② Shake Orange-Poppy Seed Dressing. Pour dressing over spinach mixture; toss gently to coat. If desired, sprinkle with almonds.

Orange-Poppy Seed Dressing: In a screw-top jar combine ¼ cup orange juice, 2 tablespoons olive oil, 1 teaspoon honey, ½ teaspoon poppy seeds, ¼ teaspoon salt, and ¼ teaspoon dry mustard. Cover and shake well.

PER SERVING 251 calories; 10 g total fat (2 g sat. fat); 43 mg cholesterol; 233 mg sodium; 22 g carbohydrate; 4 g fiber; 20 g protein

Creamy Turkey and Spinach Pie

Creamy Turkey and Spinach Pie

MAKES 8 servings **PREP** 35 minutes **BAKE** 40 minutes
STAND 10 minutes **OVEN** 350°F

    Nonstick cooking spray
- 4   ounces dried multigrain or plain angel hair pasta, broken
- 1   8-ounce package fat-free cream cheese, softened
- ¾   cup refrigerated or frozen egg product, thawed, or 3 eggs
- ½   cup light sour cream
- ¼   cup snipped fresh basil or 2 teaspoons dried basil, crushed
- ¼   teaspoon salt
- ¼   teaspoon garlic powder
- ¼   teaspoon crushed red pepper
- 2   cups chopped cooked turkey breast (10 ounces)*
- 1   10-ounce package frozen chopped spinach, thawed and well drained
- 1   cup shredded part-skim mozzarella cheese (4 ounces)
- ⅓   cup chopped roasted sweet red pepper

① Preheat oven to 350°F. Coat a 9-inch deep-dish pie plate or a 2-quart square baking dish with cooking spray; set aside. Cook pasta according to package directions; drain well.

② Meanwhile, in a large bowl beat cream cheese with an electric mixer on low to medium until smooth. Gradually beat in egg and sour cream. Stir in basil, salt, garlic powder, and crushed red pepper. Stir in cooked pasta, turkey, spinach, cheese, and roasted sweet pepper. Spread mixture in the prepared pie plate.

③ Bake for 40 to 45 minutes or until edge is slightly puffed and golden and center is heated through. Let stand for 10 minutes before serving. Cut into wedges or rectangles.

*Tip: To keep sodium in check, cook turkey breast tenderloin rather than using purchased cooked turkey breast. To cook turkey tenderloin, in a skillet bring water to boiling. Cut 1 turkey breast tenderloin in half lengthwise and add to skillet. Return to boiling; reduce heat. Simmer, covered, for 10 to 12 minutes or until no longer pink (170°F). Drain, cool slightly, and chop. Makes about 2 cups.

PER SERVING 207 calories; 4 g total fat (2 g sat. fat); 46 mg cholesterol; 488 mg sodium; 15 g carbohydrate; 2 g fiber; 25 g protein

Greek Style Turkey Burgers

Greek-Style Turkey Burgers

MAKES 4 servings **PREP** 25 minutes **GRILL** 12 minutes

- 1 egg white, lightly beaten
- ⅓ cup fine dry whole wheat bread crumbs*
- ⅓ cup crumbled reduced-fat feta cheese
- 1 tablespoon plain low-fat yogurt
- 1 teaspoon snipped fresh rosemary or ½ teaspoon dried rosemary, crushed
- 1 teaspoon snipped fresh oregano or ½ teaspoon dried oregano, crushed
- ⅛ teaspoon black pepper
- 1 pound uncooked ground turkey breast or chicken breast
   Torn mixed salad greens (optional)
   Olive-Tomato Salsa
   Plain low-fat yogurt (optional)
- 2 large whole wheat pita bread rounds, halved crosswise and lightly toasted

① In a medium bowl combine egg white, bread crumbs, 1 tablespoon of the cheese, the 1 tablespoon yogurt, rosemary, oregano, and pepper. Add ground turkey; mix well. Shape turkey mixture into four ¾-inch-thick patties.

② For a charcoal grill, grill patties on the greased rack of an uncovered grill directly over medium coals for 12 to 14 minutes or until no longer pink (165°F), turning once halfway through grilling. (For a gas grill, preheat grill. Reduce heat to medium. Place patties on greased grill rack over heat. Cover and grill as above.)

③ If desired, divide salad greens among 4 dinner plates. Top with burgers and Olive-Tomato Salsa. Sprinkle with the remaining cheese and, if desired, top with additional yogurt. Serve with pita bread.

Olive-Tomato Salsa: In a small bowl stir together 1 cup chopped, seeded tomatoes; ¼ cup chopped, seeded cucumber; ¼ cup chopped pitted kalamata or other ripe olives; ½ teaspoon snipped fresh rosemary or ¼ teaspoon dried rosemary, crushed; and ½ teaspoon snipped fresh oregano or ¼ teaspoon dried oregano, crushed. Makes about 1½ cups.

*Tip: For fine dry whole wheat bread crumbs, place 1 slice whole wheat bread, toasted, in a food processor. Cover and process until fine crumbs form. Measure ⅓ cup.

PER SERVING 265 calories; 5 g total fat (1 g sat. fat); 59 mg cholesterol; 523 mg sodium; 22 g carbohydrate; 4 g fiber; 33 g protein

Turkey and Spinach Manicotti

MAKES 14 servings **PREP** 20 minutes **COOK** 28 minutes **STAND** 10 minutes

- 1¼ pounds uncooked ground turkey
- 1 10-ounce package frozen chopped spinach, thawed and squeezed dry
- ¼ cup pine nuts
- 1 teaspoon dried Italian seasoning, crushed
- ½ teaspoon salt
- ¼ teaspoon black pepper
- 1 26-ounce jar chunky pasta sauce
- 14 dried manicotti shells
- 1 14-ounce can chicken broth
- 1 cup shredded reduced-fat mozzarella cheese (4 ounces)
   Grated Parmesan cheese (optional)

① In a large bowl combine ground turkey, spinach, pine nuts, Italian seasoning, salt, and pepper. Spread ½ cup of the pasta sauce in a 10-inch square microwave-safe dish. Fill the uncooked manicotti shells with turkey mixture and place in the dish.

② Pour broth and the remaining pasta sauce evenly over filled manicotti shells. Gently press shells into liquid. Cover with microwave-safe plastic wrap; vent 1 corner. Microwave on high for 25 minutes.

③ Sprinkle with mozzarella cheese. Microwave, uncovered, on high for 3 minutes more. Let stand for 10 minutes before serving. If desired, sprinkle with Parmesan cheese.

PER SERVING 236 calories; 9 g total fat (2 g sat. fat); 37 mg cholesterol; 579 mg sodium; 24 g carbohydrate; 2 g fiber; 14 g protein

Turkey and Spinach Manicotti

Pepper-Stuffed Burgers, page 120

Marvelous Meats

All-American Classic Meat Loaf, 120

Bagel Beef Sandwiches, 115

Beef and Black Bean Wraps, 123

Beef Sirloin Tips with Smoky Pepper Sauce, 116

Braised Sour Cream and Fennel Pork
   Tenderloins, 135

Caramelized Pork with Melon, 135

Cherry-Kissed Tacos with Feta Cheese Salsa, 132

Chops and Pineapple with Chili Slaw, 144

Dijon-Pepper Steak, 104

Eight-Layer Casserole, 124

Flank Steak with Mushrooms, 104

Floribbean Ribs with Mango Mojo, 152

Garden Pizza, 131

Gold Medal Moussaka, 123

Grilled Beef and Avocado Pitas, 111

Grilled Beef Tenderloin with Mediterranean
   Relish, 119

Grilled Filet Mignon with Portobello Relish, 116

Grilled Garden Burgers, 128

Grilled Marinated Flank Steak, 107

Honey-Lime Lamb and Melon Kabobs, 132

Indian Spiced Pork and Pineapple Kabobs, 136

Lemon-Sage Pork Taco Salad, 139

Mediterranean Beef Salad with Lemon
   Vinaigrette, 119

Mexican Ground Beef and Noodles, 124

Orange and Rosemary Pork Chops, 151

Oven Cassoulet, 152

Pan-Fried Garlic Steaks, 108

Pepper-Stuffed Burgers, 120

Pork Chops and Cherries, 147

Pork Chops and Squash, 144

Pork Chops Pizziola, 147

Pork Chops Primavera, 148

Pork Chops with Hot Pineapple Salsa, 148

Pork Chops with Sweet Onion Sauce, 151

Pork Kabobs with Onion Cakes
   and Peanut Sauce, 140

Pork Tenderloin with
   Cucumber-Mango Salad, 140

Pork Tenderloin with Green Olive
   Tapenade, 136

Salsa Beef Sandwiches, 127

Smoky-Sweet Pork, 143

Southwestern Noodle Bowl, 112

Southwestern Skirt Steak, 108

Spiced Bulgur with Beef and Mango, 127

Stuffed Spuds, 115

Sweet and Spicy Edamame-Beef Stir-Fry, 112

Taco Pizza, 131

Tenderloin Steaks with Merlot Sauce, 111

Whiskey Burgers, 128

Zucchini-Wrapped Pork, 143

Dijon-Pepper Steak

MAKES 6 servings **PREP** 20 minutes
COOK 7 to 8 hours (low) or 3½ to 4 hours (high)

- 2 pounds boneless beef sirloin steak, cut 1 inch thick
- 1 to 1½ teaspoons cracked black pepper
- 1 tablespoon vegetable oil
- 2 cups packaged peeled fresh baby carrots
- 1 medium onion, sliced
- 1 10.75-ounce can reduced-fat and reduced-sodium condensed cream of celery soup
- 2 tablespoons Dijon mustard
- 3 cups hot cooked multigrain penne pasta (optional)

  Snipped fresh parsley (optional)

① Trim fat from meat. Cut meat into 6 serving-size pieces. Sprinkle meat with pepper; press in with your fingers. In a large skillet brown meat, half at a time, in hot oil on medium-high heat until brown on both sides. Drain off fat.

② In a 3½- or 4-quart slow cooker combine carrots and onion. Add meat. In a medium bowl stir together soup and mustard. Pour soup mixture over meat.

③ Cover and cook on low-heat setting for 7 to 8 hours or on high-heat setting for 3½ to 4 hours. If desired, use a fork to slightly break up meat. If desired, serve meat mixture over hot cooked pasta and garnish with parsley.

PER SERVING 275 calories; 9 g total fat (3 g sat. fat); 65 mg cholesterol; 410 mg sodium; 10 g carbohydrate; 1 g fiber; 34 g protein

Dijon-Pepper Steak

Flank Steak with Mushrooms

MAKES 6 servings **PREP** 25 minutes **MARINATE** 1 hour
BROIL 17 minutes

- 1½ pounds beef flank steak
- ¾ cup dry red wine
- 1 tablespoon sherry vinegar or red wine vinegar
- 1 tablespoon finely shredded orange peel
- ¼ teaspoon fennel seeds, crushed
- ¼ cup chopped shallots (2 medium)
- 2 cloves garlic, minced
- 1 tablespoon butter
- 3 cups sliced fresh cremini, oyster, and/or button mushrooms (8 ounces)
- 1 tablespoon cornstarch
- ¾ cup beef broth

  Salt

  Black pepper

① Trim fat from meat. Score both sides of meat in a diamond pattern by making shallow diagonal cuts at 1-inch intervals. Place meat in a resealable plastic bag set in a shallow dish. For marinade, in a small bowl combine wine, vinegar, orange peel, and fennel seeds. Pour marinade over meat. Seal bag; turn to coat meat. Marinate in the refrigerator for 1 hour, turning bag occasionally. Drain meat, reserving ⅓ cup of the marinade.

② Preheat broiler. Place meat on the unheated rack of a broiler pan. Broil 3 to 4 inches from the heat for 17 to 21 minutes for medium (160°F), turning once halfway through broiling.

③ Meanwhile, for mushroom sauce, in a medium saucepan cook shallots and garlic in hot butter on medium heat for 2 minutes, stirring occasionally. Add mushrooms; cook and stir until tender. In a small bowl combine the reserved marinade and cornstarch; stir into mushroom mixture. Add broth. Cook and stir until thickened and bubbly. Cook and stir for 2 minutes more. Season to taste with salt and pepper.

④ To serve, thinly slice meat diagonally across the grain. Serve with mushroom sauce.

PER SERVING 240 calories; 9 g total fat (4 g sat. fat); 53 mg cholesterol; 291 mg sodium; 6 g carbohydrate; 1 g fiber; 27 g protein

Flank Steak
with Mushrooms

Grilled Marinated Flank Steak

menu

Guacamole and chips

Spinach Salad with
Dijon Vinaigrette

Grilled Marinated
Flank Steak
[below]

Apple Cake

Iced green tea

Grilled Marinated Flank Steak

MAKES 4 servings **PREP** 30 minutes **MARINATE** 30 minutes
GRILL 17 minutes

12	ounces beef flank steak
3	tablespoons red wine vinegar
1	tablespoon snipped fresh cilantro
1	tablespoon Dijon mustard
1	large clove garlic, minced
⅛	teaspoon crushed red pepper
4	8-inch whole wheat flour tortillas
	Shredded lettuce
½	cup Sweet Pepper Salsa, Artichoke-Bean Spread, and/or Quick Steak Sauce

① Trim fat from meat. Score both sides of meat in a diamond pattern by making shallow diagonal cuts at 1-inch intervals. Place meat in a resealable plastic bag set in a shallow dish. For marinade, in a small bowl combine vinegar, cilantro, mustard, garlic, and crushed red pepper. Pour marinade over meat. Seal bag; turn to coat meat. Marinate in the refrigerator for 30 minutes, turning bag once. Drain meat, discarding marinade.

② For a charcoal grill, grill meat on the rack of an uncovered grill directly over medium coals for 17 to 21 minutes for medium (160°F), turning once halfway through grilling. (For a gas grill, preheat grill. Reduce heat to medium. Place meat on grill rack over heat. Cover and grill as above.) Thinly slice meat diagonally across the grain.

③ Serve meat in tortillas with lettuce and Sweet Pepper Salsa, Artichoke-Bean Spread, and/or Quick Steak Sauce.

Sweet Pepper Salsa: In a medium bowl toss together 1½ cups finely chopped sweet green and/or yellow peppers (2 medium); ½ cup finely chopped, peeled jicama; ¼ cup finely chopped red onion; 2 tablespoons snipped fresh cilantro; 1 tablespoon red wine vinegar; 1 serrano chile, seeded and chopped;* and ¼ teaspoon salt. Cover and chill. Makes about 2½ cups.

*Tip: Because chiles contain volatile oils that can burn your skin and eyes, avoid direct contact with them as much as possible. When working with chiles, wear plastic or rubber gloves. If your bare hands do touch the peppers, wash your hands and fingernails well with soap and warm water.

PER SERVING 290 calories; 9 g total fat (3 g sat. fat); 28 mg cholesterol; 509 mg sodium; 22 g carbohydrate; 11 g fiber; 27 g protein

Artichoke-Bean Spread: Drain one 6-ounce jar marinated artichoke hearts, reserving marinade. Coarsely chop artichokes; set aside. In a food processor combine the reserved marinade; one 15-ounce can garbanzo beans (chickpeas), rinsed and drained; 2 tablespoons thinly sliced green onion (1); 1 tablespoon finely shredded lemon peel; ⅛ teaspoon salt; and ⅛ teaspoon black pepper. Cover and process until smooth. Stir in artichokes. Transfer to a medium bowl. Cover and chill. Makes about 2 cups.

Quick Steak Sauce: In a blender combine ¼ cup red wine vinegar, ¼ cup chopped onion, ¼ cup raisins, 2 tablespoons tomato paste, 1 tablespoon packed brown sugar, 1 tablespoon molasses, 1 tablespoon reduced-sodium soy sauce, and ¼ teaspoon black pepper. Cover and blend until nearly smooth. Transfer to a small bowl. Cover and chill. Makes about ¾ cup.

The recipes for each of these sauces—Sweet Pepper Salsa, Artichoke-Bean Spread, and Quick Steak Sauce—yield more than you need for just 12 ounces of steak. Use the leftover sauce with grilled chicken or to add zip to a sandwich.

Pan-Fried Garlic Steaks ⏱

MAKES 4 servings **START TO FINISH** 30 minutes

- 4 boneless beef ribeye steaks, cut ¾ inch thick (1 to 1¼ pounds total)
  Olive oil
  Salt
  Black pepper
- 6 cloves garlic, thinly sliced
- 1 15- to 19-ounce can cannellini beans (white kidney beans), rinsed and drained
- 2 tablespoons butter
- ¼ cup snipped fresh parsley

① Trim fat from steaks. Drizzle steaks lightly with oil; sprinkle with salt and pepper.

② Heat a very large heavy skillet on medium-high heat. Add steaks; reduce heat to medium. Cook for 6 to 8 minutes for medium-rare (145°F) to medium (160°F), turning once. Remove steaks from skillet; cover and keep warm.

③ Add garlic to drippings in skillet. Cook and stir about 1 minute or until softened. Remove garlic and spoon over steaks. Add beans and butter to skillet; heat through. Add parsley; cook and stir for 1 minute. Serve steaks with bean mixture.

PER SERVING 326 calories; 18 g total fat (6 g sat. fat); 81 mg cholesterol; 415 mg sodium; 16 g carbohydrate; 5 g fiber; 29 g protein

Pan-Fried Garlic Steaks

Southwestern Skirt Steak

MAKES 2 servings **PREP** 15 minutes **MARINATE** 1 to 4 hours **GRILL** 8 minutes

- 8 ounces beef skirt steak or flank steak
- ⅓ cup orange juice
- 2 tablespoons snipped fresh cilantro
- 2 tablespoons lime juice
- 1 teaspoon ground cumin
- 1 clove garlic, minced
- ¼ teaspoon salt
- ¼ teaspoon black pepper

① Trim fat from meat. Score both sides of meat in a diamond pattern by making shallow diagonal cuts at 1-inch intervals. Place meat in a resealable plastic bag set in a shallow dish. For marinade, in a small bowl combine orange juice, cilantro, lime juice, cumin, garlic, salt, and pepper. Pour marinade over meat. Seal bag; turn to coat meat. Marinate in the refrigerator for 1 to 4 hours, turning bag occasionally. Drain meat, discarding marinade.

② For a charcoal grill, grill meat on the rack of an uncovered grill directly over medium coals until desired doneness, turning once halfway through grilling. For skirt steak, allow 8 to 10 minutes or until slightly pink in center. For flank steak, allow 10 to 12 minutes for medium-rare (145°F) or 12 to 14 minutes for medium (160°F). (For a gas grill, preheat grill. Reduce heat to medium. Place meat on grill rack over heat. Cover and grill as above.)

③ To serve, thinly slice meat diagonally across the grain.

PER SERVING 196 calories; 9 g total fat (4 g sat. fat); 65 mg cholesterol; 222 mg sodium; 2 g carbohydrate; 0 g fiber; 24 g protein

Fresh-squeezed orange juice is more flavorful than bottled juice or juice made from concentrate. A medium orange yields about ⅓ cup of juice. To get the most juice from an orange (or lemon or lime), let it stand at room temperature for 30 minutes, then roll it gently on the countertop before juicing.

Southwestern Skirt Steak

Tenderloin Steaks with Merlot Sauce

menu

Italian-Style
Vegetables

Ciabatta rolls

Tenderloin Steaks
with Merlot Sauce
[below]

Tri-Color Sherbet

Lemon water

Tenderloin Steaks
with Merlot Sauce 30

MAKES 4 servings **START TO FINISH** 30 minutes

- 4   beef tenderloin steaks, cut 1 inch thick (1 to 1¼ pounds total)
- 1   to 2 teaspoons cracked black pepper
- 1   tablespoon olive oil
- ½   cup finely chopped onion (1 medium)
- 2   tablespoons finely chopped shallot (1 medium)
- 1   tablespoon snipped fresh thyme or 1 teaspoon dried thyme, crushed
- ½   cup Merlot or other dry red wine
- 2   tablespoons lower-sodium beef broth or water
- 1   tablespoon balsamic vinegar
- ⅛   teaspoon salt

① Trim fat from steaks. Sprinkle steaks with pepper; press in with your fingers. In a large skillet heat oil on medium heat. Add steaks. Cook for 10 to 13 minutes for medium-rare (145°F) to medium (160°F), turning once. Transfer steaks to a serving platter; cover and keep warm.

② For sauce, add onion, shallot, and dried thyme (if using) to drippings in skillet. Cook and stir for 4 to 6 minutes or until onion is tender. Carefully add Merlot and broth. Bring to boiling; reduce heat. Boil gently, uncovered, for 3 to 5 minutes or until mixture is reduced by about half. Stir in vinegar, salt, and fresh thyme (if using). Serve steaks with sauce.

PER SERVING 249 calories; 12 g total fat (4 g sat. fat); 70 mg cholesterol; 142 mg sodium; 5 g carbohydrate; 1 g fiber; 24 g protein

Grilled Beef and Avocado Pitas

MAKES 6 servings **PREP** 20 minutes **MARINATE** 24 hours
GRILL 17 minutes

- 12   ounces beef flank steak
- ½   cup bottled reduced-calorie Italian vinaigrette salad dressing
- ½   teaspoon finely shredded lime peel
- ¼   cup lime juice
- 2   tablespoons snipped fresh cilantro
- ¼   cup finely chopped onion
- ¼   teaspoon salt
- ¼   teaspoon black pepper
- 4   cups spring baby salad greens
- 1   cup sweet red pepper cut into thin bite-size strips (1 medium)
- 1   medium avocado, seeded, peeled, and thinly sliced
- 3   large whole wheat pita bread rounds, halved crosswise

① Trim fat from meat. Score both sides of meat in a diamond pattern by making shallow diagonal cuts at 1-inch intervals. Place meat in a resealable plastic bag set in a shallow dish.

② In a screw-top jar combine Italian dressing, lime peel, lime juice, and cilantro. Cover and shake well. Pour half of the dressing mixture into a small bowl and add onion; cover and chill until serving time. Pour the remaining dressing mixture over meat. Seal bag; turn to coat meat. Marinate in the refrigerator for 24 hours, turning bag occasionally.

③ Drain meat, discarding marinade. Sprinkle meat with salt and black pepper. For a charcoal grill, grill steak on the rack of an uncovered grill directly over medium coals for 17 to 21 minutes for medium (160°F), turning once halfway through grilling. (For a gas grill, preheat grill. Reduce heat to medium. Place steak on grill rack over heat. Cover and grill as above.)

④ To assemble, cut meat into thin bite-size strips. In a large bowl toss together meat, salad greens, sweet pepper, avocado, and the reserved dressing mixture. Fill pita halves with meat mixture.

Broiling Directions: Preheat broiler. Place meat on the unheated rack of a broiler pan. Broil 3 to 4 inches from the heat for 17 to 21 minutes for medium (160°F), turning once halfway through broiling.

PER SERVING 254 calories; 11 g total fat (3 g sat. fat); 23 mg cholesterol; 425 mg sodium; 24 g carbohydrate; 5 g fiber; 17 g protein

Southwestern Noodle Bowl ✪ ③⓪

MAKES 8 servings **START TO FINISH** 30 minutes

1½	pounds beef flank steak or boneless beef top round steak
1	teaspoon ground cumin
¼	teaspoon salt
⅛	teaspoon black pepper
2	tablespoons vegetable oil
2	cloves garlic, minced
2	14-ounce cans lower-sodium beef broth
1	14-ounce can reduced-sodium chicken broth
6	ounces dried angel hair pasta
1½	cups chopped sweet red or yellow peppers (2 medium)
6	green onions, trimmed and cut diagonally into 1-inch pieces
½	cup refrigerated hot-style salsa
¼	cup snipped fresh oregano
	Refrigerated hot-style salsa
	Garlic-pepper seasoning (optional)

① Trim fat from meat. Cut meat into thin bite-size strips. Sprinkle meat with cumin, salt, and black pepper; set aside.

② Pour 1 tablespoon of the oil into a wok or very large skillet; heat wok on medium-high heat. Add garlic; cook and stir for 15 seconds. Add half of the meat; cook and stir for 2 to 3 minutes or until slightly pink in center. Remove from wok. Repeat with the remaining 1 tablespoon oil and the remaining meat. Return all of the meat to wok.

③ Add beef and chicken broth to wok. Bring to boiling. Add pasta, sweet peppers, and green onions; return to boiling. Cook about 3 minutes or until pasta is tender, stirring occasionally. Stir in the ½ cup salsa and oregano; heat through.

④ Serve meat mixture in shallow bowls. If desired, swirl pasta into nests. Top with additional salsa and, if desired, sprinkle with garlic-pepper seasoning.

PER SERVING 260 calories; 9 g total fat (2 g sat. fat); 28 mg cholesterol; 616 mg sodium; 21 g carbohydrate; 2 g fiber; 24 g protein

Sweet and Spicy Edamame-Beef Stir-Fry ③⓪

MAKES 4 servings **START TO FINISH** 30 minutes

8	ounces boneless beef sirloin steak
3	tablespoons hoisin sauce
2	tablespoons rice vinegar
1	teaspoon red chile paste
4	teaspoons canola oil
2	teaspoons finely chopped fresh ginger
3	cups packaged fresh cut-up stir-fry vegetables
1	cup frozen shelled sweet soybeans (edamame)
1	8.8-ounce pouch cooked whole grain brown rice

① Trim fat from meat. Cut meat into thin bite-size strips; set aside. For sauce, in a small bowl combine hoisin sauce, vinegar, and chile paste. Set aside.

② Pour 2 teaspoons of the oil into a nonstick wok or skillet; heat wok on medium-high heat. Add ginger; cook and stir for 15 seconds. Add vegetables. Cook and stir about 4 minutes or until crisp-tender. Remove from wok.

③ Pour the remaining 2 teaspoons oil into wok. Add meat and soybeans; cook and stir for 2 to 3 minutes or until meat is slightly pink in center. Return vegetables to wok. Add sauce; stir all ingredients together to coat with sauce. Heat through.

④ Meanwhile, heat brown rice according to package directions. Serve meat mixture over rice.

PER SERVING 330 calories; 12 g total fat (2 g sat. fat); 24 mg cholesterol; 272 mg sodium; 34 g carbohydrate; 5 g fiber; 22 g protein

Edamame, or baby soybeans, have a sweet, nutty flavor and delightfully crunchy texture—plus they're powerfully nutritious. Soy contains isoflavones, which appears to protect against cancer, heart disease, and osteoporosis.

Stuffed Spuds

Stuffed Spuds 🕙

MAKES 4 servings **START TO FINISH** 30 minutes

4	large baking potatoes (about 2½ pounds)
12	ounces boneless beef shoulder top blade (flat-iron) steak, flank steak, or skirt steak
1	tablespoon vegetable oil
3	cups sliced fresh mushrooms (8 ounces)
2	cups broccoli florets
½	cup ginger stir-fry sauce
	Sliced sweet red peppers (optional)
	Chopped peanuts (optional)

① Arrange potatoes in a 2-quart microwave-safe dish. Microwave on high for 7 minutes. Turn potatoes; microwave for 8 minutes more. Let stand in microwave oven.

② Meanwhile, trim fat from meat. Cut meat into thin bite-size strips. In a very large skillet heat oil on medium-high heat. Add meat; cook and stir for 2 minutes. Add mushrooms and broccoli; cook and stir for 5 minutes. Add stir-fry sauce; stir all ingredients together to coat with sauce. Cook about 1 minute more or until heated through.

③ Carefully remove potatoes from microwave oven. Cut a lengthwise slit in the top of each potato. Press in and up on the ends. Serve meat mixture over potatoes. Drizzle with any remaining sauce. If desired, top with sweet peppers and peanuts.

PER SERVING 433 calories; 10 g total fat (2 g sat. fat); 51 mg cholesterol; 645 mg sodium; 60 g carbohydrate; 8 g fiber; 25 g protein

Bagel Beef Sandwiches 🕙

MAKES 4 servings **PREP** 20 minutes **BROIL** 12 minutes

¼	cup dried tomato (not oil-packed)
12	ounces boneless beef top sirloin steak, cut about ¾ inch thick
¼	teaspoon garlic salt
¼	teaspoon black pepper
½	cup chopped onion (1 medium)
2	tablespoons light mayonnaise
1	tablespoon yellow mustard
2	small whole wheat bagels, split and toasted (3 to 4 ounces total)
2	cups finely shredded romaine lettuce

① Preheat broiler. Place dried tomato in a small bowl; add enough water to cover. Microwave on high for 1 minute. Let stand for 15 minutes.

② Meanwhile, trim fat from meat. Sprinkle meat with garlic salt and pepper. Place meat on the unheated rack of a broiler pan. Broil 3 to 4 inches from the heat for 12 to 16 minutes for medium-rare (145°F), turning once halfway through broiling. Cut meat into thin bite-size strips.

③ Drain and finely chop tomato. In a small bowl combine tomato, onion, mayonnaise, and mustard. To assemble, divide meat among bagel halves. Top with lettuce and mayonnaise mixture.

PER SERVING 294 calories; 9 g total fat (2 g sat. fat); 38 mg cholesterol; 293 mg sodium; 28 g carbohydrate; 4 g fiber; 25 g protein

Beef is so flavorful, just a small amount of it—3 ounces or so—adds heft to these veggie-packed dishes.

Beef Sirloin Tips with Smoky Pepper Sauce ⊙ ⑳

MAKES 4 servings **START TO FINISH** 30 minutes

1½	pounds boneless beef bottom sirloin (tri-tip) steak
½	teaspoon smoked paprika or regular paprika
1	tablespoon vegetable oil
1	12- to 16-ounce jar roasted sweet red and/or yellow peppers
½	cup hickory- or mesquite-flavor barbecue sauce
¼	cup coarsely snipped fresh parsley

① Trim fat from meat. Cut meat into 1- to 1½-inch pieces; sprinkle with paprika. In a very large skillet cook meat in hot oil on medium-high heat until brown, stirring occasionally. Remove from skillet.

② Meanwhile, drain roasted sweet peppers, reserving liquid. Cut up peppers. Measure ½ cup of the reserved liquid (if necessary, add enough water to equal ½ cup).

③ Add roasted peppers and the reserved liquid to skillet. Stir in barbecue sauce. Cook, uncovered, for 5 to 10 minutes or until sauce is slightly thickened, stirring frequently. Return meat to skillet; heat through. Sprinkle with parsley.

PER SERVING 367 calories; 18 g total fat (6 g sat. fat); 111 mg cholesterol; 510 mg sodium; 13 g carbohydrate; 2 g fiber; 36 g protein

Grilled Filet Mignon with Portobello Relish

Grilled Filet Mignon with Portobello Relish

MAKES 4 servings **PREP** 25 minutes **GRILL** 15 minutes

4	beef tenderloin steaks, cut 1 inch thick (about 1¼ pounds total)
	Kosher salt
	Cracked black pepper
3	tablespoons snipped fresh basil
2	tablespoons olive oil
12	cloves garlic, minced
1	teaspoon kosher salt
1	teaspoon cracked black pepper
8	ounces fresh portobello mushrooms, stems removed
1	medium yellow onion, cut into ½-inch slices
4	plum tomatoes, halved lengthwise

① Trim fat from steaks. Sprinkle steaks with salt and pepper; set aside. For relish, in a medium bowl stir together basil, oil, garlic, the 1 teaspoon salt, and the 1 teaspoon pepper; set aside.

② For a charcoal grill, grill steaks, mushrooms, onion, and tomatoes on the rack of an uncovered grill directly over medium coals until steaks reach desired doneness and vegetables are tender, turning once halfway through grilling. For steaks, allow 10 to 12 minutes for medium-rare (145°F) or 12 to 15 minutes for medium (160°F). For vegetables, allow about 10 minutes for mushrooms and tomatoes and about 15 minutes for onion. (For a gas grill, preheat grill. Reduce heat to medium. Place steaks, mushrooms, onion, and tomatoes on grill rack over heat. Cover and grill as above.)

③ Cut grilled mushrooms, onion, and tomatoes into 1-inch pieces. Add vegetables to relish; toss gently to coat. Serve steaks with warm relish.

PER SERVING 329 calories; 18 g total fat (5 g sat. fat); 87 mg cholesterol; 617 mg sodium; 9 g carbohydrate; 2 g fiber; 33 g protein

Grilled Beef Tenderloin with Mediterranean Relish

Grilled Beef Tenderloin with Mediterranean Relish

MAKES 12 servings **PREP** 25 minutes **GRILL** 40 minutes
STAND 15 minutes

- 1 3- to 4-pound beef center-cut tenderloin roast
- 2 teaspoons dried oregano, crushed
- 2 teaspoons cracked black pepper
- 3 cloves garlic, minced
- 1½ teaspoons finely shredded lemon peel
- 2 Japanese eggplants, halved lengthwise, or 1 small eggplant, sliced
- 2 sweet red or yellow peppers, halved lengthwise and seeded
- 1 sweet onion (such as Vidalia or Walla Walla), cut into ½-inch slices
- 1 tablespoon olive oil
- ⅔ cup chopped plum tomatoes (2 medium)
- 2 tablespoons chopped pitted kalamata olives
- 2 tablespoons snipped fresh basil
- 1 tablespoon balsamic vinegar
- ⅛ teaspoon black pepper

① Trim fat from meat. For rub, in a small bowl stir together oregano, the cracked black pepper, 2 of the minced garlic cloves, the lemon peel, and ½ teaspoon *salt*. Sprinkle mixture evenly over meat; rub in with your fingers. Brush eggplants, sweet peppers, and onion with oil.

② For a charcoal grill, arrange hot coals around a drip pan. Test for medium-hot heat above pan. Place meat on grill rack over drip pan. Place vegetables around edge of grill rack directly over coals. Cover and grill for 10 to 12 minutes or until vegetables are tender, turning once halfway through grilling. Remove vegetables from grill. Cover and continue grilling meat for 30 to 40 minutes or until an instant-read thermometer inserted into meat registers 140°F. (For a gas grill, preheat grill. Reduce heat to medium-high. Adjust for indirect cooking. Grill as above.)

③ Remove meat from grill. Cover with foil; let stand for 15 minutes. Temperature of the meat after standing should be 145°F.

④ Meanwhile, for relish, coarsely chop grilled vegetables. In a medium bowl combine grilled vegetables, the remaining 1 minced garlic clove, tomatoes, olives, basil, vinegar, ¼ teaspoon *salt,* and the black pepper. Slice meat. Serve meat with relish.

PER SERVING 232 calories; 12 g total fat (4 g sat. fat); 70 mg cholesterol; 227 mg sodium; 6 g carbohydrate; 2 g fiber; 25 g protein

Mediterranean Beef Salad with Lemon Vinaigrette 🕥

MAKES 4 servings **START TO FINISH** 30 minutes

- 12 ounces boneless beef top sirloin steak, cut 1 inch thick
- ¼ teaspoon salt
- ⅛ teaspoon black pepper
- 4 cups torn romaine lettuce leaves
- 1 cup halved cherry or grape tomatoes
- ½ of a small red onion, thinly sliced and separated into rings
- ½ cup crumbled reduced-fat feta cheese (2 ounces)
  Lemon Vinaigrette

① Preheat broiler. Trim fat from meat. Sprinkle meat with salt and pepper. Place meat on the unheated rack of a broiler pan. Broil 3 to 4 inches from the heat for 15 to 17 minutes for medium-rare (145°F) or 20 to 22 minutes for medium (160°F), turning once halfway through broiling. Thinly slice meat.

② Divide lettuce among 4 dinner plates. Top with meat, tomatoes, and red onion; sprinkle with cheese. Drizzle salads with Lemon Vinaigrette.

Lemon Vinaigrette: In a screw-top jar combine 3 tablespoons olive oil; ½ teaspoon finely shredded lemon peel; 3 tablespoons lemon juice; 1 tablespoon snipped fresh oregano or 1 teaspoon dried oregano, crushed; 2 cloves garlic, minced; ⅛ teaspoon salt; and ⅛ teaspoon black pepper. Cover and shake well. Makes about ½ cup.

PER SERVING 256 calories; 16 g total fat (4 g sat. fat); 57 mg cholesterol; 502 mg sodium; 7 g carbohydrate; 2 g fiber; 23 g protein

Mediterranean Beef Salad with Lemon Vinaigrette

All-American Classic Meat Loaf ✪

MAKES 8 to 10 servings **PREP** 20 minutes **BAKE** 1½ hours **STAND** 25 minutes **OVEN** 350°F

- 2   eggs, lightly beaten
- ⅔   cup beef broth or dry red wine
- 1   tablespoon Worcestershire sauce
- 3   slices sourdough bread, cubed (about 2 cups)
- ¼   cup grated Parmesan or Romano cheese
- 2   tablespoons yellow mustard
- 4   cloves garlic, minced
- 1   teaspoon salt
- ½   teaspoon black pepper
- ¼   teaspoon crushed red pepper
- 1   pound ground beef sirloin
- 1   pound ground beef chuck
- ¾   cup chopped sweet green pepper (1 medium)
- ¼   cup chopped onion
- ½   cup ketchup
- 2   tablespoons packed brown sugar
- 2   teaspoons cider vinegar
-     Snipped fresh parsley, sliced green onions, and black pepper (optional)

①   Preheat oven to 350°F. In a large bowl combine eggs, broth, and Worcestershire sauce; stir in bread cubes. Let stand for 15 minutes. Using a fork, mash bread cubes into small pieces.

②   Stir cheese, mustard, garlic, salt, the ½ teaspoon black pepper, and the crushed red pepper into egg mixture. Add ground meats, sweet pepper, and onion; mix well (do not overmix). Lightly pat mixture into a 9 x 5 x 3-inch loaf pan.* (Or shape mixture into a 9 x 5-inch loaf in a shallow baking pan.) Bake for 1¼ hours.

③   For topping, in small bowl stir together ketchup, brown sugar, and vinegar. Spoon on top of loaf. Bake about 15 minutes more or until done (160°F). Let stand for 10 minutes.

④   Using 2 spatulas, transfer loaf to a serving platter. If desired, sprinkle with parsley, green onions, and additional black pepper.

*Tip: For even browning and to prevent drippings from pooling on the loaf, use your fingers to round the top while pushing the sides away from the edges of the pan.

PER SERVING 312 calories; 15 g total fat (6 g sat. fat); 113 mg cholesterol; 778 mg sodium; 16 g carbohydrate; 1 g fiber; 28 g protein

Pepper-Stuffed Burgers

MAKES 4 servings **PREP** 25 minutes **GRILL** 19 minutes

- 4   miniature sweet red, green, yellow, and/or orange peppers (about ½ ounce each)
- 1   ounce Monterey Jack cheese with jalapeños or reduced-fat Monterey Jack cheese, cut into 4 cubes
- 1   pound 90% or higher lean ground beef
- ½   teaspoon mesquite seasoning
- 4   whole grain or multigrain ciabatta rolls or hamburger buns, split and toasted
- ¼   cup green salsa (salsa verde) (optional)

①   Cut the tops off sweet peppers. Remove stems, seeds, and membranes. For a charcoal grill, grill peppers on the rack of an uncovered grill directly over medium coals for 5 to 7 minutes or just until pepper skins are lightly blistered and peppers are tender, turning occasionally. (For a gas grill, preheat grill. Reduce heat to medium. Place peppers on grill rack over heat. Cover and grill as above.) Remove peppers from grill; cool slightly. Stuff peppers with cheese.

②   In a medium bowl combine ground beef and mesquite seasoning. Divide mixture into 4 portions. Shape each portion around a stuffed pepper, enclosing pepper completely. Flatten slightly to form ¾-inch-thick patties.

③   Add patties to grill. Grill for 14 to 18 minutes or until done (160°F),* turning once halfway through grilling.

④   Place burgers on bottoms of rolls. If desired, spoon salsa on burgers. Replace tops of rolls.

*Tip: To measure the doneness of a patty, insert an instant-read thermometer through the side of the patty into the meat to the side of the pepper.

PER SERVING 374 calories; 14 g total fat (5 g sat. fat); 79 mg cholesterol; 545 mg sodium; 30 g carbohydrate; 2 g fiber; 29 g protein

Blending ground meats in meat loaf and burgers gives you the best of both worlds. In All-American Classic Meat Loaf, for example, lean ground sirloin contributes flavor while ground chuck contributes juiciness.

Gold Medal Moussaka

Gold Medal Moussaka

MAKES 4 servings **PREP** 40 minutes **BAKE** 25 minutes
STAND 5 minutes **OVEN** 350°F

  Nonstick cooking spray
1 1-pound eggplant, peeled (if desired) and cut into ¾-inch pieces
8 ounces lean ground beef or lamb
1 8-ounce can tomato sauce with basil, garlic, and oregano
⅛ teaspoon ground cinnamon
2 tablespoons all-purpose flour
2 tablespoons olive oil
¼ teaspoon salt
  Dash black pepper
½ cup fat-free milk
½ cup plain low-fat yogurt
½ cup light ricotta cheese
⅓ cup refrigerated or frozen egg product, thawed
  Ground cinnamon
  Thinly sliced Parmesan cheese (optional)

① Preheat oven to 350°F. Lightly coat a very large nonstick skillet with cooking spray; heat on medium-high heat. Add eggplant; cook about 6 minutes or until tender, stirring frequently. Set aside.

② In a large skillet cook ground meat on medium-high heat until brown, using a wooden spoon to break up meat as it cooks. Drain off fat. Stir in tomato sauce and the ⅛ teaspoon cinnamon. Bring to boiling; reduce heat. Simmer, uncovered, about 8 minutes or until mixture is thickened, stirring occasionally. Divide meat mixture among four 12- to 14-ounce gratin or baking dishes. Top with eggplant.

③ In a small saucepan combine flour, oil, salt, and pepper. Add milk and yogurt all at once. Cook and stir on medium heat until thickened and bubbly; remove from heat. Stir in ricotta cheese and egg. Spoon cheese mixture on eggplant. Sprinkle lightly with additional cinnamon.

④ Bake about 25 minutes or until heated through. If desired, top with Parmesan cheese. Let stand for 5 minutes before serving.

PER SERVING 280 calories; 14 g total fat (4 g sat. fat); 47 mg cholesterol; 582 mg sodium; 18 g carbohydrate; 4 g fiber; 20 g protein

Beef and Black Bean Wraps ③⓪

MAKES 6 servings **START TO FINISH** 25 minutes

8 ounces lean ground beef
1 cup chopped onion (1 large)
2 cloves garlic, minced
1½ teaspoons ground cumin
1 teaspoon chili powder
½ teaspoon ground coriander
1 15-ounce can black beans, rinsed and drained
1 large tomato, chopped
¼ teaspoon black pepper
6 8-inch whole wheat flour tortillas
1½ cups shredded lettuce
1 to 1½ cups shredded reduced-fat cheddar or Monterey Jack cheese (4 to 6 ounces)
  Salsa (optional)

① In a large skillet cook ground beef, onion, and garlic on medium-high heat until meat is brown, using a wooden spoon to break up meat as it cooks. Drain off fat.

② Stir in cumin, chili powder, and coriander. Cook and stir for 1 minute. Stir in black beans, tomato, and pepper. Cook, covered, for 5 minutes more, stirring occasionally.

③ To assemble, spoon meat mixture down the center of tortillas. Sprinkle with lettuce and cheese. Roll up tortillas. If desired, serve with salsa.

PER SERVING 310 calories; 11 g total fat (5 g sat. fat); 35 mg cholesterol; 651 mg sodium; 30 g carbohydrate; 15 g fiber; 24 g protein

These may be called Beef and Black Bean Wraps, but you can certainly switch up ingredients to use what you have on hand— or to create a customized wrap. Substitute ground pork or turkey for the beef and/or use pinto beans in place of the black beans.

Mexican Ground Beef and Noodles

MAKES 6 (1-cup) servings **PREP** 25 minutes
BAKE 33 minutes **OVEN** 350°F

- 4 ounces dried multigrain or regular rotini or elbow macaroni (1⅓ cups)
- 12 ounces extra-lean ground beef
- 2 cloves garlic, minced
- 1 15-ounce can black beans or pinto beans, rinsed and drained
- 1 14.5-ounce can no-salt-added diced tomatoes, undrained
- ¾ cup bottled picante sauce or salsa
- 1 teaspoon dried oregano, crushed
- ½ teaspoon ground cumin
- ½ teaspoon chili powder
- ½ cup shredded reduced-fat Colby and Monterey Jack cheese (2 ounces)
- ⅓ cup light sour cream
- 3 tablespoons sliced green onions
- 2 teaspoons coarsely chopped fresh cilantro
- ½ teaspoon finely shredded lime peel

① Preheat oven to 350°F. In a large saucepan cook pasta according to package directions; drain. Return pasta to hot saucepan; set aside.

② Meanwhile, in a large skillet cook meat and garlic until meat is brown, stirring to break up meat as it cooks. Drain off fat.

③ Stir the cooked meat into pasta in saucepan. Stir in beans, undrained tomatoes, picante sauce, oregano, cumin, and chili powder. Transfer mixture to a 1½- to 2-quart casserole or baking dish.

④ Bake, covered, about 30 minutes or until heated through. Uncover and sprinkle with cheese. Bake, uncovered, about 3 minutes more or until cheese is melted.

⑤ In a small bowl stir together sour cream, 2 tablespoons of the green onions, the cilantro, and lime peel. To serve, top each serving with a spoonful of the sour cream mixture. Sprinkle with the remaining green onions.

PER SERVING 283 calories; 10 g total fat (4 g sat. fat); 45 mg cholesterol; 520 mg sodium; 29 g carbohydrate; 7 g fiber; 23 g protein

Eight-Layer Casserole

MAKES 8 servings **PREP** 30 minutes **BAKE** 55 minutes
STAND 10 minutes **OVEN** 350°F

- 6 ounces dried medium noodles
- 1 pound ground beef
- 2 8-ounce cans tomato sauce
- 1 teaspoon dried basil, crushed
- ½ teaspoon sugar
- ½ teaspoon garlic powder
- ¼ teaspoon salt
- ¼ teaspoon black pepper
- 1 8-ounce carton sour cream
- 1 8-ounce package cream cheese, softened
- ½ cup milk
- 1 small onion, chopped (⅓ cup)
- 1 10-ounce package frozen chopped spinach, thawed and well drained
- 1 cup shredded cheddar cheese (4 ounces)

① Preheat oven to 350°F. Grease a 2-quart casserole or a 2-quart square baking dish; set aside. Cook noodles according to package directions; drain.

② Meanwhile, in a large skillet cook ground meat on medium heat until brown. Drain off fat. Stir in tomato sauce, basil, sugar, garlic powder, salt, and pepper. Bring to boiling; reduce heat. Simmer, uncovered, for 5 minutes.

③ In a medium mixing bowl combine sour cream and cream cheese. Beat with an electric mixer on medium speed until smooth. Stir in milk and onion.

④ Place half of the cooked noodles in the prepared casserole. Top with half of the meat mixture, half of the cream cheese mixture, and all of the spinach. Top with the remaining meat mixture and noodles. Cover and chill the remaining cream cheese mixture until needed.

⑤ Cover casserole with lightly greased foil. Bake about 45 minutes or until heated through. Spread with the remaining cream cheese mixture; sprinkle with cheddar cheese. Bake, uncovered, about 10 minutes more or until cheese is melted. Let stand for 10 minutes before serving.

PER SERVING 472 calories; 30 g total fat (17 g sat. fat); 127 mg cholesterol; 683 mg sodium; 25 g carbohydrate; 3 g fiber; 27 g protein

Salsa Beef Sandwiches

menu

Tomato-Ranch
Bean Dip

Fennel Apple Salad

Salsa Beef Sandwiches
[below]

Baked kettle chips

Iced tea

Salsa Beef Sandwiches ✪ ⏱

MAKES 6 servings **START TO FINISH** 20 minutes

1 **pound lean ground beef**

1 **cup chunky salsa**

¼ **cup water**

1½ **teaspoons chili powder**

6 **whole wheat hamburger buns, split and toasted**

① In a large skillet cook ground beef on medium-high heat until brown, using a wooden spoon to break up meat as it cooks. Drain off fat. Stir in salsa, the water, and chili powder.

② Bring to boiling; reduce heat. Simmer, uncovered, for 5 to 10 minutes or until mixture reaches desired consistency. Serve in buns.

PER SERVING 258 calories; 9 g total fat (3 g sat. fat); 49 mg cholesterol; 493 mg sodium; 24 g carbohydrate; 2 g fiber; 19 g protein

To add smoky flavor to Salsa Beef Sandwiches, substitute ½ teaspoon of ground chipotle chile powder for ½ teaspoon of the regular chili powder.

Spiced Bulgur with Beef and Mango ⏱

MAKES 4 servings **START TO FINISH** 30 minutes

1 **cup reduced-sodium chicken broth**

⅔ **cup bulgur**

1 **clove garlic, minced**

½ **teaspoon ground cumin**

¼ **teaspoon ground coriander**

⅛ **teaspoon ground cinnamon**

⅛ **teaspoon cayenne pepper**

6 **ounces lower-sodium deli roast beef, cut into thin strips**

½ **of a medium mango, peeled and coarsely chopped**

½ **cup fresh pea pods, halved crosswise**

¼ **cup sliced green onions (2)**

¼ **cup snipped fresh cilantro**

¼ **cup unsalted peanuts, chopped (optional)**

① In a 1½-quart microwave-safe casserole combine broth, bulgur, garlic, cumin, coriander, cinnamon, and cayenne pepper. Microwave, covered, on high about 4 minutes or until mixture is boiling. Remove from microwave oven. Let stand about 20 minutes or until bulgur is tender. Drain, if necessary.

② Divide bulgur mixture among 4 serving bowls. Top with beef, mango, pea pods, green onions, cilantro, and, if desired, peanuts.

PER SERVING 164 calories; 2 g total fat (1 g sat. fat); 26 mg cholesterol; 421 mg sodium; 25 g carbohydrate; 5 g fiber; 13 g protein

Spiced Bulgur with Beef and Mango

Grilled Garden Burgers

MAKES 4 servings **PREP** 25 minutes **GRILL** 12 minutes

- 1 egg white, lightly beaten
- ½ cup shredded carrot (1 medium)
- ¼ cup thinly sliced green onions (2)
- ¼ cup shredded zucchini
- 2 cloves garlic, minced
- ⅛ teaspoon black pepper
- 12 ounces 90% lean or higher ground beef
- 4 ½- to ¾-inch slices whole wheat baguette-style French bread, toasted
- ¾ cup fresh spinach leaves
- 1 small tomato, thinly sliced
- ½ cup very thinly sliced zucchini*

① In a large bowl combine egg white, carrot, green onions, the shredded zucchini, garlic, and pepper. Add ground beef; mix well. Shape mixture into four ¾-inch-thick patties.

② For a charcoal grill, grill patties on the rack of an uncovered grill directly over medium coals for 12 to 14 minutes or until done (160°F), turning once halfway through grilling. (For a gas grill, preheat grill. Reduce heat to medium. Place patties on grill rack over heat. Cover and grill as above.)

③ Serve burgers on baguette slices with spinach, tomato, and the thinly sliced zucchini.

*Tip: Use a vegetable peeler to cut very thin lengthwise slices from zucchini.

PER SERVING 258 calories; 10 g total fat (3 g sat. fat); 55 mg cholesterol; 229 mg sodium; 19 g carbohydrate; 3 g fiber; 21 g protein

Ground sirloin is the leanest of ground beef—at 90% to 92% lean. Cook this ground beef thoroughly for safety but avoid overcooking. And don't press burgers with a spatula as they cook: It presses out the yummy juices!

Whiskey Burgers

MAKES 4 servings **PREP** 15 minutes **GRILL** 25 minutes

- 2 garlic bulbs
- 2 teaspoons olive oil
- 1 teaspoon instant coffee crystals
- 1 teaspoon unsweetened cocoa powder
- ¾ teaspoon chili powder
- ¼ teaspoon salt
- 1 tablespoon whiskey or water
- 1 pound ground venison or lean ground beef
- 4 small whole wheat hamburger buns, split and toasted
-    Lettuce leaves (optional)
-    Thin jalapeño slices, tomato slices, thin red onion slices, and/or dill pickle slices (optional)

① Cut off the top ½ inch of garlic bulbs to expose the ends of the individual cloves. Leaving garlic bulbs whole, remove the loose, papery outer layers. Place garlic bulbs on a double thickness of foil; drizzle bulbs with oil. Bring foil up around bulbs and fold edges together to loosely enclose.

② For a charcoal grill, grill garlic packet on the greased rack of an uncovered grill directly over medium coals about 25 minutes or until garlic feels soft when squeezed. (For a gas grill, preheat grill. Reduce heat to medium. Place foil packet on greased grill rack over heat. Cover and grill as above.) Cool.

③ Meanwhile, in a medium bowl combine coffee crystals, cocoa powder, chili powder, and salt. Stir in whiskey. Add ground meat; mix well. Shape mixture into four ½-inch-thick patties. While garlic is grilling, add patties to grill. Grill for 10 to 13 minutes or until done (160°F), turning once halfway through grilling.

④ Squeeze garlic cloves from bulbs into a small bowl. Mash garlic with a fork. Spread garlic on bottoms of buns; add lettuce (if desired) and burgers. If desired, top with jalapeño, tomato, red onion, and/or pickle slices, then replace tops of buns.

PER SERVING 315 calories; 6 g total fat (1 g sat. fat); 96 mg cholesterol; 422 mg sodium; 30 g carbohydrate; 3 g fiber; 32 g protein

Taco Pizza

Taco Pizza ✪

MAKES 8 servings **PREP** 15 minutes **BAKE** 19 minutes
OVEN 425°F

Nonstick cooking spray
1 16-ounce loaf frozen whole wheat bread dough, thawed
12 ounces lean ground beef
½ cup chopped onion (1 medium)
½ cup salsa
1½ cups chopped tomatoes (3 medium)
½ cup shredded cheddar cheese (2 ounces)
½ to 1 cup shredded lettuce and/or fresh spinach leaves
1 cup baked tortilla chips, coarsely crushed
Light sour cream and/or salsa (optional)

① Preheat oven to 425°F. Lightly coat a 12- to 13-inch pizza pan with cooking spray. Pat bread dough evenly into the prepared pan, building up edges slightly. (If dough is hard to pat out, let it rest for 10 minutes.) Prick crust all over with a fork. Bake for 12 minutes.

② Meanwhile, in a large skillet cook ground beef and onion on medium-high heat until meat is brown and onion is tender, using a wooden spoon to break up meat as it cooks. Drain off fat. Stir in the ½ cup salsa. Top partially baked crust with meat mixture. Bake for 5 minutes. Sprinkle with tomatoes and cheese. Bake for 2 to 3 minutes more or until cheese is melted.

③ To serve, top pizza with lettuce; sprinkle with tortilla chips. If desired, serve with sour cream and additional salsa.

Tip: For a stuffed-crust pizza, lightly coat a 12- to 13-inch pizza pan with cooking spray. Pat bread dough evenly into the prepared pan, extending edges over pan slightly. (If dough is hard to pat out, let it rest for 10 minutes.) Sprinkle ½ cup shredded cheese in a thin strip around edges of crust. Moisten edge of dough. Fold edges over cheese; seal tightly to enclose cheese. Prick crust all over with a fork. Continue as directed.

PER SERVING 279 calories; 9 g total fat (3 g sat. fat); 35 mg cholesterol; 500 mg sodium; 33 g carbohydrate; 3 g fiber; 18 g protein

Garden Pizza

MAKES 6 servings **PREP** 30 minutes **STAND** 12 to 24 hours
BAKE 20 minutes **OVEN** 400°F

2 cups all-purpose flour
½ cup white whole wheat flour or whole wheat flour
½ cup cornmeal
1 teaspoon salt
¼ teaspoon active dry yeast
1¼ cups warm water (120°F to 130°F)
Olive oil
½ cup no-salt-added tomato sauce
½ teaspoon dried Italian seasoning, crushed
3 to 4 cups assorted fresh vegetables (such as halved cherry tomatoes, broccoli florets, and/or shredded radicchio)
1 cup fresh mushrooms, halved or sliced
2 ounces uncooked chorizo sausage, cooked and drained
½ cup crumbled feta cheese (2 ounces) or 1 cup shredded mozzarella cheese (4 ounces)

① In a large bowl combine all-purpose flour, whole wheat flour, cornmeal, salt, and yeast. Gradually stir in warm water until flour mixture is moistened (dough will be soft and sticky). Cover bowl and let stand at room temperature for 12 to 24 hours.

② Line a 15 x 10 x 1-inch baking pan with parchment paper; brush paper with oil. Turn dough out onto the prepared baking pan. Using well-oiled hands or a rubber spatula, gently push dough to edges and corners of pan. Cover and let stand for 1 to 1½ hours or until dough is puffy and pulls away slightly from edges of pan.

③ Preheat oven to 400°F. Bake crust for 10 minutes. In a small bowl combine tomato sauce and Italian seasoning; spread over hot crust. Add assorted vegetables (except radicchio, if using), mushrooms, and cooked sausage; top with cheese. Bake for 10 to 15 minutes more or until golden brown. If using, add radicchio.

PER SERVING 336 calories; 8 g total fat (3 g sat. fat); 19 mg cholesterol; 659 mg sodium; 54 g carbohydrate; 4 g fiber; 12 g protein

Cherry-Kissed Tacos with Feta Cheese Salsa ③⓪

MAKES 12 servings **START TO FINISH** 25 minutes

1   pound lean ground lamb or pork
1   cup finely chopped onion (1 large)
1   teaspoon curry powder
½   cup mango chutney
½   cup dried tart cherries, snipped
1   tablespoon lemon juice
¼   teaspoon salt
¼   teaspoon black pepper
12 taco shells, warmed
     Feta Cheese Salsa

① In a large skillet cook ground meat and onion on medium-high heat until meat is brown and onion is tender, using a wooden spoon to break up meat as it cooks. Drain off fat. Add curry powder; cook and stir for 1 minute.

② Cut up any large pieces of chutney. Stir chutney, cherries, lemon juice, salt, and pepper into meat mixture. Bring to boiling; reduce heat. Simmer, covered, for 5 minutes.

③ Spoon meat mixture into taco shells. Top with Feta Cheese Salsa.

Feta Cheese Salsa: In a medium bowl combine ½ cup seeded and finely chopped tomato (1 medium), ⅓ cup finely chopped cucumber, ¼ cup crumbled feta cheese (1 ounce), ¼ cup finely chopped red onion, ¼ cup finely chopped sweet green pepper, 1 tablespoon olive oil, and 1 tablespoon lemon juice. Season to taste with salt and black pepper. Use a slotted spoon to serve. Makes about 1½ cups.

PER SERVING 208 calories; 10 g total fat (3 g sat. fat); 27 mg cholesterol; 282 mg sodium; 21 g carbohydrate; 2 g fiber; 8 g protein

Honey-Lime Lamb and Melon Kabobs

MAKES 6 servings **PREP** 25 minutes
MARINATE 30 minutes to 2 hours **GRILL** 14 minutes

1¼ to 1½ pounds boneless lamb sirloin steak
1   tablespoon finely shredded lime peel
⅓   cup lime juice
⅓   cup honey
1   tablespoon snipped fresh tarragon or
     1½ teaspoons dried tarragon, crushed
1   clove garlic, minced
½   teaspoon salt
½   teaspoon black pepper
12 1-inch cubes cantaloupe
12 1-inch cubes honeydew melon
6   individual Italian flatbreads (focaccia)
1   6-ounce carton plain low-fat yogurt
     Fresh arugula (optional)

① Trim fat from meat. Cut meat into 1-inch pieces. Place meat in a resealable plastic bag set in a shallow dish. For marinade, in a small bowl combine 2 teaspoons of the lime peel, the lime juice, honey, 2 teaspoons of the fresh tarragon or 1 teaspoon of the dried tarragon, the garlic, salt, and pepper.

② Remove ¼ cup marinade; set aside. Pour remaining marinade over meat. Seal bag; turn to coat meat. Marinate in the refrigerator for 30 minutes to 2 hours, turning bag once or twice. Drain meat, discarding marinade.

③ On twelve 6-inch skewers,* alternately thread meat, cantaloupe, and honeydew melon. For a charcoal grill, grill kabobs on the rack of an uncovered grill directly over medium coals for 12 to 14 minutes or until meat is slightly pink in center, turning and brushing frequently with the reserved marinade. (For a gas grill, preheat grill. Reduce heat to medium. Place kabobs on grill rack over heat. Cover and grill as above.) Remove from grill.

④ Lightly brush both sides of flatbreads with *olive oil.* Add flatbreads to grill. Grill about 2 minutes or until warm, turning once halfway through grilling.

⑤ In a bowl combine yogurt, remaining lime peel, and remaining tarragon. Serve kabobs with warm flatbreads, yogurt mixture, and, if desired, arugula.

*Tip: If using wooden skewers, soak in water for at least 30 minutes; drain before using.

PER SERVING 409 calories; 6 g total fat (2 g sat. fat); 62 mg cholesterol; 616 mg sodium; 62 g carbohydrate; 3 g fiber; 27 g protein

Honey-Lime Lamb and Melon Kabobs

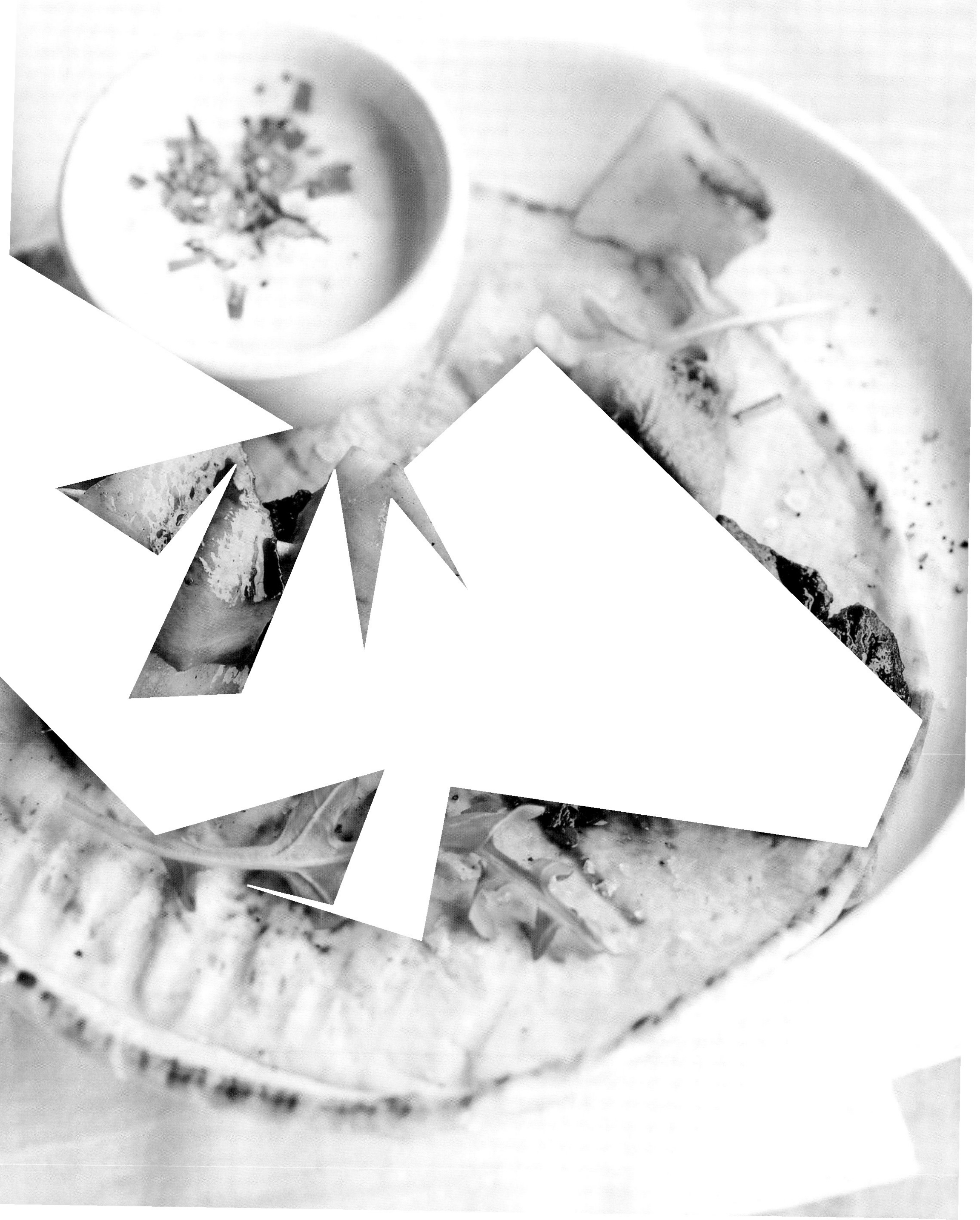

Caramelized Pork with Melon

Caramelized Pork with Melon ⑩

MAKES 4 servings **START TO FINISH** 25 minutes

- 1 small cantaloupe, peeled, seeded, and chopped (about 3½ cups)
- ¼ cup orange juice
- 3 tablespoons hoisin sauce
- ⅓ cup thinly sliced green onions
- 4 bone-in pork center-cut loin chops, cut ½ inch thick
  Salt
  Black pepper
- 1 tablespoon vegetable oil
  Shredded napa cabbage (optional)

① In a food processor or blender combine 2 cups of the cantaloupe and the orange juice. Cover and process or blend until smooth. Transfer ½ cup of the pureed mixture to a small bowl; stir in hoisin sauce.

② Press the remaining pureed mixture through a fine-mesh sieve, reserving juice and discarding solids. In a medium bowl combine the remaining 1½ cups cantaloupe, the strained juice, and green onions. Set aside.

③ Trim fat from chops. Sprinkle chops lightly with salt and pepper. Remove 2 tablespoons of the hoisin mixture; brush over both sides of chops. In a very large skillet heat oil on medium heat. Add chops; cook for 6 to 8 minutes or until meat juices run clear (160°F), turning once. Remove from skillet.

④ Add the remaining hoisin mixture to skillet. Cook and stir until heated through. Spoon warm hoisin mixture onto 4 dinner plates. Top with chops.

⑤ Add cantaloupe-green onion mixture to skillet; cook and stir until warm. Spoon over chops. If desired, serve with cabbage.

PER SERVING 327 calories; 10 g total fat (2 g sat. fat); 117 mg cholesterol; 452 mg sodium; 19 g carbohydrate; 2 g fiber; 39 g protein

Choose a cantaloupe that has a cream-color netting over a rind that is green, yellow, or gray. The blossom end should yield to gentle pressure; the rest of the melon should be firm and free from bruises and cuts. Smell it at the stem end—it should have a sweetly aromatic scent.

Braised Sour Cream and Fennel Pork Tenderloins

MAKES 8 servings **PREP** 30 minutes **ROAST** 25 minutes **STAND** 10 minutes **OVEN** 425°F

- 2 medium fennel bulbs
- 2 1- to 1½-pound pork tenderloins
- 1 tablespoon snipped fresh rosemary
- 1 tablespoon fennel seeds, coarsely crushed (optional)
- 1 teaspoon salt
- ¼ teaspoon black pepper
- 2 tablespoons olive oil
- 1 medium onion, sliced
- 6 cloves garlic, minced
- ½ cup chicken broth
- ½ cup dry vermouth or chicken broth
- ¼ cup sour cream
- 1 lemon, sliced and seeded

① Preheat oven to 425°F. Trim and core fennel bulbs, reserving some of the leafy tops for garnishing. Cut fennel bulbs into thin wedges; set aside.

② Trim fat from meat. Sprinkle meat with rosemary, fennel seeds (if desired), salt, and pepper. In a very large oven-going straight-sided skillet cook meat in hot oil on medium-high heat until brown on all sides. Remove from skillet.

③ Add fennel, onion, and garlic to skillet; cook about 4 minutes or until light brown, stirring occasionally. Remove from heat. Stir in broth, vermouth, and sour cream; return to heat. Bring to boiling. Return meat to skillet; transfer to oven.

④ Roast for 25 to 30 minutes or until an instant-read thermometer inserted into meat registers 155°F. Remove meat from skillet. Cover with foil; let stand for 10 minutes. Temperature of the meat after standing should be 160°F. Serve meat with vegetable mixture. Garnish with the reserved fennel tops and lemon slices.

PER SERVING 212 calories; 7 g total fat (2 g sat. fat); 77 mg cholesterol; 488 mg sodium; 8 g carbohydrate; 3 g fiber; 25 g protein

Pork Tenderloin with Green Olive Tapenade

MAKES 6 to 8 servings **PREP** 40 minutes **GRILL** 45 minutes
STAND 10 minutes

- 1 cup pitted green olives
- 1 tablespoon drained capers
- 1 tablespoon Dijon mustard
- 1 tablespoon olive oil
- 1 tablespoon lemon juice
- 2 teaspoons anchovy paste
- 1 teaspoon snipped fresh thyme
- 1 clove garlic, minced
- 2 12- to 16-ounce pork tenderloins

① For tapenade, in a food processor or blender combine olives, capers, mustard, oil, lemon juice, anchovy paste, thyme, and garlic. Cover and process until nearly smooth, scraping down sides as necessary. If desired, cover and chill for up to 24 hours.

② Trim fat from tenderloins. Make a lengthwise cut down the center of each tenderloin, cutting almost to, but not through, the opposite side. Spread open. Place tenderloins between 2 pieces of plastic wrap, overlapping tenderloins about 2 inches along a long side. Using the flat side of a meat mallet, pound tenderloins lightly into a 12 x 10-inch rectangle. Remove plastic wrap.

③ Spread tapenade over meat rectangle to within 1 inch of the edges. Fold in long sides just to cover edge of tapenade. Starting at one short side, roll up meat. To secure, tie at 1-inch intervals with 100%-cotton kitchen string.

④ For a charcoal grill, arrange medium-hot coals around a drip pan. Test for medium heat above pan. Place meat on grill rack over drip pan. Cover and grill for 45 to 50 minutes or until an instant-read thermometer inserted into meat registers 155°F. (For a gas grill, preheat grill. Reduce heat to medium. Adjust for indirect cooking. Grill as above, except place meat on a rack in a roasting pan; place pan on grill rack over burner that is off.)

⑤ Remove meat from grill. Cover with foil; let stand for 10 minutes before slicing. Temperature of the meat after standing should be 160°F. Remove and discard string. Slice meat.

PER SERVING 201 calories; 10 g total fat (2 g sat. fat); 83 mg cholesterol; 347 mg sodium; 1 g carbohydrate; 0 g fiber; 27 g protein

Indian Spiced Pork and Pineapple Kabobs

MAKES 4 servings **PREP** 30 minutes **MARINATE** 2 to 10 hours
GRILL 14 minutes

- 1 pound pork tenderloin
- 1 6-ounce carton plain low-fat yogurt
- 2 tablespoons honey
- 2 tablespoons lemon juice
- 1 tablespoon grated fresh ginger
- 2 teaspoons garam masala
- 2 cloves garlic, minced
- ¼ teaspoon cayenne pepper
- ½ of a medium pineapple, peeled, cored, and cut into 1-inch pieces
- 1 medium sweet red pepper, seeded and cut into 1-inch pieces
- 1 medium sweet green pepper, seeded and cut into 1-inch pieces
- 4 individual Italian flatbreads
- 2 tablespoons snipped fresh cilantro
- 2 tablespoons snipped fresh mint

① Trim fat from meat. Cut meat into 1-inch pieces. Place meat in a resealable plastic bag set in a shallow dish. In a bowl combine yogurt, honey, lemon juice, ginger, garam masala, garlic, and cayenne pepper. Remove ⅓ cup of the mixture; cover and chill. Pour remaining mixture over meat. Seal bag; turn to coat meat. Marinate in refrigerator 2 to 10 hours, turning bag occasionally. Drain meat, reserving marinade.

② On eight 8- to 10-inch skewers,* alternately thread meat, pineapple, and sweet peppers.

③ For a charcoal grill, grill kabobs on the rack of an uncovered grill directly over medium coals for 12 to 15 minutes or until meat is slightly pink in center, turning once and brushing with reserved marinade. (For a gas grill, preheat grill. Reduce heat to medium. Place kabobs on grill rack over heat. Cover and grill as above.) Remove from grill. Add flatbreads to grill. Grill 2 minutes or until light brown, turning once.

⑤ In a bowl combine cilantro, mint, and 1 teaspoon finely shredded *lemon peel;* sprinkle over kabobs. Drizzle with chilled yogurt mixture. Serve with flatbreads.

*Tip: If using wooden skewers, soak in water for at least 30 minutes; drain before using.

PER SERVING 477 calories; 10 g total fat (5 g sat. fat); 262 mg sodium; 64 g carbohydrate; 3 g fiber; 34 g protein

Indian Spiced Pork and Pineapple Kabobs

Onion Stuffed Pork Tenderloin with
Chutney-Mustard Sauce

Lemon-Sage Pork Taco Salad

MAKES 6 servings **START TO FINISH** 40 minutes **OVEN** 425°F

- 1 pound pork tenderloin
- 1 tablespoon finely shredded lemon peel
- 6 fresh sage leaves, thinly sliced
- ½ teaspoon ground cumin
- ¼ teaspoon black pepper
- ⅛ teaspoon salt
- 1 tablespoon olive oil
- 1 head green leaf lettuce, torn
- 1½ cups chopped tomatoes (3 medium)
- 1 avocado, seeded, peeled, and chopped
- 1 cup canned black beans, rinsed and drained
- ½ cup chopped green onions (4)
  Hot Red Pepper Vinaigrette

① Trim fat from meat. Cut meat into ¼-inch slices. Place meat in a large bowl. Add lemon peel, sage, cumin, pepper, and salt; toss gently to coat. Let stand for 10 minutes.

② In a very large skillet cook meat, half at a time, in hot oil on medium-high heat for 2 to 3 minutes or until meat is slightly pink in center, turning once. Remove from skillet.

③ Place lettuce on a serving platter. Top with tomatoes, avocado, beans, and green onions. Arrange meat slices over salad. Drizzle with some of the Hot Red Pepper Vinaigrette; pass the remaining vinaigrette.

Hot Red Pepper Vinaigrette: Preheat oven to 425°F. Halve 1 sweet red pepper and 1 jalapeño* lengthwise; remove stems, seeds, and membranes. Place pepper halves, cut sides down, on a foil-lined baking sheet. Bake for 20 to 25 minutes or until skin is blistered and charred. Bring foil up around peppers to enclose. Let stand about 15 minutes or until cool. Using a sharp knife, loosen edges of skin; gently pull off and discard skin. Place peppers in a blender. Add 2 tablespoons lime juice, 2 tablespoons balsamic vinegar, 2 tablespoons olive oil, and ⅛ teaspoon salt. Cover and blend or process until smooth.

*Tip: Because chiles contain volatile oils that can burn your skin and eyes, avoid direct contact with them as much as possible. When working with chiles, wear plastic or rubber gloves. If your bare hands do touch the peppers, wash your hands and fingernails well with soap and warm water.

PER SERVING 266 calories; 14 g total fat (2 g sat. fat); 49 mg cholesterol; 269 mg sodium; 17 g carbohydrate; 7 g fiber; 21 g protein

Onion-Stuffed Pork Tenderloin with Chutney-Mustard Sauce

MAKES 8 servings **PREP** 30 minutes **GRILL** 30 minutes
STAND 10 minutes

- 2 12- to 16-ounce pork tenderloins
- ¼ cup chopped golden raisins
- 2 tablespoons thinly sliced green onion (1)
- 2 tablespoons finely chopped sweet onion
- 2 tablespoons finely chopped shallot (1 medium)
- 2 tablespoons snipped fresh thyme or Italian (flat-leaf) parsley
- 2 tablespoons olive oil
- 1½ to 2 teaspoons black pepper
- 1 teaspoon kosher salt
- 1 cup mango chutney
- 1 tablespoon Dijon mustard

① Trim fat from tenderloins. Make a lengthwise cut down the center of each tenderloin, cutting almost to, but not through, the opposite side. Spread tenderloins open.

② For stuffing, in a small bowl combine raisins, green onion, sweet onion, shallot, and thyme. Spread stuffing over tenderloins. Fold each tenderloin back together. To secure, tie at 1-inch intervals with 100%-cotton kitchen string; brush with oil. For rub, in a small bowl combine pepper and salt. Sprinkle mixture evenly over tenderloins; rub in with your fingers.

③ For a charcoal grill, arrange hot coals around a drip pan. Test for medium-hot heat above pan. Place tenderloins on grill rack over drip pan. Cover and grill for 30 to 35 minutes or until an instant-read thermometer inserted into tenderloins registers 155°F. (For a gas grill, preheat grill. Reduce heat to medium-high. Adjust for indirect cooking. Grill as above, except place tenderloins on a rack in a roasting pan; place pan on grill rack over burner that is off.)

④ Remove tenderloins from grill. Cover with foil; let stand for 10 minutes before slicing. Temperature of the meat after standing should be 160°F. Meanwhile, for sauce, in a small bowl stir together chutney and mustard.

⑤ To serve, remove and discard string from tenderloins. Slice tenderloins diagonally. Serve meat with sauce.

PER SERVING 195 calories; 5 g total fat (1 g sat. fat); 55 mg cholesterol; 415 mg sodium; 18 g carbohydrate; 1 g fiber; 19 g protein

Pork Kabobs with Onion Cakes and Peanut Sauce 🥄

MAKES 4 servings **START TO FINISH** 35 minutes

1	pound pork tenderloin
1	tablespoon reduced-sodium soy sauce
2	teaspoons Thai seasoning
½	cup all-purpose flour
½	teaspoon baking powder
1	bunch green onions, chopped
½	cup water
1	egg, lightly beaten
2	teaspoons vegetable oil
¼	cup peanut butter
1	tablespoon honey
⅓	cup water
½	cup shredded carrot (1 medium)
	Fresh cilantro and lime wedges (optional)

① Preheat broiler. Trim fat from meat. Cut meat into ½-inch slices. Thread meat onto 8 skewers,* leaving ¼ inch between pieces. Brush meat with 1 teaspoon of the soy sauce and sprinkle with 1 teaspoon of the Thai seasoning. Place kabobs on the unheated rack of a broiler pan. Broil 3 to 4 inches from the heat about 8 minutes or until meat is slightly pink in center, turning once halfway through broiling.

② Meanwhile, for onion cakes, in a medium bowl stir together flour, baking powder, and the remaining 1 teaspoon Thai seasoning. Stir in green onions, the ½ cup water, and egg. In a very large skillet heat oil on medium-high heat. Spread batter in skillet; cook for 10 to 12 minutes or until golden brown, turning once. Remove from heat. Cut into wedges.

③ For sauce, in a small microwave-safe bowl combine peanut butter, honey, and the remaining 2 teaspoons soy sauce; gradually stir in the ⅓ cup water. Microwave on high for 30 seconds. Whisk mixture; microwave for 15 seconds more.

④ Serve kabobs with onion cakes, sauce, carrot, and, if desired, cilantro and lime wedges.

*Tip: If using wooden skewers, soak in water for at least 30 minutes; drain before using.

PER SERVING 346 calories; 14 g total fat (3 g sat. fat); 127 mg cholesterol; 515 mg sodium; 23 g carbohydrate; 3 g fiber; 32 g protein

Pork Tenderloin with Cucumber-Mango Salad 🥄

MAKES 4 servings **PREP** 10 minutes **ROAST** 25 minutes
STAND 10 minutes **OVEN** 425°F

1½	pounds pork tenderloin
2	tablespoons packed brown sugar
2	teaspoons five-spice powder
½	teaspoon salt
4	green onions
1	small English cucumber, sliced and/or chopped
1	mango, seeded, peeled, and chopped
1	jalapeño, seeded and sliced* (optional)

① Preheat oven to 425°F. Line a shallow roasting pan with foil; set aside. Trim fat from meat. In a small bowl combine brown sugar, five-spice powder, and salt. Remove 1 teaspoon of the mixture; set aside. Sprinkle the remaining mixture over meat; rub in with your fingers. Place meat in the prepared roasting pan.

② Roast about 25 minutes or until an instant-read thermometer inserted into meat registers 155°F. Remove from oven. Cover with foil; let stand for 10 minutes. Temperature of the meat after standing should be 160°F.

③ Meanwhile, for Cucumber-Mango Salad, slice the green portions of the green onions into thin strips; chop the white portions. In a medium bowl combine green onions, cucumber, mango, jalapeño (if desired), and the reserved brown sugar mixture.

④ Slice meat. Serve meat with Cucumber-Mango Salad.

*Tip: Because chiles contain volatile oils that can burn your skin and eyes, avoid direct contact with them as much as possible. When working with chiles, wear plastic or rubber gloves. If your bare hands do touch the peppers, wash your hands and fingernails well with soap and warm water.

PER SERVING 258 calories; 3 g total fat (1 g sat. fat); 110 mg cholesterol; 370 mg sodium; 19 g carbohydrate; 2 g fiber; 37 g protein

Five-spice powder, a blend of ground cinnamon, cloves, fennel seeds, star anise, and Szechuan peppercorns, is widely used in Chinese cooking.

Pork Kabobs with Onion Cakes and Peanut Sauce

Zucchini-Wrapped Pork

menu

Layered Asian Salad

Blood Orange and Toasted Almond Couscous

Zucchini-Wrapped Pork [below]

Almond Sandwich Cookies

Zucchini-Wrapped Pork ③⓪

MAKES 4 servings **START TO FINISH** 30 minutes **OVEN** 450°F

1	small zucchini
12	to 16 ounces pork tenderloin
	Olive oil
	Salt
	Black pepper
⅓	cup basil pesto
	Small fresh basil leaves (optional)
	Watercress or arugula (optional)

① Preheat oven to 450°F. Line a 15 x 10 x 1-inch baking pan with foil; set aside. Using a vegetable peeler, cut 8 very thin slices from the zucchini. Trim fat from meat. Cut meat crosswise into 4 equal portions. Press each portion with the palm of your hand to flatten slightly.

② Wrap 2 of the zucchini slices around each portion of meat. If necessary, secure with wooden toothpicks. (Reserve any remaining zucchini for another use.) Place wrapped meat in the prepared baking pan. Brush meat lightly with oil; sprinkle with salt and pepper. Roast for 18 to 25 minutes or until meat juices run clear (160°F).

③ Spoon some of the pesto on meat. If desired, sprinkle with basil and serve with watercress. Pass the remaining pesto.

PER SERVING 203 calories; 11 g total fat (2 g sat. fat); 62 mg cholesterol; 382 mg sodium; 4 g carbohydrate; 1 g fiber; 21 g protein

Smoky-Sweet Pork

MAKES 8 servings **PREP** 25 minutes **COOK** 1½ hours

1½	pounds boneless pork top loin roast (single loin) or loin blade roast
2	teaspoons vegetable oil
1½	cups water
1	cup chopped red onion (1 large)
½	cup chopped celery (1 stalk)
½	cup ketchup
½	cup barbecue sauce
¼	cup packed brown sugar
¼	cup snipped pitted whole dates
2	tablespoons finely chopped canned chipotle chiles in adobo sauce (see tip, page 140)
2	cloves garlic, minced
1	teaspoon dry mustard
8	1-inch slices bread (optional)
8	lettuce leaves (optional)

① Trim fat from meat. In a large saucepan cook meat in hot oil on medium-high heat until brown on all sides. Drain off fat. Add the water, red onion, celery, ketchup, barbecue sauce, brown sugar, dates, chipotle chiles, garlic, and dry mustard. Bring to boiling; reduce heat. Simmer, covered, for 1½ to 2 hours or until meat is fork tender, stirring occasionally.

② Remove meat from ketchup mixture. Pour ketchup mixture into a large glass measuring cup or bowl. If necessary, skim fat from ketchup mixture. Using 2 forks, pull meat apart into shreds. Return meat to saucepan; stir in enough of the ketchup mixture to moisten. Heat through.

③ If desired, line bread slices with lettuce and top with meat mixture.

PER SERVING 335 calories; 8 g total fat (2 g sat. fat); 50 mg cholesterol; 606 mg sodium; 41 g carbohydrate; 3 g fiber; 23 g protein

Find pesto in jars on grocery store shelves and in containers in the refrigerated section. If you can find it, buy the refrigerated variety—its flavor and color is superior. The best option, of course, is to make your own—when you have time and fresh basil.

Pork Chops and Squash 🕒

MAKES 4 servings **START TO FINISH** 20 minutes

- ½ cup chipotle salsa
- 1 orange, peeled and chopped
- 4 bone-in pork loin or rib chops, cut ¾ inch thick
- 4 small zucchini and/or yellow summer squash, halved lengthwise
- 1 tablespoon olive oil
-   Salt
-   Black pepper

① In a small bowl combine salsa and orange; set aside. Trim fat from chops. Brush chops and squash lightly with oil and sprinkle with salt and pepper.

② For a charcoal grill, grill chops on the rack of an uncovered grill directly over medium coals for 11 to 13 minutes or until meat juices run clear (160°F), turning once halfway through grilling. (For a gas grill, preheat grill. Reduce heat to medium. Place chops on grill rack over heat. Cover and grill as above.)

③ While chops are grilling, add squash, cut sides down, to grill. Grill for 6 to 8 minutes or until squash is tender, turning once halfway through grilling.

④ Cut squash into bite-size pieces. Serve chops and squash with salsa mixture.

PER SERVING 268 calories; 14 g total fat (4 g sat. fat); 78 mg cholesterol; 340 mg sodium; 10 g carbohydrate; 3 g fiber; 26 g protein

Pork Chops and Squash

Chops and Pineapple with Chili Slaw 🕒

MAKES 4 servings **PREP** 20 minutes **GRILL** 6 minutes

- 8 boneless pork top loin chops, cut ½ inch thick
- 1½ teaspoons chili powder
- ¼ teaspoon salt
- 3 tablespoons cider vinegar
- 2 tablespoons orange juice
- 2 tablespoons olive oil
- 1 tablespoon sugar
- 5 cups shredded green cabbage
- ¾ cup sweet red pepper strips (1 small)
- ½ of a small red onion, thinly sliced
-   Salt
-   Black pepper
- ½ of a medium pineapple, cored, sliced, and cut into wedges

① Trim fat from chops. Sprinkle chops with 1 teaspoon of the chili powder and the ¼ teaspoon salt. Set aside.

② For Chili Slaw, in a large bowl combine vinegar, orange juice, oil, sugar, and the remaining ½ teaspoon chili powder. Add cabbage, sweet pepper, and red onion; toss gently to coat. Season to taste with additional salt and black pepper.

③ For a charcoal grill, grill chops and pineapple on the rack of an uncovered grill directly over medium coals for 6 to 8 minutes or until meat juices run clear (160°F), turning once halfway through grilling. (For a gas grill, preheat grill. Reduce heat to medium. Place chops and pineapple on grill rack over heat. Cover and grill as above.) Serve chops with pineapple and chili slaw.

PER SERVING 357 calories; 12 g total fat (3 g sat. fat); 112 mg cholesterol; 392 mg sodium; 20 g carbohydrate; 4 g fiber; 40 g protein

Chops and Pineapple with Chili Slaw

Pork Chops and Cherries

menu

Spring greens with
balsamic vinaigrette

Loaded Mashed
Sweet Potatoes

Pork Chops
and Cherries
[below]

Seven-grain rolls

Pork Chops and Cherries ✪ ③⓪

MAKES 2 servings **START TO FINISH** 20 minutes

- 2   **bone-in pork loin or rib chops, cut ¾ inch thick**
- ⅛   **teaspoon salt**
- ⅛   **teaspoon black pepper**
      Nonstick cooking spray
- ½   **cup low-calorie cranberry juice**
- 1½   **teaspoons spicy brown mustard**
- ¾   **teaspoon cornstarch**
- ½   **cup halved, pitted fresh sweet cherries or frozen unsweetened pitted dark sweet cherries, thawed**

① Trim fat from chops. Sprinkle chops with salt and pepper.

② Lightly coat a medium skillet with cooking spray; heat skillet on medium-high heat. Add chops; reduce heat to medium. Cook for 8 to 10 minutes or until meat juices run clear (160°F), turning once. Remove from skillet; cover and keep warm.

③ For cherry sauce, in a small bowl stir together cranberry juice, mustard, and cornstarch; add to drippings in skillet. Cook and stir until thickened and bubbly. Cook and stir for 2 minutes more. Stir in cherries. Serve chops with cherry sauce.

PER SERVING 222 calories; 5 g total fat (2 g sat. fat); 97 mg cholesterol; 291 mg sodium; 10 g carbohydrate; 1 g fiber; 31 g protein

Pork Chops Pizziola ✪

MAKES 4 servings **PREP** 20 minutes **COOK** 30 minutes

- 4   **bone-in pork loin or rib chops, cut ½ inch thick**
- 1   **tablespoon canola oil**
- 1   **tablespoon snipped fresh oregano or 1 teaspoon dried oregano, crushed**
- 2   **cloves garlic, minced**
- 1   **14.5-ounce can no-salt-added diced tomatoes, undrained**
- ¼   **cup dry red wine or low-sodium tomato juice**
- 1   **tablespoon tomato paste**

① Trim fat from chops. In a large skillet cook chops in hot oil on medium-high heat until brown on both sides. Remove from skillet.

② Add dried oregano (if using) and garlic to skillet; cook and stir for 15 seconds. Stir in tomatoes, wine, and tomato paste. Bring to boiling. Return chops to skillet; reduce heat. Simmer, covered, for 30 minutes.

③ Transfer chops to a serving dish. Skim off any fat from tomato mixture. Stir fresh oregano (if using) into tomato mixture. If desired, cook, uncovered, for 1 to 2 minutes more or until mixture reaches desired consistency, stirring occasionally. Serve chops with tomato mixture.

PER SERVING 210 calories; 10 g total fat (3 g sat. fat); 58 mg cholesterol; 130 mg sodium; 7 g carbohydrate; 2 g fiber; 19 g protein

Pork Chops Pizziola

Pork Chops Primavera 30

MAKES 4 servings **START TO FINISH** 30 minutes

- 12 ounces fresh young green beans, trimmed
- 2 tablespoons water
- 4 slices peppered bacon, cut into 1-inch pieces
- 4 bone-in pork loin or rib chops, cut ½ inch thick
- 1 tablespoon soy sauce
- ⅓ cup apple butter
- ¼ cup water
- 1 cup red or yellow cherry or grape tomatoes

① In a 2-quart microwave-safe dish combine green beans and the 2 tablespoons water. Microwave, covered, on high for 4 minutes, stirring once. Drain and set aside.

② In a very large skillet cook bacon on medium heat until crisp. Using a slotted spoon, remove bacon and drain on paper towels, reserving 1 tablespoon drippings in skillet.

③ Meanwhile, trim fat from chops. Brush chops with soy sauce. Add chops to the reserved drippings in skillet. Cook on medium-high heat until brown on both sides. Add apple butter and the ¼ cup water. Simmer, covered, for 5 minutes. Add green beans, bacon, and tomatoes. Cook, uncovered, for 3 to 5 minutes more or until apple butter mixture is thickened.

PER SERVING 402 calories; 16 g total fat (5 g sat. fat); 80 mg cholesterol; 534 mg sodium; 39 g carbohydrate; 5 g fiber; 27 g protein

Although bone-in pork chops take a little longer to cook than boneless chops, cooking them on the bone results in a juicier and more flavorful dish. The same is true of roasts and chicken pieces.

Pork Chops with Hot Pineapple Salsa 30

MAKES 4 servings **PREP** 20 minutes **GRILL** 8 minutes

- 1 20-ounce can crushed pineapple (juice pack), undrained
- 1 15-ounce can black-eyed peas, rinsed and drained
- ½ cup finely chopped red onion (1 medium)
- ⅓ cup finely chopped sweet red pepper
- ¼ cup snipped fresh parsley
- 2 jalapeños, seeded and finely chopped*
- ½ teaspoon salt
- ¼ teaspoon ground cumin
- 4 boneless pork top loin chops, cut 1 inch thick
- 1 tablespoon olive oil
- ½ teaspoon dried thyme, crushed
- ½ teaspoon black pepper
- ½ teaspoon lemon juice

① For salsa, in a medium saucepan combine pineapple, black-eyed peas, red onion, sweet pepper, parsley, jalapeños, salt, and cumin. Cook on medium heat about 5 minutes or until heated through, stirring occasionally. Remove from heat; cover and keep warm.

② Meanwhile, trim fat from chops. In a small bowl combine oil, thyme, black pepper, and lemon juice. Brush both sides of chops with lemon mixture.

③ For a charcoal grill, grill chops on the rack of an uncovered grill directly over medium coals for 8 to 10 minutes or until meat juices run clear (160°F), turning once halfway through grilling. (For a gas grill, preheat grill. Reduce heat to medium. Place chops on grill rack over heat. Cover and grill as above.) Serve chops with warm salsa.

*Tip: Because chiles contain volatile oils that can burn your skin and eyes, avoid direct contact with them as much as possible. When working with chiles, wear plastic or rubber gloves. If your bare hands do touch the peppers, wash your hands and fingernails well with soap and warm water.

PER SERVING 466 calories; 12 g total fat (3 g sat. fat); 93 mg cholesterol; 661 mg sodium; 43 g carbohydrate; 7 g fiber; 44 g protein

Pork Chops Primavera

Orange and Rosemary Pork Chops

Pork Chops with Sweet Onion Sauce

MAKES 6 servings **PREP** 20 minutes
COOK 6 to 7 hours (low) or 3 to 3½ hours (high)

- 2 medium onions, thinly sliced and separated into rings
- 6 boneless pork top loin chops, cut 1 inch thick
- ¾ cup ketchup
- ¼ cup grape jelly
- 2 tablespoons quick-cooking tapioca, crushed
- 2 tablespoons red wine vinegar
- 1 teaspoon dried Italian seasoning, crushed
- ¼ teaspoon salt
- ¼ teaspoon black pepper
- 1 24-ounce package frozen potatoes for steaming and mashing

① Place onions in a 3½- or 4-quart slow cooker. Trim fat from chops. Arrange chops in cooker, overlapping as necessary. In a medium bowl combine ketchup, jelly, tapioca, vinegar, Italian seasoning, salt, and pepper; pour over chops.

② Cover and cook on low-heat setting for 6 to 7 hours or on high-heat setting for 3 to 3½ hours.

③ Meanwhile, prepare potatoes according to package directions. Serve chops with onion mixture and potatoes.

PER SERVING 458 calories; 9 g total fat (3 g sat. fat); 131 mg cholesterol; 854 mg sodium; 44 g carbohydrate; 3 g fiber; 47 g protein

Although white and yellow onions are similar in quality, they have different uses. White onions are stronger and the onion of choice for Mexican salsas, such as pico de gallo. Yellow onions are milder and have a higher sugar content—ideal for slow cooking which develops a rich, sweet flavor.

Orange and Rosemary Pork Chops

MAKES 4 servings **PREP** 15 minutes **MARINATE** 4 to 24 hours
GRILL 20 minutes

- 4 boneless pork top loin chops, cut 1 inch thick
- 2 teaspoons finely shredded orange peel
- ½ cup orange juice
- 2 tablespoons snipped fresh rosemary or 2 teaspoons dried rosemary, crushed
- 2 tablespoons Worcestershire-style marinade for chicken
- 1 tablespoon olive oil
- 1 tablespoon mild-flavor molasses or maple syrup
- ⅛ teaspoon black pepper
- 2 cups orange, apple, or peach wood chips
  Fresh rosemary sprigs (optional)

① Trim fat from chops. Place chops in a resealable plastic bag set in a shallow dish. For marinade, in a small bowl combine orange peel, orange juice, the snipped or dried rosemary, Worcestershire-style marinade, oil, molasses, and pepper.

② Pour marinade over chops. Seal bag; turn to coat chops. Marinate in the refrigerator for 4 to 24 hours, turning bag occasionally.

③ At least 1 hour before grilling, soak wood chips in enough water to cover. Drain before using. Drain chops, reserving marinade.

④ For a charcoal grill, arrange medium-hot coals around a drip pan. Test for medium heat above pan. Sprinkle drained chips over coals. Place chops on grill rack over drip pan. Cover and grill for 20 to 24 minutes or until meat juices run clear (160°F), brushing once with the reserved marinade halfway through grilling. (For a gas grill, preheat grill. Reduce heat to medium. Adjust for indirect cooking. Add drained chips according to the manufacturer's directions. Place chops on a rack in a roasting pan; place pan on grill rack over burner that is off. Grill as above.) Discard any remaining marinade. If desired, garnish chops with rosemary sprigs.

PER SERVING 178 calories; 6 g total fat (2 g sat. fat); 62 mg cholesterol; 86 mg sodium; 3 g carbohydrate; 0 g fiber; 25 g protein

Oven Cassoulet

MAKES 6 servings **PREP** 30 minutes **STAND** 1 hour
COOK 1 hour 20 minutes **BAKE** 25 minutes **OVEN** 350°F

- 8 ounces dried Great Northern beans (1¼ cups)
- 1 tablespoon canola oil or olive oil
- 6 bone-in chicken thighs (about 2¼ pounds total), skinned
- 1 cup thinly sliced carrots (2 medium)
- 1 medium onion, cut into thin wedges
- ½ cup sliced celery (1 stalk)
- 2 cloves garlic, minced
- 1 14.5-ounce can no-salt-added diced tomatoes, undrained
- 6 ounces cooked light, smoked sausage, cut into bite-size pieces
- ½ teaspoon dried thyme, crushed
- ¼ teaspoon salt
- ⅛ to ¼ teaspoon cayenne pepper (optional)

① Rinse beans. In a large saucepan combine beans and 4 cups *water*. Bring to boiling; reduce heat. Simmer, uncovered, for 2 minutes. Remove from heat. Cover and let stand for 1 hour. (Or place beans in water in saucepan. Cover and let soak in a cool place overnight.) Drain and rinse beans. Return beans to saucepan. Stir in 4 cups fresh *water*. Bring to boiling; reduce heat. Simmer, covered, for 1 to 1½ hours or until beans are tender. Drain beans.

② Preheat oven to 350°F. In a large skillet heat oil on medium-high heat. Add chicken; reduce heat to medium-low. Cook about 10 minutes or until chicken is brown on both sides. Remove chicken from skillet. Drain all but 1 tablespoon of the drippings from skillet.

③ Add carrots, onion, celery, and garlic to drippings in skillet. Cook, covered, about 10 minutes or just until vegetables are tender, stirring occasionally. Stir in beans, tomatoes, sausage, thyme, salt, and, if desired, cayenne pepper. Bring to boiling.

④ Transfer mixture to a 2-quart rectangular baking dish. Arrange chicken on top. Bake about 25 minutes or until chicken is no longer pink (180°F).

Tip: Save time by using two 15-ounce cans Great Northern beans, rinsed and drained, instead of the dried beans (omit Step 1) and use bottled minced garlic; omit the salt.

PER SERVING 347 calories; 10 g total fat (3 g sat. fat); 98 mg cholesterol; 481 mg sodium; 32 g carbohydrate; 10 g fiber; 33 g protein

Floribbean Ribs with Mango Mojo ✪

MAKES 6 servings **PREP** 20 minutes **BAKE** 2 hours
GRILL 10 minutes **OVEN** 350°F

- 1 tablespoon whole allspice
- 1 tablespoon cumin seeds
- 2 teaspoons fennel seeds
- 1 teaspoon mustard seeds
- 1 teaspoon salt
- 4 to 5 pounds meaty pork spareribs or pork loin back ribs
- 2 cups hickory or oak wood chips
- 2 medium mangoes, seeded, peeled, and chopped
- 2 tablespoons honey
- 2 tablespoons grated fresh ginger
- 2 tablespoons key lime juice or lime juice
- 2 tablespoons bourbon (optional)
- ¼ cup chopped green onions (2)
- 1 jalapeño, seeded and finely chopped (see tip, page 148)

① Preheat oven to 350°F. Heat a medium skillet on medium heat. Add allspice, cumin seeds, fennel seeds, and mustard seeds to skillet. Cook about 3 minutes or until seeds are fragrant, stirring occasionally. Crush seeds with a mortar and pestle or in a clean coffee grinder. Stir in salt.

② Trim fat from ribs. Place ribs in a shallow roasting pan. Generously sprinkle allspice mixture over both sides of ribs; rub in with your fingers. Bake, covered, for 2 to 2½ hours or until ribs are very tender. Drain off fat.

③ At least 1 hour before grilling, soak wood chips in enough water to cover. Drain before using.

④ For Mango Mojo, in a food processor or blender combine mangoes, honey, ginger, lime juice, and, if desired, bourbon. Cover and process until smooth. Stir in green onions and jalapeño.

⑤ For a charcoal grill, sprinkle wood chips over medium coals. Place ribs on grill rack directly over coals. Cover and grill about 10 minutes or until ribs are brown, turning once halfway through grilling and brushing occasionally with some of the Mango Mojo. (For a gas grill, preheat grill. Reduce heat to medium. Add wood chips according to the manufacturer's directions. Place ribs on grill rack over heat. Cover and grill as above.) Drizzle ribs with the remaining Mango Mojo.

PER SERVING 239 calories; 7 g total fat (2 g sat. fat); 84 mg cholesterol; 454 mg sodium; 20 g carbohydrate; 2 g fiber; 25 g protein

Mexican-Style Shrimp Pizza, page 179

Fresh Fish & Seafood

Open-Face Barbecue Tilapia Sandwiches ㉚

MAKES 4 servings **PREP** 15 minutes
GRILL 4 to 6 minutes per ½-inch thickness

- 4 4- to 5-ounce fresh or frozen skinless tilapia or flounder fillets

   Nonstick cooking spray
- 2 tablespoons light mayonnaise or salad dressing
- 2 teaspoons lemon juice
- 2 cups packaged shredded cabbage with carrot (coleslaw mix)
- 4 slices whole wheat bread, toasted
- 2 tablespoons bottled low-calorie barbecue sauce

① Thaw fish, if frozen. Rinse fish; pat dry with paper towels. Measure thickness of fish. Lightly coat both sides of fish fillets with cooking spray.

② For a charcoal grill, place fish on the greased rack of an uncovered grill directly over medium coals. Grill 4 to 6 minutes per ½-inch thickness or until fish flakes easily when tested with a fork. (For a gas grill, preheat grill. Reduce heat to medium. Place fish on greased grill rack over heat. Cover and grill as above.)

③ In a medium bowl stir together mayonnaise and lemon juice. Add cabbage; toss to coat.

④ To assemble, spoon cabbage mixture onto bread slices. Top with fish fillets. Drizzle fish with barbecue sauce.

PER SERVING 206 calories; 5 g total fat (1 g sat. fat); 59 mg cholesterol; 339 mg sodium; 13 g carbohydrate; 2 g fiber; 26 g protein

Herbed Fish and Vegetables with Lemon Mayo

Herbed Fish and Vegetables with Lemon Mayo ㉚

MAKES 2 servings **PREP** 20 minutes **COOK** 6 minutes

- 2 6-ounce fresh or frozen skinless flounder, sole, cod, or perch fillets, ½ to ¾ inch thick
- 2 tablespoons assorted snipped fresh herbs (such as parsley, basil, oregano, and thyme)
- 1 cup thin bite-size strips carrots
- 1 cup thin bite-size strips zucchini and/or yellow summer squash
- ½ of a lemon, thinly sliced
- 3 tablespoons light mayonnaise or salad dressing
- 1 tablespoon thinly sliced green onion
- ¼ teaspoon finely shredded lemon peel
- 1 teaspoon lemon juice

① Thaw fish, if frozen. Rinse fish; pat dry with paper towels. Using a sharp knife, make shallow bias cuts into both sides of fish fillets, spacing cuts ¾ inch apart. Sprinkle herbs over fillets, tucking into cuts.

② Place a steamer insert in a large deep saucepan or large skillet with a tight-fitting lid. Add water to the saucepan or skillet to just below the steamer insert. Bring water to boiling. Place carrots and zucchini in the steamer basket. Place fish on top of vegetables. Arrange lemon slices on top of fish. Cover and steam on medium heat for 6 to 8 minutes or until fish flakes easily when tested with a fork, adding more water as needed to maintain steam.

③ Meanwhile, in a small bowl stir together mayonnaise, green onion, lemon peel, and lemon juice.

④ Serve mayonnaise mixture with fish and vegetables.

PER SERVING 270 calories; 10 g total fat (2 g sat. fat); 90 mg cholesterol; 340 mg sodium; 13 g carbohydrate; 4 g fiber; 34 g protein

When you can find it, buy U.S. raised tilapia. The domestic fish has better texture and flavor than tilapia imported from overseas.

Grilled Jamaican Jerk Fish Wraps

Gazpacho Fish Fillets 30

MAKES 4 servings **START TO FINISH** 30 minutes

- 1 pound fresh or frozen fish fillets (such as orange roughy, cod, or other fish), ½ to ¾ inch thick
- ½ teaspoon salt
- ⅛ teaspoon black pepper
- 1 8.8-ounce pouch cooked whole grain brown rice or 1½ cups hot cooked brown rice
- 1 large tomato, chopped
- ¼ cup chopped, seeded cucumber
- ¼ cup chopped sweet green pepper
- ¼ cup chopped celery
- 2 tablespoons chopped onion
- 2 tablespoons tomato paste
- 1 tablespoon snipped fresh thyme or 1 teaspoon dried thyme, crushed
   Fresh thyme sprigs (optional)

① Thaw fish, if frozen. Rinse fish; pat dry with paper towels. Cut fish into serving-size portions. Sprinkle both sides of fish fillets with ¼ teaspoon of the salt and the black pepper; set aside. If using, heat cooked whole grain brown rice according to package directions; set aside.

② In a 2-quart microwave-safe casserole or baking dish stir together tomato, cucumber, sweet pepper, celery, onion, tomato paste, the 1 tablespoon fresh thyme, and the remaining ¼ teaspoon salt. Cover tightly with lid or plastic wrap. Microwave on high for 4 to 6 minutes or until celery is crisp-tender. Transfer tomato mixture to a medium bowl; cover and keep warm.

③ Arrange fish in the same microwave-safe casserole or baking dish, turning under any thin portions of fish to make an even thickness. Cover and microwave on high for 3 to 5 minutes or until fish flakes easily when tested with a fork.

④ Serve fish and tomato mixture with rice. If desired, garnish with fresh thyme sprigs.

PER SERVING 197 calories; 3 g total fat (0 g sat. fat); 22 mg cholesterol; 378 mg sodium; 23 g carbohydrate; 2 g fiber; 20 g protein

Grilled Jamaican Jerk Fish Wraps 30

MAKES 4 servings **START TO FINISH** 30 minutes

- 1 pound fresh or frozen skinless flounder, cod, or sole fillets
- 1½ teaspoons Jamaican jerk seasoning
- 4 7- to 8-inch whole grain flour tortillas
- 2 cups packaged fresh baby spinach
- ¾ cup chopped, seeded tomato
- ¾ cup chopped fresh mango or pineapple
- 2 tablespoons snipped fresh cilantro
- 1 tablespoon finely chopped, seeded fresh jalapeño*
- 1 tablespoon lime juice

① Thaw fish, if frozen. Rinse fish; pat dry with paper towels. Sprinkle both sides of fish fillets with Jamaican jerk seasoning; rub in with your fingers. Measure thickness of fish.

② For a charcoal grill, grill tortillas on the greased rack of an uncovered grill directly over medium coals about 1 minute or until bottoms of tortillas have grill marks. (For a gas grill, preheat grill. Reduce heat to medium. Place tortillas on greased grill rack over heat. Cover; grill as above.) Remove from grill and set aside.

③ For a charcoal grill, place fish on the grill rack directly over medium coals. Grill fish for 4 to 6 minutes per ½-inch thickness or until fish flakes easily when tested with a fork, carefully turning once halfway through grilling. (For a gas grill, add fish; cover and grill as above.) Coarsely flake the fish.

④ Meanwhile, in a medium bowl toss together spinach, tomato, mango, cilantro, jalapeño, and lime juice.

⑤ To serve, place tortillas, grill mark sides down, on a flat work surface. Divide spinach mixture and fish among tortillas. Fold tortillas over to enclose filling. Cut each in half to serve.

*Tip: Because chiles contain volatile oils that can burn your skin and eyes, avoid direct contract with them as much as possible. When working with chiles, wear plastic or rubber gloves. If your bare hands do touch the peppers, wash your hands and fingernails well with soap and warm water.

PER SERVING 254 calories; 4 g total fat (1 g sat. fat); 48 mg cholesterol; 509 mg sodium; 23 g carbohydrate; 11 g fiber; 29 g protein

Crispy Fish and Peppers

MAKES 4 servings **START TO FINISH** 20 minutes

- 1 pound fresh or frozen small fish fillets (such as grouper, catfish, or tilapia)
- ¾ cup buttermilk or sour milk*
- 1 egg
- 1 teaspoon Cajun seasoning
- 1 cup all-purpose flour
- 3 to 4 tablespoons vegetable oil
- 1 cup sliced and/or chopped miniature sweet peppers
- 1 lemon, cut up

① Thaw fish, if frozen. Rinse fish and pat dry with paper towels.

② In a shallow dish whisk together buttermilk, egg, and Cajun seasoning. Place flour in another shallow dish. Dip fish in buttermilk mixture and then into flour, turning to coat. Repeat dipping and coating once more.

③ In a large heavy skillet heat 3 tablespoons of the oil on medium-high heat. Carefully add fish to hot oil (working in batches, if necessary). Cook for 6 to 10 minutes or until golden and fish flakes easily when tested with a fork, turning fish once halfway through cooking. Add more of the remaining 1 tablespoon oil, if needed. Drain fish on paper towels.

④ Drain oil from skillet; wipe clean with paper towels. Add sweet peppers to skillet and cook and stir about 2 minutes or until crisp tender.

⑤ Serve fish with sweet peppers and lemon.

*Tip: To make ¾ cup sour milk, place 2 teaspoons lemon juice or vinegar in a glass measuring cup. Add enough milk to equal ¾ cup liquid; stir. Let stand for 5 minutes before using.

PER SERVING 251 calories; 13 g total fat (2 g sat. fat); 97 mg cholesterol; 188 mg sodium; 8 g carbohydrate; 2 g fiber; 26 g protein

When frying fish—or anything else—it's important not to crowd the pan. When there is too much food in the pan, the temperature of the oil drops. When that happens, more oil is absorbed into the food and the coating gets soggy, not crispy.

Grilled Halibut with Corn and Pepper Relish

MAKES 4 servings **PREP** 45 minutes **GRILL** 8 minutes

- 4 5- to 6-ounce fresh or frozen halibut steaks, cut 1 inch thick
  - Kosher salt
  - Black pepper
- 3 tablespoons olive oil
- 1 tablespoon snipped fresh parsley
- 1 tablespoon snipped fresh oregano
- 1½ cups fresh cut corn or frozen whole kernel corn
- 1 cup finely snipped sweet red pepper
- 1 cup finely snipped sweet green pepper
- 2 cloves garlic, minced
- ¼ teaspoon kosher salt
- ⅛ teaspoon cayenne pepper
- ½ cup seeded and chopped tomato
- ¼ cup finely chopped red onion
- 3 tablespoons snipped fresh parsley
- 1 tablespoon white wine vinegar
  - Fresh oregano (optional)

① Thaw fish, if frozen. Rinse fish; pat dry with paper towels. Sprinkle both sides of fish steaks with salt and black pepper. In a bowl combine 1 tablespoon of olive oil, 1 tablespoon parsley, and oregano. Rub on both sides of fish steaks; set aside.

② In a large skillet heat 1 tablespoon of the remaining oil on medium-high heat. Add corn; cook about 4 minutes or just until starting to brown, stirring occasionally. Add sweet peppers; cook and stir for 2 minutes more. Stir in garlic, the ¼ teaspoon salt, and cayenne pepper. Cook and stir for 1 minute more. Remove from heat; cool slightly.

③ For a charcoal grill, place fish on the rack of an uncovered grill directly over medium coals. Grill for 8 to 12 minutes or until fish flakes easily when tested with a fork, carefully turning once halfway through grilling. (For a gas grill, preheat grill. Reduce heat to medium. Place fish on grill rack over heat. Cover and grill as above.)

④ Meanwhile, for relish, in a medium bowl combine corn mixture, tomato, red onion, the 3 tablespoons parsley, vinegar, and the remaining 1 tablespoon oil; toss well.

⑤ Serve each fish steak with ½ cup of the relish. Cover and chill the remaining relish for another use. If desired, garnish with additional fresh oregano.

PER SERVING 282 calories; 12 g total fat (2 g sat. fat); 45 mg cholesterol; 283 mg sodium; 13 g carbohydrate; 2 g fiber; 32 g protein

Chile-Lime Catfish with Corn Sauté

menu

Broccoli and
Cauliflower Saute

Tomato and Red
Onion Salad

Grilled Bass with
Lemon and Herbs
[below]

Corn bread

Grilled Bass with Lemon and Herbs 🜵

MAKES 4 servings **PREP** 15 minutes
GRILL 4 to 6 minutes per ½-inch thickness

- 1 **pound fresh or frozen striped bass fillets**
- 2 **teaspoons olive oil**
- ¼ **teaspoon salt**
- ⅛ **teaspoon black pepper**
- 2 **tablespoons snipped fresh parsley**
- 1 **tablespoon snipped fresh basil and/or chives**
- 2 **teaspoons finely shredded lemon peel**
- 1 **teaspoon snipped fresh rosemary**

① Thaw fish, if frozen. Rinse; pat dry with paper towels. Cut into serving-size portions. Brush both sides of fish fillets with oil; sprinkle with salt and pepper. Measure thickness of fish.

② For a charcoal grill, place fish on greased rack of uncovered grill directly over medium coals. Grill 4 to 6 minutes per ½-inch thickness of fish or until fish flakes easily when tested with fork, carefully turning once halfway through grilling. (For a gas grill, preheat grill. Reduce heat to medium. Place fish on greased grill rack over heat; cover. Grill as above.)

③ In a bowl combine parsley, basil, lemon peel, and rosemary. Sprinkle over fish.

PER SERVING 131 calories; 5 g total fat (1 g sat. fat); 90 mg cholesterol; 225 mg sodium; 0 g carbohydrate; 0 g fiber; 20 g protein

Chile-Lime Catfish with Corn Saute 🜵

MAKES 4 servings **PREP** 25 minutes
COOK 4 to 6 minutes per ½-inch thickness

- 4 **4- to 5-ounce fresh or frozen skinless catfish, sole, or tilapia fillets**
- 1 **tablespoon lime juice**
- 1 **teaspoon ground ancho chile or chili powder**
- ¼ **teaspoon salt**
- 1 **tablespoon canola oil**
- 2⅔ **cups frozen gold and white whole kernel corn, thawed**
- ¼ **cup finely chopped red onion**
- 2 **teaspoons finely chopped, seeded fresh jalapeño***
- 2 **cloves garlic, minced**
- 1 **tablespoon snipped fresh cilantro**
   Lime wedges (optional)

① Thaw fish, if frozen. Rinse fish; pat dry with paper towels. In a small bowl stir together lime juice, ground ancho chile, and salt. Brush mixture evenly on both sides of fish fillets. Measure thickness of fish.

② In a large nonstick skillet heat 2 teaspoons of the oil on medium-high heat. Add fish; cook for 4 to 6 minutes per ½-inch thickness or until fish flakes easily when tested with a fork, turning once halfway through cooking. Remove from skillet. Cover and keep warm.

③ In the same skillet heat the remaining 1 teaspoon oil on medium heat. Add corn, red onion, jalapeño, and garlic; cook about 2 minutes or until vegetables are heated through and just starting to soften, stirring occasionally. Remove from heat. Stir in cilantro.

④ Serve corn mixture with fish and, if desired, lime wedges.

***Tip:** Because chiles contain volatile oils that can burn your skin and eyes, avoid direct contact with them as much as possible. When working with chiles, wear plastic or rubber gloves. If your bare hands do touch the peppers, wash your hands and fingernails well with soap and warm water.

PER SERVING 288 calories; 13 g total fat (2 g sat. fat); 53 mg cholesterol; 216 mg sodium; 25 g carbohydrate; 3 g fiber; 21 g protein

Catfish and Turkey Sausage Jambalaya

MAKES 4 servings **PREP** 30 minutes **COOK** 20 minutes **STAND** 5 minutes

- 8 ounces fresh or frozen skinless catfish fillets
- 1 teaspoon olive oil or vegetable oil
- 4 ounces uncooked turkey hot Italian sausage links, cut into ½-inch pieces
- ½ cup chopped onion (1 medium)
- ½ cup chopped sweet green pepper (1 small)
- ½ cup chopped celery (1 stalk)
- 3 cloves garlic, minced
- 1 14.5-ounce can no-salt-added diced tomatoes, drained
- 1 14-ounce can reduced-sodium chicken broth
- 1½ cups instant brown rice
- 1½ teaspoons paprika
- 1 teaspoon dried oregano, crushed, or 1 tablespoon snipped fresh oregano
- ½ teaspoon dried thyme, crushed, or 1½ teaspoons snipped fresh thyme
- ⅛ to ¼ teaspoon cayenne pepper
  Fresh oregano

① Thaw fish, if frozen. Rinse fish; pat dry with paper towels. Cut fish into ¾-inch chunks. Set aside.

② In a large saucepan heat oil on medium heat. Add sausage; cook and stir for 3 to 4 minutes or until browned. Add onion, sweet pepper, celery, and garlic; cook about 10 minutes or until vegetables are tender and sausage is cooked through, stirring occasionally.

③ Stir in tomatoes, broth, uncooked rice, paprika, dried oregano (if using), dried thyme (if using), and cayenne pepper. Bring to boiling; reduce heat to medium-low. Cover and simmer for 5 minutes. Stir in fish, fresh oregano (if using), and fresh thyme (if using); cook about 5 minutes more or until liquid is nearly absorbed and rice is tender. Remove from heat. Cover and let stand for 5 minutes.

④ To serve, use a slotted spoon to transfer mixture to shallow bowls. If desired, garnish with fresh oregano.

PER SERVING 263 calories; 9 g total fat (2 g sat. fat); 44 mg cholesterol; 548 mg sodium; 29 g carbohydrate; 4 g fiber; 18 g protein

Grilled Tuna and Cannellini Bean Salad

MAKES 4 servings **PREP** 25 minutes **GRILL** 8 minutes

- 2 5- to 6-ounce fresh or frozen tuna steaks, cut 1 inch thick
- 2 tablespoons lemon juice
- 2 tablespoons olive oil
- 1 tablespoon balsamic vinegar
- 1 tablespoon Dijon mustard
- 4 cups fresh baby spinach leaves
- 2 15-ounce cans cannellini beans (white kidney beans), rinsed and drained
- 1 cup thinly sliced red onion
- 1 cup sliced celery
- ¼ cup oil-packed dried tomatoes, drained and chopped
- 2 tablespoons snipped fresh parsley

① Thaw fish, if frozen. Rinse fish; pat dry with paper towels.

② For a charcoal grill, place fish on the greased rack of an uncovered grill directly over medium coals. Grill for 8 to 12 minutes or until fish flakes easily when tested with a fork, carefully turning once halfway through grilling. (For a gas grill, preheat grill. Reduce heat to medium. Place fish on greased grill rack over heat. Cover and grill as above.)

③ Meanwhile, for dressing, in a screw-top jar combine lemon juice, oil, vinegar, and mustard. Cover and shake well. Set aside 1 tablespoon of the dressing to drizzle over grilled fish.

④ In a large bowl combine spinach, beans, red onion, celery, tomatoes, and parsley. Drizzle with remaining dressing; toss gently to coat.

⑤ To serve, arrange spinach mixture on a serving platter. Slice fish; place on top of spinach mixture. Drizzle fish with the reserved dressing.

PER SERVING 306 calories; 9 g total fat (1 g sat. fat); 32 mg cholesterol; 515 mg sodium; 38 g carbohydrate; 12 g fiber; 31 g protein

Grilled Tuna and Cannellini Bean Salad

Curried Tuna Sandwiches

Curried Tuna Sandwiches ③⓪

MAKES 4 servings **START TO FINISH** 15 minutes

1½	cups creamy deli coleslaw
1	small tomato, seeded and chopped
1	teaspoon curry powder
1	6-ounce can tuna, drained and flaked
¼	cup chopped peanuts
4	ciabatta rolls, cut in half
4	large butterhead (Bibb or Boston) lettuce leaves
	Light sour cream dip with chives (optional)

① In a small bowl stir together coleslaw, tomato, and curry powder. Fold in tuna and peanuts.

② Spoon tuna mixture onto bottoms of ciabatta rolls; top with lettuce leaves. If desired, top with sour cream dip. Add roll tops.

PER SERVING 254 calories; 9 g total fat (2 g sat. fat); 21 mg cholesterol; 434 mg sodium; 28 g carbohydrate; 3 g fiber; 17 g protein

Use either mild or hot curry powder in the filling for Curried Tuna Sandwiches, depending on your taste.

Tuna-Red Pepper Salad Wraps ③⓪

MAKES 2 servings **START TO FINISH** 15 minutes

1	5-ounce pouch chunk light tuna
¼	cup light mayonnaise or salad dressing
¼	cup chopped bottled roasted sweet red pepper
1	tablespoon chopped sweet gherkin
6	Bibb lettuce leaves
1	slice whole wheat bread, toasted and cut into 6 strips

① In a small bowl combine tuna, mayonnaise, roasted sweet pepper, and gherkin. Spoon some of the tuna mixture onto each lettuce leaf near one edge. Top each with a strip of toast. Roll up lettuce, starting from the edge with the tuna mixture.

PER SERVING 216 calories; 11 g total fat (2 g sat. fat); 48 mg cholesterol; 599 mg sodium; 10 g carbohydrate; 2 g fiber; 19 g protein

Seasoned Tuna Sandwiches ✪③⓪

MAKES 4 sandwiches **START TO FINISH** 15 minutes

2	6-ounce cans low-sodium chunk (light or white) tuna, drained and flaked
2	teaspoons lemon juice
1	tablespoon olive oil
1	teaspoon capers, drained
⅛	teaspoon black pepper
2	tablespoons light mayonnaise or salad dressing
8	slices whole wheat bread
4	romaine lettuce leaves, ribs removed
4	large tomato slices

① In a small bowl combine tuna, lemon juice, oil, capers, and pepper.

② To assemble, spread mayonnaise on 4 of the bread slices. Top with lettuce, tomato, tuna mixture, and remaining bread slices.

PER SANDWICH 277 calories; 8 g total fat (1 g sat. fat); 48 mg cholesterol; 446 mg sodium; 23 g carbohydrate; 4 g fiber; 28 g protein

Seasoned Tuna Sandwiches

Tuna Salad Pockets

MAKES 4 servings **START TO FINISH** 15 minutes

- 1   12-ounce can solid white tuna (water pack), drained and broken into chunks
- ¼   cup finely chopped onion
- ¼   cup thinly sliced celery
- ¼   cup purchased coarsely shredded fresh carrot
- 1   tablespoon capers, rinsed and drained
- 2   tablespoons olive oil
- 2   tablespoons lime juice
- 1   tablespoon Dijon mustard
- 1   tablespoon champagne vinegar or white wine vinegar
- 1½   cups torn mixed salad greens
- 2   large whole wheat or regular pita bread rounds, halved crosswise

① In a medium bowl combine tuna, onion, celery, carrot, and capers. Set aside.

② For vinaigrette, in a small screw-top jar combine olive oil, lime juice, mustard, and vinegar. Cover and shake well to combine. Pour vinaigrette over tuna mixture, tossing gently to coat. Add salad greens and toss gently to combine.

③ Place a pita bread half in each of 4 shallow salad bowls. Fill pita bread halves with tuna mixture.

PER SERVING 268 calories; 9 g total fat (1 g sat. fat); 38 mg cholesterol; 713 mg sodium; 21 g carbohydrate; 3 g fiber; 26 g protein

If you don't like the strings in celery, getting rid of them is easy. Simply run a vegetable peeler down the back of each stalk. The strings will come right off—and you'll be left with crunchy, string-free stalks of celery.

Tuna Salad Niçoise

MAKES 4 servings **PREP** 30 minutes **BROIL** 8 minutes

- 1   pound fresh or frozen tuna steaks, cut 1 inch thick
- 3   tablespoons sherry vinegar or white wine vinegar
- 2   tablespoons finely chopped shallot or onion
- 1   tablespoon Dijon mustard
- 2   tablespoons olive oil
- 1   anchovy fillet, rinsed and mashed (optional)
-     Salt and black pepper
- 8   ounces tiny new potatoes, quartered
- 6   ounces fresh green beans
- 6   cups butterhead (Bibb or Boston) lettuce leaves
- ¾   cup thinly sliced radishes
- ½   cup niçoise olives or black ripe olives, pitted

① Thaw fish, if frozen. Rinse fish and pat dry with paper towels. For dressing, in a small bowl combine vinegar and shallot. Whisk in mustard. Add oil in a thin, steady stream, whisking constantly. If desired, stir in the anchovy; season to taste with salt and pepper. Remove 1 tablespoon of the dressing for brushing tuna steaks; set aside remaining dressing.

② Brush the 1 tablespoon dressing over both sides of tuna steaks. Place fish on the greased unheated rack of a broiler pan. Broil 4 inches from the heat for 8 to 12 minutes or until fish begins to flake when tested with a fork, gently turning once halfway through broiling time. Cut fish into slices.

③ Meanwhile, in a covered medium saucepan cook potatoes in enough boiling water to cover for 6 minutes. Add green beans; cook for 4 to 9 minutes more or until potatoes are tender. Drain and cool slightly.

④ To serve, arrange fish, potatoes, green beans, lettuce leaves, radishes, and olives on 4 serving plates. Serve with remaining dressing.

PER SERVING 354 calories; 16 g total fat (2 g sat. fat); 51 mg cholesterol; 475 mg sodium; 22 g carbohydrate; 6 g fiber; 30 g protein

Tuna and Fruit Salsa

menu

Fiesta Corn Salad

Brown rice pilaf

Tuna and Fruit Salsa
[below]

Almond Sandwich
Cookies

Ginger tea

Tuna and Fruit Salsa 30

MAKES 4 servings   **START TO FINISH** 25 minutes

- 4   5 to 6-ounces fresh or frozen tuna steaks, 1-inch thick
- 2   fresh peaches, halved and pitted
- 2   tablespoons olive oil
      Salt
      Cracked black pepper
- 2   tablespoons apricot preserves
- 1   tablespoon vinegar
- ½   cup fresh raspberries
- 6   tablespoons thinly sliced green onions (3)

① Thaw fish, if frozen. Rinse fish; pat dry with paper towels. Lightly brush fish steaks and peach halves with oil; sprinkle with salt and pepper.

② In a large skillet cook fish and peach halves on medium-high heat for 5 minutes. Remove peaches; set aside. Turn fish over and cook 6 to 7 minutes more or until fish flakes easily when tested with a fork. Remove fish to a platter and cover to keep warm.

③ Coarsely chop peach halves. In a medium microwave-safe bowl heat apricot preserves on high for 15 seconds. Stir in vinegar; gently fold in raspberries and peaches.

④ Serve fruit mixture with fish. Sprinkle with green onions.

PER SERVING 333 calories; 14 g total fat (3 g sat. fat); 54 mg cholesterol; 133 mg sodium; 17 g carbohydrate; 3 g fiber; 34 g protein

Pepper Jelly- and Soy-Glazed Salmon

MAKES 8 servings   **PREP** 30 minutes
MARINATE 1 hour   **GRILL** 15 minutes

- 1   2-pound fresh or frozen skinless salmon fillet, about 1 inch thick
- ⅔   cup green jalapeño jelly
- ⅓   cup rice vinegar
- ⅓   cup soy sauce
- 6   tablespoons sliced green onions (3)
- 1   tablespoon grated fresh ginger
- 2   teaspoons toasted sesame oil
- 3   cloves garlic, minced
- ¼   teaspoon crushed red pepper
- ¼   teaspoon snipped fresh cilantro
- ¼   cup sliced fresh jalapeños* and/or sliced green onions

① Thaw fish, if frozen. Rinse fish; pat dry. For marinade, in a small saucepan melt jelly on low heat; remove from heat. Stir in vinegar, soy sauce, the 6 tablespoons green onions, ginger, oil, garlic, and crushed red pepper. Place salmon in a shallow dish and pour marinade over fish. Cover; chill in the refrigerator for 1 to 2 hours, turning fish occasionally.

② Remove salmon from marinade, reserving marinade. For a charcoal grill, arrange medium-hot coals around edge of grill. Test for medium heat in center of grill. Place fish on a greased piece of foil. Place fish on foil in center of the grill. Cover; grill for 15 to 18 minutes or until fish flakes easily when tested with a fork. (For a gas grill, preheat grill. Reduce heat to medium. Adjust for indirect cooking. Grill as above.)

③ Meanwhile, for sauce, in a small saucepan bring reserved marinade to boiling; reduce heat. Simmer, uncovered, for 10 to 15 minutes or until reduced to ½ cup. Drizzle over fish. Sprinkle fish with cilantro and jalapeños and/or additional green onions.

*Tip: Because chiles contain volatile oils that can burn your skin and eyes, avoid direct contact with them as much as possible. When working with chiles, wear plastic or rubber gloves. If your bare hands do touch the peppers, wash your hands and fingernails well with soap and warm water.

PER SERVING 302 calories; 13 g total fat (3 g sat. fat); 67 mg cholesterol; 753 mg sodium; 19 g carbohydrate; 0 g fiber; 24 g protein

Herbed Salmon Loaf with Creamed Peas

MAKES 8 servings **PREP** 25 minutes **BAKE** 1 hour
STAND 10 minutes **OVEN** 350°F

- 2 14- to 15-ounce cans salmon, drained
- 1 cup cooked barley
- ½ cup finely chopped celery (1 stalk)
- ⅓ cup finely chopped onion (1 small)
- ¼ cup fine dry bread crumbs
- 2 tablespoons snipped fresh parsley or 2 teaspoons dried parsley flakes
- 2 tablespoons lemon juice
- 1 tablespoon snipped fresh dill or 1 teaspoon dried dill
- ¼ teaspoon black pepper
- 4 egg whites; ½ cup refrigerated or frozen egg product, thawed; or 2 eggs, lightly beaten
   Nonstick cooking spray
   Creamed Peas
   Fresh dill sprigs (optional)

① Preheat oven to 350°F. Remove skin and bones from salmon. Flake salmon. In a large bowl combine salmon, cooked barley, celery, onion, bread crumbs, parsley, lemon juice, snipped or dried dill, and pepper. Stir in egg whites.

② Lightly coat an 8 x 4 x 2-inch loaf pan with cooking spray. Press salmon mixture into pan. Bake about 1 hour or until an instant-read thermometer inserted into center of the loaf registers 160°F. Cover and let stand for 10 minutes.

③ To serve, carefully invert pan onto a cutting board to remove loaf. Invert loaf again and transfer to a serving platter. Cut into 12 slices. Serve warm with Creamed Peas. If desired, garnish with fresh dill sprigs.

Creamed Peas: In a small saucepan stir together 1 cup fat-free milk, 2½ teaspoons cornstarch, ¼ teaspoon salt, and a dash black pepper. Cook and stir until thickened and bubbly. Cook and stir for 2 minutes more. Stir in ½ cup cooked fresh or frozen peas and ⅛ teaspoon finely shredded lemon peel. Heat through. Makes about 1 cup.

PER SERVING 206 calories; 5 g total fat (1 g sat. fat); 82 mg cholesterol; 561 mg sodium; 13 g carbohydrate; 2 g fiber; 27 g protein

Salmon Alfredo ③⓪

MAKES 6 servings **START TO FINISH** 30 minutes

- 3 cups wide noodles
- 3 cups fresh broccoli florets
- 1 14.75-ounce can salmon, drained
- 1½ cups fat-free milk
- 3 tablespoons all-purpose flour
- 1 tablespoon dried chives
- 2 cloves garlic, minced
- ½ teaspoon finely shredded lemon peel
- 2 tablespoons coarsely shredded Parmesan cheese
   Black pepper (optional)

① Cook noodles according to package directions, adding broccoli for the last 3 minutes of cooking; drain and keep warm. Meanwhile, remove skin and bones from salmon and break into chunks; set aside.

② In a medium saucepan whisk together milk and flour; add chives and garlic. Cook and stir on medium heat until thickened and bubbly. Add salmon and lemon peel. Heat through.

③ Serve salmon mixture over noodle mixture. Sprinkle with Parmesan cheese and, if desired, pepper.

PER SERVING 227 calories; 5 g total fat (1 g sat. fat); 76 mg cholesterol; 351 mg sodium; 23 g carbohydrate; 2 g fiber; 23 g protein

Quick Salmon Alfredo: Prepare as directed, except use 1 teaspoon bottled minced garlic in place of the fresh garlic; use purchased broccoli florets for the regular broccoli; and use two 7.1-ounce pouches skinless, boneless pink salmon instead of the 14.75-ounce can salmon.

Swap an equal amount of tuna for the salmon in Salmon Alfredo to make Tuna Alfredo. Chunk or solid white Albacore tuna works best because either stays in chunks rather than flaking, as light tuna tends to do.

Seafood Enchiladas

Chile-Dusted Salmon with Pineapple-Jicama Salsa ③⓪

MAKES 4 servings **PREP** 25 minutes
GRILL 4 to 6 minutes per ½-inch thickness

4	6-ounce fresh or frozen salmon steaks, ½ to 1 inch thick
2	teaspoons chili powder
½	teaspoon salt
1½	cups chopped fresh pineapple
1	cup chopped, peeled jicama
½	cup chopped red onion
1	large Anaheim chile, seeded and finely chopped*
3	tablespoons snipped fresh cilantro
3	tablespoons lime juice

① Thaw fish, if frozen. Rinse fish; pat dry with paper towels. Sprinkle both sides of fish steaks with chili powder and salt. Measure thickness of fish. Cover and chill in the refrigerator.

② For pineapple salsa, in a medium bowl combine pineapple, jicama, red onion, Anaheim chile, cilantro, and lime juice. Mix well and let stand at room temperature while grilling fish.

③ For a charcoal grill, grill fish on the greased rack of an uncovered grill directly over medium coals for 4 to 6 minutes per ½-inch thickness or until fish flakes easily when tested with a fork, carefully turning once halfway through grilling. (For a gas grill, preheat grill. Reduce heat to medium. Place fish on a greased grill rack over heat. Cover and grill as above.)

④ Serve immediately with pineapple salsa.

*Tip: Because chiles contain volatile oils that can burn your skin and eyes, avoid direct contact with them as much as possible. When working with chiles, wear plastic or rubber gloves. If your bare hands do touch the peppers, wash your hands and fingernails well with soap and warm water.

PER SERVING 367 calories; 19 g total fat (4 g sat. fat); 100 mg cholesterol; 408 mg sodium; 14 g carbohydrate; 3 g fiber; 35 g protein

Seafood Enchiladas

MAKES 10 enchiladas **PREP** 1 hour
STAND 45 minutes **BAKE** 25 minutes **OVEN** 350°F

2	to 3 dried ancho chiles or mulato chiles*
2	cups shredded Chihuahua cheese, Monterey Jack cheese, or farmer cheese (8 ounces)
12	ounces chopped cooked shrimp; 12 ounces chopped cooked crabmeat; two 6-ounce packages frozen peeled cooked shrimp, thawed and chopped; or 12 ounces frozen crabmeat, thawed and flaked
10	6-inch corn tortillas
1	tablespoon olive oil or vegetable oil
½	cup chopped onion (1 medium)
⅓	cup all-purpose flour
¼	teaspoon salt
¼	teaspoon black pepper
3	cups milk

① For filling, cut dried chiles open; discard stems and seeds. Place chiles in a small bowl and cover with boiling water. Let stand for 45 to 60 minutes to soften; drain well. Cut 1 of the chiles into thin slivers; cut remaining chile(s) into small pieces. Set chile slivers aside to use as a garnish. In a medium bowl combine 1½ cups of the cheese, the shrimp, and the chile pieces. Set filling aside.

② Preheat oven to 350°F. Stack tortillas and wrap tightly in foil. Bake about 10 minutes or until heated through.

③ Spoon about ¼ cup filling onto each tortilla near one end; roll up. Place filled tortillas, seam sides down, in a 3-quart rectangular baking dish.

④ For sauce, in a medium saucepan heat oil on medium heat. Add onion; cook and stir until tender. Stir in flour, salt, and black pepper. Add milk all at once. Cook and stir until thickened and bubbly. Pour sauce over filled tortillas.

⑤ Cover; bake about 20 minutes or until heated through. Remove cover; sprinkle with the remaining cheese. Place chile slivers diagonally over enchiladas. Bake about 5 minutes more or until cheese melts.

PER ENCHILADA 241 calories; 11 g total fat (6 g sat. fat); 92 mg cholesterol; 334 mg sodium; 19 g carbohydrate; 0 g fiber; 17 g protein

Scallop Salad with Basil Vinaigrette ③⓪

MAKES 4 servings **START TO FINISH** 25 minutes

- 1 pound fresh or frozen sea scallops
- ¼ cup snipped fresh basil
- 3 tablespoons balsamic vinegar
- 2 tablespoons lemon juice
- 2 tablespoons olive oil
- 2 teaspoons Dijon mustard
- ½ teaspoon black pepper
  Nonstick cooking spray
- 6 cups torn mixed salad greens
- 3 plum tomatoes, seeded and chopped
- 1 cup fresh cut corn or frozen whole kernel corn, thawed
- ¾ cup chopped, seeded sweet red pepper (1 medium)
- ½ of a medium English cucumber, chopped
- 2 tablespoons finely shredded Parmesan cheese (optional)

① Thaw scallops, if frozen. Rinse scallops; pat dry with paper towels. For vinaigrette, in a screw-top jar combine basil, vinegar, lemon juice, oil, mustard, and ¼ teaspoon of the black pepper. Cover and shake well. Set aside.

② Sprinkle scallops with the remaining ¼ teaspoon black pepper. Coat an unheated large nonstick skillet with cooking spray. Preheat on medium-high heat. Add scallops. Cook for 2 to 4 minutes or until scallops are opaque, turning once halfway through cooking.

③ Meanwhile, divide salad greens among 4 serving plates. In a large bowl combine tomatoes, corn, sweet pepper, and cucumber. Add half of the vinaigrette; toss to coat. Add tomato mixture to serving plates with greens. Add scallops to salads and brush with some of the remaining vinaigrette. Pass the remaining vinaigrette. If desired, sprinkle with Parmesan cheese.

PER SERVING 256 calories; 9 g total fat (1 g sat. fat); 37 mg cholesterol; 241 mg sodium; 22 g carbohydrate; 4 g fiber; 23 g protein

English cucumbers on produce shelves are usually wrapped in plastic. They're longer and thinner than regular cucumbers, have a sweeter flavor, and are nearly seedless.

Pacific Northwest Paella

MAKES 6 servings **START TO FINISH** 45 minutes

- 1¼ pounds fresh or frozen skinless salmon fillet, 1 inch thick
- ¼ teaspoon cracked black pepper
- 4 slices apple wood-smoked bacon
- 8 ounces fresh cremini or button mushrooms, sliced
- 1 cup chopped onion (1 large)
- 2 cloves garlic, minced
- 1 cup uncooked long grain white rice
- 2½ cups chicken broth
- 2 teaspoons snipped fresh thyme or ½ teaspoon dried thyme, crushed
- 1 pound fresh asparagus spears or one 10-ounce package frozen cut asparagus, thawed
- 1 plum tomato, chopped (⅓ cup)

① Thaw fish, if frozen. Rinse fish; pat dry with paper towels Cut salmon into 1-inch pieces. Toss with pepper; set aside.

② In a large deep skillet or paella pan cook the bacon on medium heat until crisp, turning occasionally. Drain bacon on paper towels. Crumble bacon and set aside. Reserve drippings in skillet.

③ Add mushrooms, onion, and garlic to drippings in skillet. Cook and stir about 5 minutes or until the onion is tender. Stir in uncooked rice. Add broth and thyme. Bring mixture to boiling; reduce heat. Cover and simmer for 10 minutes.

④ Meanwhile, if using, snap off and discard woody bases from fresh asparagus; cut asparagus into 1-inch pieces. Set aside.

⑤ Place fish pieces on rice mixture. Sprinkle asparagus over all. Cover and simmer for 10 to 12 minutes more or until asparagus is crisp-tender and fish flakes easily when tested with a fork.

⑥ Sprinkle with tomato and crumbled bacon before serving.

PER SERVING 320 calories; 10 g total fat (3 g sat. fat); 56 mg cholesterol; 569 mg sodium; 31 g carbohydrate; 2 g fiber; 27 g protein

Scallop Salad with Basil Vinaigrette

Mexican-Style Shrimp Pizza

menu

Kickoff Pepper Dip

Shrimp and
Watermelon Salad
[below]

Whole grain rolls

Hint-of-Herb Butter
Cookies

Shrimp and Watermelon Salad 🕥

MAKES 4 servings **START TO FINISH** 20 minutes

1 **pound fresh or frozen peeled, deveined medium shrimp**
2 **tablespoons olive oil**
2 **teaspoons snipped fresh thyme**
4 **cups sliced bok choy or napa cabbage**
1 **cup grape tomatoes, halved**
   Salt
   Black pepper
2 **1-inch slices seedless watermelon, halved**
   Small limes, halved
   Feta cheese (optional)
   Fresh thyme sprigs (optional)

① Thaw shrimp, if frozen. Rinse shrimp; pat dry with paper towels.

② In a large skillet heat 1 tablespoon of the oil on medium-high heat. Add shrimp; cook and stir for 3 to 4 minutes or until shrimp are opaque. Transfer shrimp to bowl; stir in the snipped thyme.

③ Add the remaining 1 tablespoon oil, bok choy, and tomatoes to skillet; cook and stir for 1 minute. Return shrimp to skillet; cook and stir for 1 minute more. Season with salt and pepper.

④ Serve shrimp and vegetables with watermelon. Squeeze lime juice on salads. If desired, sprinkle salads with cheese and garnish with the thyme sprigs.

PER SERVING 241 calories; 9 g total fat (1 g sat. fat); 172 mg cholesterol; 363 mg sodium; 16 g carbohydrate; 2 g fiber; 25 g protein

Mexican-Style Shrimp Pizza ⭐ 🕥

MAKES 2 servings **START TO FINISH** 30 minutes **OVEN** 400°F

4 **ounces fresh or frozen cooked, peeled, and deveined medium shrimp**
2 **8-inch multigrain, whole wheat, or regular flour tortillas**
1 **teaspoon olive oil**
   Nonstick cooking spray
1 **cup thin bite-size assorted sweet pepper strips**
⅓ **cup thinly sliced green onions**
½ **of a medium fresh jalapeño, seeded and thinly sliced* (optional)**
1 **tablespoon water**
2 **to 3 tablespoons green salsa**
⅓ **cup shredded reduced-fat Monterey Jack cheese**
1 **to 2 tablespoons snipped fresh cilantro**

① Thaw shrimp, if frozen. Rinse shrimp; pat dry with paper towels. Set aside.

② Preheat oven to 400°F. Brush both sides of tortillas with oil; place on an ungreased baking sheet. Bake about 10 minutes or until crisp, turning once.

③ Meanwhile, coat an unheated medium nonstick skillet with cooking spray. Preheat skillet on medium heat. Add sweet pepper, green onions, and, if desired, jalapeño. Cook about 5 minutes or until nearly crisp-tender, stirring occasionally. Add the water; cover and cook for 2 minutes more.

④ Spread each tortilla with some of the green salsa. Top with cooked vegetable mixture and shrimp. Sprinkle with cheese. Bake about 3 minutes or until cheese is melted and shrimp is heated through. Sprinkle with cilantro.

*Tip: Because chiles contain volatile oils that can burn your skin and eyes, avoid direct contact with them as much as possible. When working with chiles, wear plastic or rubber gloves. If your bare hands do touch the peppers, wash your hands and nails well with soap and warm water.

PER SERVING 300 calories; 11 g total fat (4 g sat. fat); 126 mg cholesterol; 689 mg sodium; 23 g carbohydrate; 12 g fiber; 26 g protein

Dilled Shrimp with Beans and Carrots

MAKES 4 servings **PREP** 25 minutes **COOK** 40 minutes

- 1 pound fresh or frozen large shrimp in shells
- 1⅓ cups water
- ⅔ cup regular brown rice
- 1 tablespoon butter
- 3 medium carrots, cut into thin bite-size strips
- 8 ounces fresh green beans, trimmed and cut into 1-inch pieces
- ¼ cup water
- 1 teaspoon instant chicken bouillon granules
- 1 teaspoon finely shredded lemon peel
- ½ teaspoon dried dill

① Thaw shrimp, if frozen. Peel and devein shrimp, leaving tails intact if desired. Rinse shrimp; pat dry with paper towels. Set aside. In a medium saucepan bring the 1⅓ cups water and uncooked brown rice to boiling. Reduce heat; simmer, covered, about 40 minutes or until rice is tender and most of the liquid is absorbed.

② Meanwhile, in a large skillet melt butter on medium heat. Add carrots and green beans; cook and stir for 4 to 5 minutes or until vegetables are crisp-tender. In a small bowl stir together the ¼ cup water and bouillon granules until granules are dissolved. Add bouillon mixture, shrimp, lemon peel, and dill to bean mixture. Cook, uncovered, on medium heat for 3 to 4 minutes or until shrimp are opaque, stirring occasionally.

③ Serve shrimp and vegetable mixture over rice in bowls.

PER SERVING 268 calories; 5 g total fat (2 g sat. fat); 137 mg cholesterol; 381 mg sodium; 33 g carbohydrate; 4 g fiber; 21 g protein

Easy Shrimp with Beans and Carrots: Prepare as directed, except use cooked, peeled shrimp in place of the shrimp in shells. Add shrimp to bean mixture with bouillon mixture, lemon peel, and dill and cook just until heated through. Also, omit regular brown rice and the 1½ cups water and use one 8.8-ounce pouch cooked brown rice heated according to package directions. Replace the 3 medium carrots with 1½ cups purchased thin bite-size carrot strips.

Grilled Shrimp and Pineapple Kabobs ⭐ 30

MAKES 4 servings **START TO FINISH** 30 minutes

- 1 pound fresh or frozen jumbo shrimp
- ½ of a fresh pineapple
- ½ cup water
- 6 tablespoons orange marmalade
- 1 tablespoon soy sauce
- 1 8.8-ounce pouch cooked long grain rice
- ¼ cup snipped fresh cilantro

① Thaw shrimp, if frozen. Peel and devein shrimp. Rinse shrimp; pat dry with paper towels. Thread shrimp onto 4 skewers.* Cut pineapple crosswise into 4 slices; if desired, core pineapple. Cut each slice into quarters, making 16 small wedges total. Thread wedges onto 4 additional skewers.*

② In a small saucepan combine the water, 4 tablespoons of the marmalade, and the soy sauce. Brush some of the mixture on shrimp and pineapple wedges. Set remaining mixture aside.

③ For a charcoal grill, place skewers on the rack of an uncovered grill directly over medium coals. Grill for 8 to 10 minutes or until shrimp are opaque and pineapple is heated through, carefully turning once halfway through grilling. (For gas grill, preheat grill. Reduce heat to medium. Place fish on grill rack over heat; cover. Grill as above.) Remove from heat; cover to keep warm.

④ Heat rice according to package directions. Transfer rice to serving bowl; stir in the remaining 2 tablespoons marmalade and the cilantro.

⑤ Bring the remaining marmalade-soy sauce mixture to a full boil. Serve skewers with rice and marmalade-soy sauce mixture.

***Tip:** If using wooden skewers, soak skewers in water for 30 minutes before threading on shrimp and pineapple.

PER SERVING 322 calories; 3 g total fat (0 g sat. fat); 172 mg cholesterol; 451 mg sodium; 49 g carbohydrate; 2 g fiber; 25 g protein

Quick Shrimp Jambalaya

Quick Shrimp Jambalaya ③⓪

MAKES 6 servings **START TO FINISH** 30 minutes

- 8 ounces fresh or frozen cooked, peeled, and deveined shrimp, thawed
- 2 teaspoons canola oil or vegetable oil
- 1 cup sliced celery (2 stalks)
- 2 cloves garlic, minced
- ½ teaspoon Creole seasoning or Cajun seasoning
- ⅛ to ¼ teaspoon crushed red pepper
- 4 cups coarsely chopped, trimmed collard greens or kale
- ½ of a 16-ounce package frozen (yellow, green, and red) peppers and onion stir-fry vegetables (2 cups)
- 1 cup cubed cooked ham (5 ounces)
- 2 tablespoons water
- 1 14.5-ounce can no-salt-added stewed tomatoes, undrained, cut up
- 1 8.8-ounce pouch cooked brown rice
- 1 cup frozen cut okra

① Thaw shrimp, if frozen. Rinse shrimp; pat dry with paper towels. Set aside.

② In a 4-quart Dutch oven heat oil on medium heat. Add celery; cook for 5 minutes, stirring occasionally. Stir in garlic, Creole seasoning, and crushed red pepper. Add collard greens, stir-fry vegetables, ham, and the water. Bring to boiling; reduce heat. Cover and simmer for 8 minutes, stirring occasionally.

③ Stir shrimp, tomatoes, rice, and okra into Dutch oven. Cook, uncovered, about 5 minutes or until heated through and flavors are blended, stirring occasionally.

PER SERVING 190 calories; 4 g total fat (1 g sat. fat); 84 mg cholesterol; 572 mg sodium; 23 g carbohydrate; 4 g fiber; 17 g protein

For a smoky touch to Quick Shrimp Jambalaya, substitute a can of diced fire-roasted tomatoes for the stewed tomatoes.

Garlic Shrimp on Spinach ③⓪

MAKES 2 servings **START TO FINISH** 20 minutes

- 8 ounces fresh or frozen medium shrimp in shells
- 2 teaspoons olive oil
- 2 cloves garlic, minced
- ½ teaspoon finely shredded lemon peel
- ⅛ teaspoon black pepper
- 4 cups fresh spinach
- 1 tablespoon shredded Parmesan cheese
  Lemon wedges

① Thaw shrimp, if frozen. Peel and devein shrimp, leaving tails on if desired. In a small bowl, toss together shrimp, oil, garlic, lemon peel, and pepper. Place a steamer basket in a wok or large skillet with a tight-fitting lid. Add water to just below the basket.

② Place shrimp in a single layer in steamer basket. Cover and place on medium-high heat. Steam for 5 to 6 minutes or until shrimp are opaque (start timing when wok is placed on the burner). Remove shrimp and keep warm.

③ Meanwhile, wash spinach. Arrange spinach evenly in steamer basket. Cover and steam about 2 minutes or until wilted. Divide spinach between 2 serving plates. If desired, thread shrimp onto 6- to 8-inch wooden skewers. Place shrimp on top of spinach. Sprinkle with Parmesan cheese. Serve with lemon wedges.

PER SERVING 159 calories; 7 g total fat (1 g sat. fat); 131 mg cholesterol; 216 mg sodium; 4 g carbohydrate; 1 g fiber; 20 g protein

Garlic Shrimp on Spinach

Shrimp and Grits

MAKES 6 servings **PREP** 30 minutes **COOK** 15 minutes

1¼	pounds fresh or frozen medium shrimp in shells
1	14-ounce can reduced-sodium chicken broth
1½	cups fat-free milk
1	cup regular grits
2	teaspoons olive oil
1	large onion, thinly sliced and separated into rings
2	cloves garlic, minced
1	tablespoon snipped fresh parsley
½	cup shredded reduced-fat cheddar cheese (2 ounces)
¼	cup sliced green onions (2)

① Thaw shrimp, if frozen. Peel and devein shrimp, leaving tails intact if desired; set aside. In a medium saucepan, combine broth, milk, and grits. Bring to boiling; reduce heat. Cover and simmer for 4 minutes or until grits are desired consistency, stirring occasionally.

② In a large skillet heat olive oil on medium heat. Add onion and garlic; cook and stir about 5 minutes or until onion is tender and lightly browned. Remove onion mixture from skillet and set aside. Add shrimp to hot skillet; cook on medium heat for 2 minutes or until shrimp are opaque, turning occasionally. Stir in onion mixture and parsley.

③ Divide grits among 6 shallow bowls; top with shrimp mixture. Sprinkle with cheese and green onions.

PER SERVING 274 calories; 6 g total fat (2 g sat. fat); 152 mg cholesterol; 384 mg sodium; 30 g carbohydrate; 2 g fiber; 27 g protein

Seafood-Corn Chowder

MAKES 6 servings **PREP** 25 minutes **COOK** 12 minutes

8	ounces fresh or frozen skinless halibut fillets
4	fresh or frozen sea scallops (about 8 ounces total)
1	tablespoon vegetable oil
1	medium onion, chopped
1	medium green sweet pepper, seeded and chopped
2	cloves garlic, minced
4	medium tomatoes, cored and coarsely chopped (about 3 cups)
2	cups lower-sodium vegetable broth
1	cup water
1	cup fresh or frozen whole kernel corn
1	teaspoon ground cumin
¼	teaspoon black pepper
1	10-ounce can or two 3.53-ounce packages whole baby clams, drained
¼	cup snipped fresh cilantro
	Cracked black pepper (optional)

① Thaw halibut and scallops, if frozen. Cut halibut into 1-inch pieces and cut large scallops in half or quarters; set aside. In a large saucepan heat oil on medium heat. Add onion, sweet pepper, and garlic; cook about 5 minutes or until tender, stirring occasionally. Stir in tomatoes, vegetable broth, the water, corn, cumin, and black pepper. Bring to boiling; reduce heat. Cover and simmer 10 minutes.

② Add halibut and scallops to tomato mixture. Return to boiling; reduce heat. Simmer, uncovered, for 2 to 3 minutes more or until scallops are opaque and halibut flakes easily when tested with a fork.

③ Stir in clams and cilantro just before serving. If desired, sprinkle with cracked black pepper.

PER SERVING 205 calories; 5 g total fat (0 g sat. fat); 50 mg cholesterol; 319 mg sodium; 15 g carbohydrate; 2 g fiber; 26 g protein

Serving seafood always makes a meal feel just a little bit special.

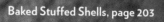
Baked Stuffed Shells, page 203

Make-'em-Meatless Main Dishes

Cannellini Bean Burgers

MAKES 4 servings **PREP** 25 minutes **COOK** 10 minutes

- 1 15-ounce can cannellini beans (white kidney beans), rinsed and drained
- ¾ cup soft whole wheat bread crumbs (1 slice)
- ½ cup chopped onion (1 medium)
- ¼ cup broken walnuts, toasted if desired
- 2 tablespoons coarsely snipped fresh basil or 1 teaspoon dried basil, crushed
- 2 cloves garlic, quartered
- 1 tablespoon olive oil
- 4 slices whole grain bread, toasted
- 2 tablespoons bottled reduced-calorie ranch salad dressing
- 2 cups fresh spinach leaves
- 4 tomato slices, halved

① In a food processor combine cannellini beans, ¼ cup of the bread crumbs, the onion, walnuts, basil, and garlic. Cover and process until mixture is coarsely chopped and holds together.

② Shape bean mixture into four ½-inch-thick patties. Place the remaining ½ cup bread crumbs in a shallow dish. Carefully brush both sides of patties with oil. Dip patties into bread crumbs, turning to coat.

③ Heat a grill pan or large skillet on medium heat. Add patties. Cook for 10 to 12 minutes or until heated through, turning once. (Reduce heat to medium-low if patties brown too quickly.)

④ Spread one side of bread slices with salad dressing. Top with spinach, burgers, and tomato.

PER SERVING 280 calories; 12 g total fat (1 g sat. fat); 2 mg cholesterol; 394 mg sodium; 37 g carbohydrate; 11 g fiber; 14 g protein

Cheesy Eggplant Burgers ㉚

MAKES 6 servings **PREP** 15 minutes **GRILL** 6 minutes

- 1 teaspoon garlic powder
- ½ teaspoon black pepper
- ⅛ teaspoon salt
- ½ cup chopped, seeded tomato (1 medium)
- 2 tablespoons olive oil
- 1 tablespoon snipped fresh oregano
- 2 teaspoons snipped fresh thyme
- 2 teaspoons cider vinegar
- 6 ½-inch slices eggplant
- 6 ¾-ounce slices smoked Gouda cheese
- 6 ½-inch slices whole grain baguette-style French bread, toasted

① In a small bowl combine garlic powder, pepper, and salt. In another small bowl combine half of the garlic powder mixture, the tomato, 1 tablespoon of the oil, the oregano, thyme, and vinegar. Set aside.

② Brush both sides of eggplant slices with the remaining 1 tablespoon oil. Sprinkle with the remaining garlic powder mixture.

③ For a charcoal grill, grill eggplant on the rack of an uncovered grill directly over medium coals for 6 to 8 minutes or just until tender and golden brown, turning once halfway through grilling and topping with cheese during the last 2 minutes of grilling. (For a gas grill, preheat grill. Reduce heat to medium. Place eggplant on grill rack over heat. Cover and grill as above.)

④ Serve grilled eggplant on toasted bread. Top with tomato and herb mixture.

PER SERVING 201 calories; 11 g total fat (4 g sat. fat); 17 mg cholesterol; 506 mg sodium; 19 g carbohydrate; 4 g fiber; 7 g protein

Use fresh herbs, flavorful cheeses, and lots of fresh veggies, and no one will miss the meat.

Vegetable Salad Wraps

menu

Cheese tortellini soup

Ciabatta rolls

Vegetable Salad
Wraps [below]

Red grapes

Must-Have Chocolate
Chip Cookies

Vegetable Salad Wraps 🔵

MAKES 2 servings **START TO FINISH** 20 minutes

1	cup frozen shelled sweet soybeans (edamame)
1	cup chopped, peeled jicama and/or chopped cauliflower
¼	cup carrot cut into thin bite-size strips
⅛	teaspoon black pepper
¼	cup bottled reduced-calorie cucumber ranch salad dressing or reduced-fat ginger vinaigrette salad dressing
6	butterhead (Boston or bibb) lettuce leaves

① Cook soybeans according to package directions; drain. Transfer soybeans to a large bowl. Add jicama and/or cauliflower, carrot, and pepper. Drizzle with salad dressing; toss gently to coat.

② Spoon soybean mixture into lettuce leaves.

PER SERVING 296 calories; 15 g total fat (2 g sat. fat); 0 mg cholesterol; 451 mg sodium; 26 g carbohydrate; 10 g fiber; 19 g protein

Panini without the Press

MAKES 4 sandwiches **START TO FINISH** 30 minutes

8	slices sourdough bread
2	tablespoons olive oil
¼	cup mayonnaise
2	medium tomatoes, thinly sliced
1	medium zucchini, thinly sliced diagonally
1	small red onion, thinly sliced
¼	cup oil-packed dried tomatoes, drained and snipped
½	to ¾ cup fresh basil leaves
½	to ¾ cup shredded mozzarella cheese (2 to 3 ounces)

① Brush one side of bread slices with olive oil. Spread the other side of 4 of the bread slices with mayonnaise. Layer the mayonnaise-topped bread with tomato slices, zucchini, red onion, and dried tomatoes. Sprinkle with basil and cheese. Top with the remaining 4 bread slices, oiled sides up.

② Heat a very large skillet on medium-low heat. Place sandwiches in skillet. Weight sandwiches down with a heavy skillet. Cook until bread is lightly toasted. Turn sandwiches over, weight down, and cook until bread is lightly toasted and cheese is melted.

PER SANDWICH 386 calories; 23 g total fat (5 g sat. fat); 13 mg cholesterol; 526 mg sodium; 37 g carbohydrate; 3 g fiber; 11 g protein

The popularity of panini probably owes in part to the fact that they're delightfully crunchy, toasted on the outside and gooey with melted cheese on the inside. Switch up the cheese in this version—try smoked Gouda, Muenster, or provolone.

Mushroom and Poblano Vegetarian Enchiladas ③⓪

MAKES 4 servings **START TO FINISH** 30 minutes

- 1 tablespoon vegetable oil
- 6 ounces firm, tub-style tofu (fresh bean curd), drained and cubed
- 1 8-ounce package sliced fresh cremini mushrooms
- 1 small poblano chile, seeded and cut into strips*
- 1 teaspoon ground cumin
- ½ teaspoon salt
- 1 cup shredded cheddar and Monterey Jack cheese (4 ounces)
- ¼ cup sour cream
  Nonstick cooking spray
- 8 corn tortillas
  Chopped tomato (optional)
  Chopped green onion (optional)

① Preheat broiler. In a large skillet heat oil on medium heat. Add tofu, mushrooms, poblano chile, cumin, and salt. Cook for 8 to 10 minutes or until mushrooms and chile are tender, stirring occasionally. Stir in ½ cup of the cheese and the sour cream.

② Lightly coat a 13 x 9 x 2-inch baking pan with cooking spray; set aside. Stack tortillas and wrap in dampened paper towels. Microwave on high about 30 seconds or until warm and softened. Spoon warm mushroom mixture onto each tortilla; fold opposite sides over filling. Place in the prepared baking pan. Sprinkle with the remaining ½ cup cheese.

③ Broil 4 to 5 inches from the heat for 1 to 2 minutes or until cheese is melted. If desired, top with tomato and green onion.

*Tip: Because chiles contain volatile oils that can burn your skin and eyes, avoid direct contact with them as much as possible. When working with chiles, wear plastic or rubber gloves. If your bare hands do touch the peppers, wash your hands and fingernails well with soap and warm water.

PER SERVING 335 calories; 18 g total fat (8 g sat. fat); 36 mg cholesterol; 521 mg sodium; 29 g carbohydrate; 4 g fiber; 15 g protein

Tomato-Edamame Grilled Cheese

MAKES 4 servings plus 1 cup spread **PREP** 20 minutes
ROAST 15 minutes **OVEN** 425°F

- 1 garlic bulb
- 1 teaspoon canola oil
- 1 12-ounce package frozen shelled sweet soybeans (edamame)
- ¼ cup lemon juice
- ¼ cup water
- ½ teaspoon salt
- ½ teaspoon ground cumin
- ⅓ cup snipped fresh parsley
- 8 slices whole grain bread
- 4 1-ounce slices reduced-fat Monterey Jack cheese
- 1 tomato, thinly sliced

① Preheat oven to 425°F. Cut off the top ½ inch of garlic bulb to expose the ends of the individual cloves. Leaving garlic bulb whole, remove any loose, papery outer layers. Place bulb, cut side up, in a custard cup. Drizzle with oil. Cover with foil; roast about 15 minutes or until garlic feels soft when squeezed. Cool.

② Meanwhile, cook soybeans according to package directions; drain. Rinse with cold water; drain again.

③ Squeeze 3 of the garlic cloves from bulb into a food processor. Wrap and chill the remaining garlic cloves for another use. Add cooked soybeans, lemon juice, the water, salt, and cumin to garlic in food processor. Cover and process until smooth. Transfer to a small bowl. Stir in parsley.

④ To assemble, spread one side of each bread slice with 2 tablespoons of the soybean mixture. Top 4 of the bread slices with cheese and tomato. Add the remaining 4 bread slices, spread sides down.

⑤ Heat a nonstick griddle or skillet on medium-high heat. Add sandwiches; cook until toasted, turning once.

PER SERVING 332 calories; 12 g total fat (4 g sat. fat); 20 mg cholesterol; 685 mg sodium; 38 g carbohydrate; 11 g fiber; 22 g protein

Puree the leftover roasted garlic from the Tomato-Edamame Grilled Cheese with some olive oil and use it as a sauce to toss with steamed or roasted vegetables or pasta or to spread on a pizza crust.

Summer Ratatouille Tart

Summer Ratatouille Tart

MAKES 6 servings **PREP** 50 minutes **BAKE** 25 minutes
STAND 20 minutes **OVEN** 400°F/350°F

- ½ of a 15-ounce package (1 crust) rolled refrigerated unbaked piecrust
- ¼ cup chopped yellow onion
- 2 cloves garlic, minced
- 1 tablespoon olive oil
- 4 cups cubed, peeled eggplant (1 small)
- 1¼ cups sliced zucchini (1 medium)
- ¾ cup sweet red pepper cut into bite-size pieces (1 medium)
- 1½ cups chopped, peeled tomatoes (3 medium)
- ½ teaspoon sea salt or salt
- ½ teaspoon herbes de Provence or dried Italian seasoning, crushed
- ½ teaspoon black pepper
- 8 ounces asparagus spears, trimmed and cut into 2-inch pieces
- ¼ cup finely shredded Parmesan cheese (1 ounce)

① Preheat oven to 400°F. Let piecrust stand according to package directions. Line the bottom and sides of a 9- to 10-inch tart pan that has a removable bottom with piecrust. Line piecrust with foil. Bake for 10 minutes. Remove foil; bake for 5 minutes more. Cool on a wire rack. Reduce oven temperature to 350°F.

② Meanwhile, in a large saucepan cook onion and garlic in hot oil on medium heat about 3 minutes or until onion is tender. Add eggplant, zucchini, and half of the sweet pepper. Cook and stir about 10 minutes or until vegetables are tender. Stir in tomatoes, salt, herbes de Provence, and black pepper. Simmer, covered, for 10 minutes. Simmer, uncovered, about 10 minutes more or until mixture is thickened and most of the liquid is evaporated.

③ Spoon vegetable mixture into the partially baked tart shell. Bake for 10 minutes. Top with the remaining sweet pepper and the asparagus. Bake for 15 minutes more. Sprinkle with cheese. Let stand for 20 minutes before serving.

PER SERVING 237 calories; 13 g total fat (4 g sat. fat); 6 mg cholesterol; 344 mg sodium; 27 g carbohydrate; 4 g fiber; 4 g protein

Nutty Meatless Loaf

MAKES 8 servings **PREP** 30 minutes **BAKE** 35 minutes
STAND 15 minutes **OVEN** 350°F

- Nonstick cooking spray
- 3 cups water
- 1¼ cups red or yellow lentils, rinsed and drained
- 1 cup shredded carrots (2 medium)
- ¾ cup snipped dried apricots and/or golden raisins
- ½ cup chopped onion (1 medium)
- ½ cup chopped celery (1 stalk)
- 1½ teaspoons garam masala or 2 teaspoons Jamaican jerk seasoning
- 2 cloves garlic, minced
- 1 tablespoon vegetable oil
- 3 eggs, lightly beaten
- 1½ cups cooked brown rice
- ¾ cup pecans, toasted and chopped
- ½ cup mango chutney
- 1 teaspoon salt
- ¼ cup chopped sweet red pepper
- ¼ cup chopped, peeled mango
- Fresh cilantro leaves (optional)

① Preheat oven to 350°F. Lightly coat a 9- or 9½-inch deep-dish pie plate with cooking spray; set aside. In a medium saucepan combine the water and lentils. Bring to boiling; reduce heat. Simmer, covered, for 10 to 15 minutes or until tender. Drain; set aside.

② Meanwhile, in a medium skillet cook carrots, apricots and/or raisins, onion, celery, garam masala, and garlic in hot oil on medium heat about 5 minutes or until onion is tender, stirring occasionally.

③ In a large bowl combine eggs, brown rice, ⅔ cup of the pecans, ¼ cup of the chutney, and the salt. Stir in cooked lentils and carrot mixture. Press mixture firmly into the prepared pie plate. Bake for 25 minutes.

④ For topping, in a small bowl combine the remaining pecans, the remaining ¼ cup chutney, sweet pepper, and mango. Spoon topping over lentil loaf.

⑤ Bake about 10 minutes more or until topping is heated through and an instant-read thermometer inserted into the center of the loaf registers 160°F. If desired, sprinkle with cilantro. Let stand for 15 minutes before cutting into wedges.

PER SERVING 367 calories; 12 g total fat (1 g sat. fat); 79 mg cholesterol; 496 mg sodium; 53 g carbohydrate; 13 g fiber; 14 g protein

Asparagus-Leek Risotto

MAKES 4 servings **START TO FINISH** 45 minutes **OVEN** 450°F

12	ounces asparagus spears, trimmed
2	tablespoons olive oil
	Salt
	Coarse black pepper
1½	cups sliced leeks
1	cup uncooked arborio rice
3	cups reduced-sodium chicken broth
⅓	cup freshly grated Parmesan cheese
2	tablespoons snipped fresh parsley
½	teaspoon finely shredded lemon peel
1	tablespoon lemon juice
¼	teaspoon coarse black pepper
	Lemon slices
	Finely shredded lemon peel

① Preheat oven to 450°F. Place asparagus in a single layer on a baking sheet. Brush with 1 tablespoon of the oil; sprinkle lightly with salt and pepper. Roast about 10 minutes or until crisp-tender. Cool slightly. Cut two-thirds of the asparagus into 2-inch pieces. Set all of the asparagus aside.

② In a large saucepan cook leeks in the remaining 1 tablespoon oil on medium heat until tender, stirring occasionally. Add rice. Cook and stir about 5 minutes or until rice starts to brown.

③ Meanwhile, in a medium saucepan bring broth to boiling. Reduce heat and simmer. Gradually add 1 cup of the broth to rice mixture, stirring constantly. Continue to cook and stir on medium heat until liquid is absorbed. Add another ½ cup of the broth to rice mixture, stirring constantly. Continue to cook and stir until liquid is absorbed. Add the remaining broth, ½ cup at a time, stirring constantly just until liquid is absorbed and rice is tender and creamy. (This should take about 20 minutes.)

④ Stir in the asparagus pieces, cheese, parsley, the ½ teaspoon lemon peel, lemon juice, and the ¼ teaspoon pepper. Garnish with the asparagus spears, lemon slices, and additional lemon peel.

PER SERVING 256 calories; 9 g total fat (2 g sat. fat); 6 mg cholesterol; 683 mg sodium; 36 g carbohydrate; 3 g fiber; 10 g protein

Zucchini Pilaf

MAKES 8 servings **PREP** 20 minutes
COOK 25 minutes **BAKE** 35 minutes **OVEN** 350°F

	Nonstick cooking spray
1	cup chopped onion (1 large)
3	cloves garlic, minced
2	teaspoons olive oil
4½	cups water
2	6-ounce packages long grain and wild rice mix or rice pilaf mix
8	ounces semisoft goat cheese (chèvre), cubed
1	pound zucchini or yellow summer squash, quartered lengthwise and sliced ½ inch thick
3	to 4 medium red, yellow, and/or orange tomatoes, seeded and coarsely chopped
2	teaspoons snipped fresh rosemary
¼	teaspoon salt
⅛	teaspoon black pepper
½	cup coarsely chopped walnuts, toasted

① Preheat oven to 350°F. Lightly coat a 3-quart rectangular baking dish with cooking spray; set aside. In a large saucepan cook onion and garlic in hot oil on medium heat about 5 minutes or until tender, stirring occasionally. Add the water.

② Bring to boiling. Stir in rice mix (including seasoning packets); reduce heat. Simmer, covered, about 25 minutes or until most of the water is absorbed. Stir in cheese until melted.

③ Transfer rice mixture to a large bowl. Stir in zucchini, tomatoes, rosemary, salt, and pepper. Transfer mixture to the prepared baking dish.

④ Bake, covered, for 35 to 45 minutes or until heated through. Sprinkle with walnuts before serving.

Make-Ahead Directions: Prepare as directed through Step 3. Cover and chill for 2 to 24 hours. To serve, preheat oven to 350°F. Bake, covered, for 50 to 60 minutes or until heated through. Sprinkle with walnuts before serving.

PER SERVING 311 calories; 12 g total fat (5 g sat. fat); 13 mg cholesterol; 688 mg sodium; 37 g carbohydrate; 3 g fiber; 12 g protein

Confetti Barley Salad

menu

Corn bread sticks

Sliced melon

Sesame-Ginger
Wheat Berry Salad
[below]

Key Lime Phyllo Tarts

Iced tea

Sesame-Ginger Wheat Berry Salad

MAKES 4 servings **PREP** 15 minutes **COOK** 45 minutes

1¼ cups water
½ cup wheat berries
1 15-ounce can black beans, rinsed and drained
1 medium mango, pitted, peeled, and chopped
¾ cup carrots cut into thin bite-size strips
¼ cup mango chutney
2 tablespoons rice vinegar
2 teaspoons toasted sesame oil
¼ teaspoon ground ginger
  Salt
1 small head napa cabbage, coarsely shredded

① In a small saucepan combine the water and wheat berries. Bring to boiling; reduce heat. Simmer, covered, for 45 to 60 minutes or until tender. Drain off any liquid.

② Stir black beans, mango, carrots, chutney, vinegar, oil, and ginger into cooked wheat berries. Season to taste with salt. Serve with napa cabbage.

PER SERVING 265 calories; 3 g total fat (0.4 g sat. fat); 0 mg cholesterol; 419 mg sodium; 54 g carbohydrate; 10 g fiber; 11 g protein

Confetti Barley Salad

MAKES 4 servings **PREP** 15 minutes **COOK** 45 minutes

5 cups water
1 cup regular barley
2 cups frozen succotash,* thawed
¼ cup white wine vinegar
3 tablespoons olive oil
1 tablespoon Dijon mustard
2 teaspoons snipped fresh oregano or ½ teaspoon dried oregano, crushed
2 cloves garlic, minced
½ teaspoon salt
¼ teaspoon black pepper
1 cup finely chopped sweet red pepper
⅓ cup sliced pitted ripe olives
  Fresh herb sprigs (optional)

① In a large saucepan bring the water to boiling. Stir in barley; reduce heat. Simmer, covered, for 45 to 50 minutes or just until barley is tender, adding succotash during the last 10 minutes of cooking; drain. Rinse with cold water; drain again.

② Meanwhile, for dressing, in a screw-top jar combine vinegar, oil, mustard, oregano, garlic, salt, and black pepper. Cover and shake well.

③ In a large bowl combine barley mixture, sweet pepper, and olives. Shake dressing. Pour dressing over barley mixture; toss gently to coat. Serve immediately or cover and chill for up to 24 hours. If desired, garnish with herb sprigs.

*Tip: If you can't find frozen succotash, substitute 1 cup thawed frozen corn and 1 cup thawed frozen lima beans.

PER SERVING 332 calories; 13 g total fat (2 g sat. fat); 0 mg cholesterol; 724 mg sodium; 49 g carbohydrate; 8 g fiber; 9 g protein

Cheesy Red Pepper Pizza 30

MAKES 8 (1-slice) servings **PREP** 15 minutes **BAKE** 15 minutes
OVEN 425°F

Nonstick cooking spray

1 **13.8-ounce package refrigerated pizza dough**

1 **tablespoon olive oil**

½ **cup sliced roasted red and/or yellow sweet peppers**

2 **medium plum tomatoes, thinly sliced**

2 **tablespoons shredded fresh spinach (optional)**

1 **cup shredded mozzarella cheese (4 ounces)**

¼ **teaspoon coarsely ground black pepper**

2 **tablespoons snipped fresh basil**

① Preheat oven to 425°F. Coat a 12-inch pizza pan with nonstick spray. Press refrigerated dough into prepared pan, building up edges. Brush with olive oil. Bake for 10 minutes.

② Remove crust from oven. Arrange sweet peppers, tomato slices, and, if using, spinach on the crust. Sprinkle with cheese and black pepper.

③ Bake for 5 to 10 minutes more or until cheese is bubbly. Sprinkle with basil.

PER SERVING 182 calories; 6 g total fat (2 g sat. fat); 9 mg cholesterol; 359 mg sodium; 25 g carbohydrate; 1 g fiber; 8 g protein

Sweet peppers can be pricey. When they're on sale, stock up. Roast them, then cut them into strips and store in the freezer in ½ to 1-cup portions.

Italian Beans with Pesto 30

MAKES 6 servings **PREP** 15 minutes **COOK** 15 minutes

1 **14-ounce can reduced-sodium chicken broth or vegetable broth**

¾ **cup bulgur**

¾ **cup chopped sweet red pepper (1 medium)**

⅓ **cup basil pesto**

¼ **cup thinly sliced green onions (2)**

2 **tablespoons balsamic vinegar**

2 **cups cooked or canned red kidney beans, pinto beans, Christmas lima beans, and/or other white beans***

Black pepper

12 **butterhead (Boston or bibb) lettuce leaves**

① In a large saucepan combine broth and bulgur. Bring to boiling; reduce heat. Simmer, covered, about 15 minutes or until bulgur is tender. Remove from heat.

② Stir in sweet pepper, pesto, green onions, and vinegar. Stir in beans. Season to taste with black pepper.

③ To assemble, spoon bean mixture onto lettuce leaves; wrap lettuce around filling.

***Tip:** To cook dried beans, rinse ¾ cup dried beans. In a large saucepan combine rinsed beans and 5 cups water. Bring to boiling; reduce heat. Simmer, uncovered, for 2 minutes. Remove from heat. Cover and let stand at room temperature for 1 hour; drain. Rinse beans; drain again and return to saucepan. Add 5 cups fresh water. Bring to boiling; reduce heat. Simmer, covered, for 1¼ to 1½ hours or until beans are tender; drain.

PER SERVING 251 calories; 10 g total fat (0 g sat. fat); 2 mg cholesterol; 267 mg sodium; 33 g carbohydrate; 8 g fiber; 10 g protein

Italian Beans with Pesto serves up grains, beans, and vegetables— in each delicious bite.

Cheesy Red Pepper Pizza

Baked Stuffed Shells

Baked Stuffed Shells ✪

MAKES 6 servings PREP 40 minutes BAKE 37 minutes
STAND 10 minutes OVEN 350°F

- 1 teaspoon olive oil
- ½ cup chopped onion (1 medium)
- 2 cloves garlic, minced
- 1 14.5-ounce can no-salt-added diced tomatoes, undrained
- 1 8-ounce can no-salt-added tomato sauce
- 1 tablespoon snipped fresh basil or ½ teaspoon dried basil, crushed
- 2 teaspoons snipped fresh oregano or ½ teaspoon dried oregano, crushed
- ¼ teaspoon salt
- 12 dried jumbo shell macaroni
- 1 12.3-ounce package extra-firm, silken-style tofu (fresh bean curd)
- ½ cup finely shredded Parmesan or Romano cheese (2 ounces)
- ¼ cup refrigerated or frozen egg product, thawed, or 1 egg
- ¼ teaspoon black pepper
- ½ cup shredded reduced-fat mozzarella cheese (2 ounces)

① Preheat oven to 350°F. For sauce, in a saucepan heat oil on medium heat. Add onion and garlic; cook 5 minutes or until onion is tender, stirring occasionally. Add tomatoes, tomato sauce, dried basil and oregano (if using), and salt. Bring to boiling; reduce heat. Simmer, uncovered, about 15 minutes or until desired consistency. Remove from heat; stir in snipped fresh basil and oregano (if using). Set aside ¾ cup of the sauce; spread the remaining sauce in the bottom of a 2-quart rectangular baking dish. Set aside.

② Meanwhile, cook pasta shells according to package directions; drain. Rinse with cold water; drain again.

③ For filling, place tofu in a blender or food processor. Cover and blend or process until smooth. Add Parmesan cheese, egg, and pepper; cover and blend or process just until combined. Spoon 3 tablespoons filling into each pasta shell. Arrange filled shells, filling sides up, on sauce in baking dish. Spoon the reserved sauce over shells.

④ Bake, covered, about 35 minutes or until heated through. Sprinkle with mozzarella cheese. Bake, uncovered, 2 minutes more or until cheese is melted. Let stand for 10 minutes before serving.

PER SERVING 234 calories; 5 g total fat (2 g sat. fat); 10 mg cholesterol; 357 mg sodium; 32 g carbohydrate; 3 g fiber; 14 g protein

Broccoli Spaghetti ③⓪

MAKES 4 servings START TO FINISH 25 minutes

- 6 ounces dried spaghetti
- 3 cups broccoli florets
- 1 15- or 19-ounce can cannellini beans (white kidney beans), rinsed and drained
- 1 10-ounce container refrigerated light Alfredo pasta sauce
- 3 cloves garlic, minced
- ½ cup croutons, coarsely crushed
- ¼ teaspoon crushed red pepper
  Olive oil

① Cook spaghetti according to package directions, adding broccoli during the last 3 to 4 minutes of cooking. Drain, reserving ½ cup of the cooking water. Return spaghetti mixture to hot pan; cover and keep warm.

② Meanwhile, in a blender or food processor combine the reserved pasta cooking water, beans, Alfredo sauce, and garlic. Cover and blend or process until nearly smooth. Transfer mixture to a small saucepan; heat through on medium heat, stirring frequently.

③ Spoon sauce onto 4 dinner plates. Top each serving with spaghetti mixture, croutons, crushed red pepper, and a drizzle of oil.

PER SERVING 402 calories; 12 g total fat (5 g sat. fat); 18 mg cholesterol; 659 mg sodium; 60 g carbohydrate; 8 g fiber; 19 g protein

Broccoli Spaghetti

Macaroni and Cheese ✪

MAKES 6 servings **PREP** 25 minutes **BAKE** 10 minutes
OVEN 425°F

- 7 ounces dried multigrain or whole grain rotini pasta
- 1½ cups broccoli florets, finely chopped carrots, or ½-inch pieces green beans
- ¼ cup finely chopped onion
- 4 teaspoons olive oil
- 1 6.5-ounce container light semisoft cheese with garlic and herb
- 1⅔ cups fat-free milk
- 1 tablespoon all-purpose flour
- ½ cup shredded reduced-fat cheddar cheese (2 ounces)
- ½ cup shredded Asiago, Gruyère, or Manchego cheese (2 ounces)
- ½ cup crumbled whole wheat baguette-style French bread or panko (Japanese-style bread crumbs)

  Fresh parsley or oregano

① Preheat oven to 425°F. In a medium saucepan cook pasta according to package directions, adding broccoli during the last 3 minutes of cooking; drain. Return pasta mixture to hot pan; cover and keep warm.

② Meanwhile, in a large saucepan cook onion in 2 teaspoons of the oil on medium heat about 5 minutes or until tender, stirring occasionally. Remove from heat. Stir in semisoft cheese until melted.

③ In a medium bowl whisk together milk and flour until smooth. Add all at once to onion mixture. Cook and stir on medium heat until thickened and bubbly. Reduce heat to low. Stir in cheddar cheese and Asiago cheese until melted. Add pasta mixture; stir gently to coat. Transfer pasta mixture to an ungreased 2-quart casserole.

④ In a small bowl combine crumbled bread and the remaining 2 teaspoons oil; sprinkle on pasta mixture. Bake for 10 to 15 minutes or until top is browned. Sprinkle with parsley.

PER SERVING 332 calories; 15 g total fat (7 g sat. fat); 39 mg cholesterol; 455 mg sodium; 34 g carbohydrate; 3 g fiber; 17 g protein

Penne with Walnuts and Peppers ③⓪

MAKES 4 servings **START TO FINISH** 30 minutes

- 6 ounces dried whole wheat or multigrain penne or wagon wheel pasta
- 1 tablespoon olive oil
- ¼ cup walnuts, coarsely chopped
- 4 large cloves garlic, thinly sliced
- 2 cups sweet green, red, and/or yellow pepper strips (2 medium)
- 1 small red onion, cut into thin wedges
- 1 cup halved red or yellow cherry or grape tomatoes
- ¼ cup snipped fresh parsley
- 2 teaspoons snipped fresh rosemary or ½ teaspoon dried rosemary, crushed
- ¼ teaspoon coarse black pepper
- 2 tablespoons grated Parmesan cheese (optional)

① Cook pasta according to package directions; drain. Return to hot pan; cover and keep warm.

② Meanwhile, in a large skillet heat oil on medium heat. Add walnuts and garlic. Cook and stir about 2 minutes or until light brown. Add sweet peppers and red onion. Cook for 5 to 7 minutes or until vegetables are crisp-tender, stirring occasionally. Add tomatoes; cook and stir until heated through. Stir in parsley, rosemary, and black pepper.

③ Transfer cooked pasta to a large shallow bowl. Top with pepper mixture; toss gently to coat. If desired, sprinkle with cheese.

PER SERVING 268 calories; 10 g total fat (1 g sat. fat); 0 mg cholesterol; 7 mg sodium; 40 g carbohydrate; 5 g fiber; 9 g protein

Almonds or shelled pistachios work well in place of the walnuts, if you like.

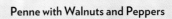

Fresh-Herb Pasta Primavera

Rigatoni with Broccoli, Beans, and Basil ③⓪

MAKES 4 servings **START TO FINISH** 25 minutes

- 8 ounces dried rigatoni pasta
- 2 cups broccoli florets
- 1 19-ounce can cannellini beans (white kidney beans), rinsed and drained
- ¼ cup olive oil
- 4 cloves garlic, minced
- ¼ cup snipped fresh basil
- ½ teaspoon salt
- 2 slices bread, cut into small cubes
- ¼ teaspoon crushed red pepper
  Snipped fresh basil (optional)

① In a 4-quart Dutch oven cook pasta according to package directions, adding broccoli during the last 3 to 4 minutes of cooking. Drain, reserving ¾ cup of the cooking water. Return pasta mixture to hot pan; cover and keep warm.

② Meanwhile, in a large bowl combine beans, 3 tablespoons of the oil, and the garlic. Mash about ½ cup of the bean mixture. Stir in the reserved pasta cooking water, the ¼ cup basil, and salt. Add bean mixture to pasta mixture; toss gently to coat. Cover and keep warm.

③ For croutons, in a medium skillet heat the remaining 1 tablespoon oil on medium heat. Add bread cubes and crushed red pepper. Cook and stir for 1 to 2 minutes or until bread is crisp. Top pasta mixture with croutons and, if desired, additional basil.

PER SERVING 456 calories; 15 g total fat (2 g sat. fat); 0 mg cholesterol; 601 mg sodium; 70 g carbohydrate; 9 g fiber; 17 g protein

When cooking pasta, it's always a good idea to reserve a cup or so of the cooking water to thin the sauce and moisten the pasta, if necessary. It's better than using water out of the tap because it has starch in it, which helps coat the pasta—and it's hot.

Fresh-Herb Pasta Primavera

MAKES 6 servings **START TO FINISH** 35 minutes

- 8 ounces dried multigrain or whole grain penne or mostaccioli
- 3 cups assorted fresh vegetables (such as sweet red pepper strips, trimmed sugar snap peas, 2-inch-long pieces trimmed asparagus, and/or quartered lengthwise packaged peeled baby carrots)
- 1 cup halved cherry tomatoes
- ½ cup reduced-sodium chicken broth
- 3 tablespoons all-purpose flour
- ½ teaspoon salt
- 1¼ cups low-fat milk
- ¼ cup dry sherry or reduced-sodium chicken broth
- 3 ounces Parmesan or Asiago cheese, finely shredded (¾ cup)
- ½ cup lightly packed fresh basil, coarsely chopped
- 4 teaspoons snipped fresh thyme or oregano
- ⅓ cup sliced green onions (optional)

① In a 4-quart Dutch oven cook pasta according to package directions; add the 3 cups assorted vegetables for the last 2 minutes of cooking. Drain well. Return to hot Dutch oven. Add cherry tomatoes.

② In a medium saucepan whisk together chicken broth, flour, and salt until smooth. Stir in milk and sherry. Cook and stir until thickened and bubbly; cook and stir for 2 minutes more. Remove from heat; stir in finely shredded Parmesan cheese, basil, and thyme.

③ Add herb sauce to pasta mixture; toss gently to coat. Divide among 6 serving plates. If desired, sprinkle with green onions.

PER SERVING 253 calories; 5 g total fat (3 g sat. fat); 12 mg cholesterol; 496 mg sodium; 41 g carbohydrate; 6 g fiber; 13 g protein

menu

Italian-Style
Vegetables

Italian baguette

Tricolor Tomato
Ravioli
[below]

Milk Chocolate-Berry
Ice Cream

Tricolor Tomato Ravioli

MAKES 4 servings **START TO FINISH** 35 minutes

1   24- to 25-ounce package frozen cheese-filled ravioli

4   large tomatoes (such as Green Zebra, yellow, and/or red), cut into thin wedges and seeded (about 4 cups)

¾   cup small fresh basil leaves

¼   cup capers, drained

½   teaspoon black pepper

¼   teaspoon salt

2   tablespoons butter

6   cloves garlic, minced

2   cups fresh baby spinach

½   cup shredded Parmesan cheese

① Cook pasta according to package directions; drain. Return pasta to hot pan; cover and keep warm.

② Meanwhile, in a large bowl combine tomatoes, basil, capers, pepper, and salt; set aside.

③ For sauce in a large skillet melt butter on medium heat. Add garlic and cook for 30 seconds. Add tomato mixture; cook just until heated through. Remove from heat; gently stir in spinach.

④ To serve place cooked ravioli on a large serving platter. Spoon sauce over ravioli. Sprinkle with Parmesan cheese.

PER SERVING 480 calories; 18 g total fat (11 g sat. fat); 93 mg cholesterol; 914 mg sodium; 57 g carbohydrate; 5 g fiber; 22 g protein

Three-Cheese Manicotti ✪

MAKES 10 to 12 servings **PREP** 30 minutes **BAKE** 40 minutes
STAND 10 minutes **OVEN** 350°F

20   dried manicotti shells

2½   cups light ricotta cheese (24 ounces)

2   cups shredded part-skim mozzarella cheese (8 ounces)

½   cup refrigerated or frozen egg product, thawed, or 2 eggs

⅓   cup grated Romano or Asiago cheese

¼   cup snipped fresh parsley

¼   teaspoon black pepper

4   cups light tomato-basil pasta sauce

  Snipped fresh parsley (optional)

① Cook manicotti shells according to package directions; drain. Meanwhile, preheat oven to 350°F. For filling, in a large bowl combine ricotta cheese, 1 cup of the mozzarella cheese, the egg, Romano cheese, the ¼ cup parsley, and pepper.

② Spread 1 cup of the pasta sauce in the bottom of a 3-quart rectangular baking dish. Spoon about 3 tablespoons of the filling into each cooked manicotti shell and place in the dish. Spoon the remaining pasta sauce evenly over filled manicotti shells.

③ Bake for 35 to 40 minutes or until heated through. Sprinkle with the remaining 1 cup mozzarella cheese. Bake about 5 minutes more or until cheese is melted. Let stand for 10 minutes before serving. If desired, sprinkle with additional parsley.

Make-Ahead Directions: Prepare as directed through Step 2. Cover and chill for 2 to 24 hours. To serve, preheat oven to 350°F. Bake, uncovered, for 40 to 45 minutes or until heated through. Sprinkle with the remaining 1 cup mozzarella cheese. Bake about 5 minutes more or until cheese is melted. Let stand for 10 minutes before serving. If desired, sprinkle with additional parsley.

PER SERVING 293 calories; 8 g total fat (4 g sat. fat); 36 mg cholesterol; 640 mg sodium; 37 g carbohydrate; 3 g fiber; 20 g protein

Mustard-Herb Beef Stew, page 227

Satisfying Soups & Stews

Squash and Quinoa Soup 30

MAKES 6 servings **START TO FINISH** 30 minutes

12	ounces skinless, boneless chicken breast halves, cut into 1-inch pieces
⅓	cup finely chopped shallots or onion
2	teaspoons olive or canola oil
2	14-ounce cans reduced-sodium chicken broth
1	5.5-ounce can apricot nectar
1	pound butternut squash, peeled, halved, seeded, and cut into 1-inch cubes
¾	cup quinoa, rinsed and drained
1	teaspoon ground cumin
2	small zucchini, halved lengthwise and cut into 1-inch pieces
	Salt
	Black pepper

① In a large saucepan cook chicken and shallots in hot oil on medium heat for 2 to 3 minutes or until shallots are tender, stirring occasionally. Carefully add broth, apricot nectar, squash, quinoa, and cumin. Bring to boiling; reduce heat. Cover and simmer for 5 minutes.

② Add zucchini. Cover and simmer about 10 minutes more or until squash and quinoa are tender. Season to taste with salt and pepper.

PER SERVING 226 calories; 4 g total fat (1 g sat. fat); 33 mg cholesterol; 454 mg sodium; 31 g carbohydrate; 3 g fiber; 19 g protein

Quinoa, an ancient grain that originated in South America, is a bit of a nutritional marvel. Lower in carbohydrates than most grains and considered to be a complete protein because it contains all eight essential amino acids, it also cooks in half the time as rice and expands to four times its volume. Use it as you would rice in almost any dish.

Chicken Minestrone Soup

MAKES 8 servings **START TO FINISH** 40 minutes

1	cup sliced carrots (2 medium)
½	cup chopped celery (1 stalk)
½	cup chopped onion (1 medium)
2	cloves garlic, minced
1	tablespoon olive oil
3	14-ounce cans reduced-sodium chicken broth
1	15- to 19-ounce can cannellini beans (white kidney beans), rinsed and drained
8	to 10 ounces skinless, boneless chicken breast halves, cut into ¾-inch pieces
1	cup fresh green beans cut into ½-inch pieces (4 ounces)
1	teaspoon dried Italian seasoning, crushed
¼	teaspoon black pepper
⅔	cup dried bow tie pasta
1	medium zucchini, quartered lengthwise and cut into ½-inch slices (1¼ cups)
1	14.5-ounce can no-salt-added diced tomatoes, undrained

① In a 4-quart Dutch oven cook carrots, celery, onion, and garlic in hot oil on medium heat for 5 minutes, stirring frequently. Add broth, cannellini beans, chicken, green beans, Italian seasoning, and pepper. Bring to boiling; reduce heat. Add pasta. Simmer, uncovered, for 5 minutes, stirring occasionally.

② Stir in zucchini. Return to boiling; reduce heat. Simmer, uncovered, for 10 minutes more or until pasta is tender, stirring occasionally. Stir in tomatoes; heat through.

PER SERVING 212 calories; 2 g total fat (0 g sat. fat); 16 mg cholesterol; 707 mg sodium; 37 g carbohydrate; 11 g fiber; 16 g protein

Although classic minestrone is an all-vegetable soup that may or may not contain legumes, the addition of chicken makes it a hearty main-dish soup.

Chicken Tortellini Soup

Sage-Chicken Dumpling Soup ✪

MAKES 8 servings **START TO FINISH** 45 minutes

- 2 cups sliced fresh mushrooms
- 1 cup chopped onion (1 large)
- 1 tablespoon olive oil
- ¼ cup all-purpose flour
- 6 cups reduced-sodium chicken broth
- 1 2- to 2½-pound purchased roasted chicken, skinned, boned, and cut into bite-size pieces
- 2 cups fresh or frozen peas
- ½ cup pitted kalamata olives, halved
- 1 tablespoon lemon juice
- 1 teaspoon ground sage
  Buttermilk Dumplings
  Thinly sliced green onions (optional)
  Fried Sage Sprigs (optional)

① In a 4-quart Dutch oven cook mushrooms and onion in hot oil on medium heat for 6 to 8 minutes or until mushrooms are tender and liquid has evaporated.

② Stir in flour until combined. Add broth all at once. Cook and stir until thickened and bubbly. Stir in chicken, peas, olives, lemon juice, and sage. Return to boiling.

③ Drop the Buttermilk Dumpling batter from a tablespoon to make 8 mounds on top of the soup. Cover and simmer about 10 minutes or until a toothpick inserted near the center comes out clean.

④ Remove from heat. If desired, sprinkle with green onions and top with Fried Sage Leaves.

Buttermilk Dumplings: In a medium bowl stir together 2 cups all-purpose flour, ½ teaspoon baking powder, ¼ teaspoon baking soda, and ¼ teaspoon salt. Stir in ¼ cup sliced green onions and 1 tablespoon snipped fresh parsley. Add 1 cup buttermilk and 2 tablespoons olive oil, stirring with a fork until just moistened and combined.

PER SERVING 367 calories; 12 g total fat (2 g sat. fat); 56 mg cholesterol; 776 mg sodium; 37 g carbohydrate; 4 g fiber; 25 g protein

Fried Sage Sprigs: In a medium saucepan heat ¼ cup olive oil on medium heat until hot but not smoky. Add 8 small sage sprigs, 2 at a time, and cook for 30 to 60 seconds or until crisp. Remove with slotted spoon and drain sage sprigs on paper towels.

Chicken Tortellini Soup ✪

MAKES 6 servings **START TO FINISH** 40 minutes

- 2 teaspoons olive oil
- 12 ounces skinless, boneless chicken breast halves, cut into ¾-inch pieces
- 3 cloves garlic, minced
- 3 cups sliced fresh mushrooms (about 8 ounces)
- 2 14-ounce cans reduced-sodium chicken broth
- 1¾ cups water
- 1 9-ounce package refrigerated cheese-filled tortellini
- 2 cups torn fresh purple kale or spinach
- 2 medium carrots, cut into thin bite-size sticks
- 1 teaspoon dried tarragon, crushed

① In a 4- to 6-quart Dutch oven heat olive oil on medium-high heat. Add chicken and garlic; cook and stir 4 minutes or until outsides of chicken pieces are no longer pink. Remove chicken from pan using a slotted spoon. Add mushrooms to the same pan. Cook about 5 minutes or just until tender, stirring frequently. Carefully add chicken broth and the water; bring to boiling.

② Add tortellini, kale (if using), carrots, tarragon, and partially cooked chicken to broth mixture. Return to boiling; reduce heat. Cover and simmer for 7 to 9 minutes or until tortellini is tender, stirring occasionally. Stir in spinach (if using).

PER SERVING 274 calories; 6 g total fat (2 g sat. fat); 53 mg cholesterol; 616 mg sodium; 31 g carbohydrate; 3 g fiber; 25 g protein

Kale takes longer to cook than fresh spinach, which just needs to be wilted in the hot soup right before serving. That accounts for the different points in the recipe at which you add the type of green you're using.

Chicken-Squash Noodle Soup ③⓪

MAKES 6 servings **START TO FINISH** 30 minutes

½	cup chopped onion (1 medium)
½	cup chopped celery (1 stalk)
½	cup chopped carrot (1 medium)
2	cloves garlic, minced
½	teaspoon poultry seasoning
1	tablespoon canola oil
3	14-ounce cans reduced-sodium chicken broth
1½	cups dried medium noodles
1	medium zucchini or yellow summer squash, quartered lengthwise and cut into 1-inch-thick pieces
1¾	cups fat-free milk
¼	cup all-purpose flour
2	cups cubed cooked chicken breast
¼	cup snipped fresh parsley

① In 4-quart Dutch oven cook onion, celery, carrot, garlic, and poultry seasoning in hot oil on medium heat about 5 minutes or just until tender, stirring occasionally. Add chicken broth; bring to boiling. Add noodles and zucchini. Return to boiling; reduce heat. Cover and simmer for 5 minutes.

② In a medium bowl whisk together milk and flour; stir into vegetable mixture. Add chicken. Cook and stir until thickened and bubbly. Cook and stir for 1 minute more. Sprinkle with parsley just before serving.

PER SERVING 210 calories; 5 g total fat (1 g sat. fat); 49 mg cholesterol; 555 mg sodium; 20 g carbohydrate; 2 g fiber; 22 g protein

5-Spice Chicken Noodle Soup ③⓪

MAKES 4 servings **START TO FINISH** 20 minutes

2	cups water
1	14-ounce can reduced-sodium chicken broth
¼	cup thinly bias-sliced green onions (2)
2	teaspoons reduced-sodium soy sauce
2	cloves garlic, minced
¼	teaspoon five-spice powder
⅛	teaspoon ground ginger
2	cups chopped bok choy
1	medium sweet red pepper, cut into thin bite-size strips
2	ounces somen, broken into 2-inch lengths, or 2 ounces dried fine noodles
1½	cups cubed cooked chicken breast (about 8 ounces)

① In a large saucepan combine the water, broth, green onions, soy sauce, garlic, five-spice powder, and ginger. Bring to boiling. Stir in bok choy, sweet pepper strips, and somen. Return to boiling; reduce heat. Simmer, uncovered, for 3 to 5 minutes or until noodles are just tender. Stir in cooked chicken. Heat through. Serve immediately.

PER SERVING 181 calories; 4 g total fat (1 g sat. fat); 51 mg cholesterol; 556 mg sodium; 14 g carbohydrate; 1 g fiber; 20 g protein

Somen are thin white Japanese noodles made from wheat flour. Look for them in the Asian section of your supermarket or at an Asian market.

Cooks all over the world are well aware of the restorative properties of chicken noodle soup.

French Chicken Stew

menu

Mixed green salad
with vinaigrette

Chipotle-Chicken
Chowder [below]

Wheat tortillas,
warmed

Lemon-Cherry Oat
Cookies

Chipotle-Chicken Chowder 30

MAKES 4 servings **START TO FINISH** 20 minutes

- 1   14-ounce can reduced-sodium chicken broth
- ½   cup water
- ¼   teaspoon ground cumin
- 2   cups refrigerated diced potatoes
- 1¼   cups chopped sweet red or green pepper (1 large)
- 1   teaspoon chopped canned chipotle peppers in adobo sauce (see note, page 220)
- 1   9-ounce package frozen chopped cooked chicken breast
- 1   12-ounce can (1½ cups) evaporated fat-free milk
- 3   tablespoons cornstarch
      Sliced green onions (optional)

① In a large saucepan bring chicken broth, the water, and cumin to boiling. Carefully add potatoes, sweet pepper, and chipotle peppers. Return to boiling; reduce heat. Cover and simmer about 4 minutes or until potatoes are tender. Stir in chicken.

② In a small bowl whisk together ⅓ cup of the evaporated milk into cornstarch; stir into the broth mixture. Add the remaining milk. Cook and stir over medium heat until thickened and bubbly. Cook and stir for 2 minutes more. If desired, garnish with green onions just before serving.

PER SERVING 214 calories; 1 g total fat (0 g sat. fat); 38 mg cholesterol; 722 mg sodium; 29 g carbohydrate; 2 g fiber; 23 g protein

French Chicken Stew ✪

MAKES 8 servings **PREP** 30 minutes
SLOW COOKER 6 to 7 hours (low) or 3 to 4 hours (high)

- 4   cups sliced fresh button and/or shiitake mushrooms
- 1   14.5-ounce can diced tomatoes, undrained
- 1   cup thinly bias-sliced carrots (2 medium)
- ½   cup chopped onion
- ½   cup cubed red potato
- ½   cup fresh green beans cut into 1-inch pieces
- ½   cup pitted ripe olives, halved
- 1   cup reduced-sodium chicken broth
- ½   cup dry white wine or chicken broth
- 2   tablespoons quick-cooking tapioca
- 1   teaspoon herbes de Provence or dried Italian seasoning, crushed
- ¾   teaspoon dried thyme, crushed
- ¼   teaspoon coarsely ground black pepper
- 8   skinless, boneless chicken thighs (1¾ to 2 pounds total)
- ½   teaspoon seasoned salt
- 1   14-ounce jar tomato pasta sauce or one 16-ounce jar Alfredo pasta sauce
      French bread (optional)

① In a 5- to 6-quart slow cooker combine mushrooms, tomatoes, carrots, onion, potato, green beans, and olives. Stir in broth, wine, tapioca, herbes de Provence, thyme, and pepper. Place chicken on top; sprinkle chicken with seasoned salt.

② Cover and cook on low-heat setting for 6 to 7 hours or on high-heat setting for 3 to 4 hours. Stir in pasta sauce. Cover and cook about 5 minutes more or until heated through. If desired, serve with French bread.

PER SERVING 219 calories; 5 g total fat (1 g sat. fat); 83 mg cholesterol; 629 mg sodium; 17 g carbohydrate; 3 g fiber; 23 g protein

Spring Chicken Stew ㉚

MAKES 4 servings **START TO FINISH** 30 minutes

- 1   lemon
- 1¼ pounds skinless, boneless chicken thighs
     Salt
     Black pepper
- 1   tablespoon olive oil
- 8   ounces baby carrots with tops, scrubbed, trimmed, and halved lengthwise
- 1½ cups water
- 1   12-ounce jar chicken gravy
- 1   tablespoon Dijon mustard
- 2   heads baby bok choy, quartered
     Fresh lemon thyme (optional)

① Finely shred peel from lemon; set peel aside. Juice lemon; set juice aside. Sprinkle chicken lightly with salt and pepper.

② In a Dutch oven heat olive oil on medium-high heat; add chicken. Cook for 2 to 3 minutes or until chicken is browned on both sides, turning occasionally.

③ Add carrots, the water, and gravy to Dutch oven. Stir in mustard. Bring to boiling. Add bok choy. Reduce heat. Cover and simmer about 10 minutes or until chicken is no longer pink and vegetables are tender. Season to taste with the reserved lemon juice. Sprinkle with lemon peel and, if desired, lemon thyme.

PER SERVING 273 calories; 12 g total fat (2 g sat. fat); 117 mg cholesterol; 909 mg sodium; 13 g carbohydrate; 3 g fiber; 31 g protein

Rarely do you have a need for an entire can of chipotle peppers in a single recipe. Freeze leftovers—in 1- and 2-pepper portions—in small freezer bags for future use.

Yucatan-Style Turkey and Vegetable Soup

MAKES 6 servings **PREP** 35 minutes **COOK** 15 minutes

- 1   medium onion, thinly sliced
- 3   or 4 cloves garlic
- 1   tablespoon vegetable oil
- 2   canned chipotle chile peppers in adobo sauce, drained and chopped*
- 1   cup chopped carrots (2 medium)
- 5   cups reduced-sodium chicken broth or turkey stock
- 2   cups coarsely chopped tomatoes (4 medium)
- ⅛   teaspoon salt
- 3   cups cubed cooked turkey or chicken
- 2   cups chopped zucchini (2 medium)
- 2   tablespoons snipped fresh cilantro
- ⅓   cup crumbled queso fresco or feta cheese
- 1   avocado, halved, seeded, peeled, and chopped
- 1   lime, cut into wedges
- 6   fresh cilantro sprigs

① In a dry medium skillet combine onion slices and unpeeled garlic cloves; cook and stir for 3 to 5 minutes or until edges are brown. Chop onion. Peel and slice garlic cloves.

② In a 4-quart Dutch oven heat oil on medium-high heat. Add chopped onion, sliced garlic, and chipotle peppers; cook and stir for 3 minutes. Add carrots; cook and stir for 3 minutes more.

③ Add broth, tomatoes, and salt. Bring to boiling; reduce heat. Cover and simmer for 10 minutes. Add turkey, zucchini, and snipped cilantro. Cover and simmer for 5 minutes more.

④ Serve with queso fresco, avocado, lime wedges, and cilantro sprigs.

*Tip: Because hot chile peppers contain volatile oils that can burn your skin and eyes, avoid direct contact with chiles as much as possible. When working with chile peppers, wear plastic or rubber gloves. If your bare hands do touch the chile peppers, wash your hands and fingernails well with soap and warm water when you are done.

PER SERVING 229 calories; 8 g total fat (2 g sat. fat); 65 mg cholesterol; 609 mg sodium; 12 g carbohydrate; 4 g fiber; 27 g protein

German Potato-Sausage Soup

German Potato-Sausage Soup ⏱

MAKES 6 servings **START TO FINISH** 30 minutes

12	ounces uncooked bulk turkey sausage
8	ounces sliced fresh mushrooms
½	cup chopped onion (1 medium)
½	cup chopped celery (1 stalk)
1	teaspoon caraway seeds, crushed
¼	teaspoon black pepper
1	14-ounce can lower-sodium beef broth
½	cup light beer or nonalcoholic beer
2	cups cubed potatoes (2 medium)
1	cup small broccoli florets
2	cups shredded cabbage
1½	cups fat-free milk

① In a 4-quart Dutch oven cook sausage, mushrooms, onion, and celery on medium heat until sausage is brown, using a wooden spoon to break up sausage as it cooks. Drain off fat.

② Stir caraway seeds and pepper into sausage mixture in Dutch oven. Add beef broth and beer; bring to boiling. Add potatoes. Return to boiling; reduce heat. Cover and simmer for 10 minutes. Add broccoli. Cover and simmer about 5 minutes more or until potatoes and broccoli are tender.

③ Stir cabbage and milk into sausage-broccoli mixture. Cook for 2 to 3 minutes more or just until cabbage is tender and soup is heated through.

PER SERVING 179 calories; 5 g total fat (1 g sat. fat); 44 mg cholesterol; 522 mg sodium; 16 g carbohydrate; 3 g fiber; 17 g protein

Mexican-Style Turkey Soup ⏱

MAKES 6 servings **START TO FINISH** 30 minutes

	Nonstick cooking spray
1¼	cups chopped sweet red pepper (1 large)
1	cup chopped onion (1 large)
1	teaspoon ground cumin
1	teaspoon chili powder
½	teaspoon paprika
5	cups reduced-sodium chicken broth
1½	cups peeled, cubed winter squash
1	large tomato, chopped
¼	teaspoon salt
¼	teaspoon black pepper
2	cups cubed cooked turkey or chicken breast (about 10 ounces)
1	cup fresh or frozen whole kernel corn
2	tablespoons snipped fresh cilantro

① Coat an unheated Dutch oven with cooking spray. Preheat on medium heat. Add sweet pepper and onion to hot Dutch oven. Cook about 5 minutes or until vegetables are tender, stirring occasionally. Stir in cumin, chili powder, and paprika; cook and stir for 1 minute.

② Carefully add broth, squash, tomato, salt, and black pepper. Bring to boiling; reduce heat. Cover and simmer about 20 minutes or until squash is tender, stirring occasionally. Stir in turkey, corn, and cilantro; heat through.

PER SERVING 153 calories; 3 g total fat (1 g sat. fat); 35 mg cholesterol; 615 mg sodium; 15 g carbohydrate; 3 g fiber; 17 g protein

These soups serve up quick comfort—they're ready from start to finish in 30 minutes or less.

Creamy Potato and Asparagus Soup

MAKES 4 servings **PREP** 15 minutes **COOK** 15 minutes

- 1¼ pounds fresh asparagus, trimmed
- 1¼ pounds potatoes, peeled and cut into ½-inch pieces
- 1 12-ounce can (1½ cups) evaporated milk
- 1¼ cups water
- ½ teaspoon salt
- ½ teaspoon black pepper
- 6 slices bacon
- 1 tablespoon honey

  Soup toppings (such as shredded lemon peel, snipped fresh parsley, coarse salt, and/or freshly ground black pepper)

① Set aside about one-third of the asparagus; set aside. In a large saucepan combine the remaining asparagus, the potatoes, evaporated milk, the water, salt, and pepper. Bring to boiling; reduce heat. Cover and simmer about 10 minutes or until potatoes are tender. Cool slightly.

② In a blender or food processor blend or process asparagus mixture, half at a time, until smooth.

③ Meanwhile, in a large skillet cook bacon on medium heat until crisp. Remove bacon and drain on paper towels; reserve 1 tablespoon bacon drippings in skillet. Set bacon aside.

④ Add the reserved asparagus spears to the drippings in skillet. Cook for 5 to 6 minutes or until asparagus is crisp-tender, stirring occasionally.

⑤ Just before serving, coarsely chop bacon and place in a microwave-safe pie plate. Drizzle with honey; cover with vented lid or plastic wrap. Microwave on high for 30 seconds.

⑥ To serve, ladle soup into bowls and top with asparagus, bacon, and desired soup toppings.

PER SERVING 356 calories; 15 g total fat (7 g sat. fat); 41 mg cholesterol; 673 mg sodium; 43 g carbohydrate; 4 g fiber; 15 g protein

menu

Greek Vegetable Salad

Stone-ground crackers

Ham and Pea Soup [below]

Zucchini-Banana Snack Cake

Ham and Pea Soup

MAKES 4 servings **START TO FINISH** 35 minutes

- 1 cup low-fat, reduced-sodium cooked ham sliced into bite-size pieces
- 2 teaspoons canola oil
- 12 ounces fresh peas or one 10-ounce package frozen baby peas
- 2 cups water
- 1 14-ounce can reduced-sodium chicken broth
- 1 cup sliced carrots (2 medium)
- 1 cup sliced celery (2 stalks)
- 6 green onions, bias-sliced
- 1 tablespoon snipped fresh tarragon or ½ teaspoon dried tarragon

  Lemon wedges
- ½ of a 6-ounce carton plain fat-free yogurt

① In large saucepan cook ham in hot oil on medium heat without stirring for 3 minutes. Stir ham and cook for 2 to 3 minutes more or until browned.

② Add peas, the water, broth, carrots, celery, green onions, and tarragon to the ham in saucepan. Bring to boiling; reduce heat. Cover and simmer for 5 to 10 minutes or until peas and carrots are tender.

③ To serve, pass lemon wedges and yogurt.

PER SERVING 176 calories; 4 g total fat (1 g sat. fat); 19 mg cholesterol; 586 mg sodium; 21 g carbohydrate; 6 g fiber; 14 g protein

Buffalo Vegetable Soup

Buffalo Vegetable Soup

MAKES 6 to 8 servings **START TO FINISH** 50 minutes

- 1 teaspoon olive oil
- 1 pound ground bison (buffalo) or 90% or higher lean ground beef*
- 1 cup chopped onion (1 large)
- 1 fresh poblano chile,** chopped
- 4 cups reduced-sodium chicken broth
- 2 cups chopped potatoes (2 medium)
- 1 cup fresh or frozen whole kernel corn
- ¾ cup chopped sweet red pepper (1 medium)
- 1 tablespoon snipped fresh sage or 1 teaspoon dried leaf sage, crushed
- 2 teaspoons snipped fresh rosemary or ½ teaspoon dried rosemary, crushed
- 2½ cups chopped zucchini (2 medium)
- ½ teaspoon black pepper
  Snipped fresh rosemary (optional)

① In a 4- to 5-quart Dutch oven heat olive oil on medium heat. Add the bison, onion, and poblano. Cook until meat is brown and onion is tender, using a wooden spoon to break up meat as it cooks. Drain off fat if necessary.

② Add the chicken broth, potatoes, corn, sweet pepper, dried sage (if using), and dried rosemary (if using). Bring just to boiling; reduce heat. Cover and simmer for 15 minutes.

③ Add zucchini, fresh sage (if using), fresh rosemary (if using), and black pepper to the soup. Return to boiling; reduce heat. Cover and simmer for 5 to 10 minutes or until vegetables are tender. If desired, sprinkle with additional snipped fresh rosemary before serving.

*Tip: If using the ground beef option, omit the olive oil.

**Tip: Because hot chile peppers contain volatile oils that can burn your skin and eyes, avoid direct contact with chiles as much as possible. When working with chile peppers, wear plastic or rubber gloves. If your bare hands do touch the chile peppers, wash your hands and fingernails well with soap and water when you are done.

PER SERVING 277 calories; 13 g total fat (5 g sat. fat); 53 mg cholesterol; 443 mg sodium; 21 g carbohydrate; 3 g fiber; 19 g protein

Mustard-Herb Beef Stew

MAKES 8 servings **PREP** 30 minutes **COOK** 1 hour

- ⅓ cup all-purpose flour
- 1 tablespoon snipped fresh parsley
- 1 teaspoon snipped fresh thyme or ½ teaspoon dried thyme, crushed
- 1 teaspoon black pepper
- ¼ teaspoon salt
- 1½ pounds boneless beef chuck roast, cut into 1- to 1½-inch pieces
- 2 tablespoons olive oil
- 1 8- to 10-ounce package cipolini onions, peeled, or 1 medium onion, peeled and cut in thin wedges
- 4 carrots, peeled and cut into 1-inch pieces
- 1 8-ounce package fresh cremini mushrooms, halved if large
- 8 tiny new Yukon gold potatoes, halved
- 3 tablespoons tomato paste
- 2 tablespoons spicy brown mustard
- 1 14-ounce can lower-sodium beef broth
- 1 12-ounce bottle dark porter beer or nonalcoholic beer
- 1 bay leaf
  Crusty bread slices

① In a large bowl or plastic bag combine flour, parsley, thyme, pepper, and salt. Add meat, a few pieces at a time; stir or shake to coat. Reserve leftover flour mixture.

② In 6-quart Dutch oven heat oil on medium-high heat. Cook meat, half at a time, in hot oil until brown on all sides. Stir in onions, carrots, mushrooms, and potatoes. Cook and stir for 3 minutes. Stir in tomato paste, mustard, and the remaining flour mixture. Add broth, beer, and bay leaf. Bring to boiling; reduce heat. Cover and simmer for 1 to 1¼ hours or until beef is tender. Discard bay leaf. Serve stew with crusty bread.

PER SERVING 338 calories; 8 g total fat (2 g sat. fat); 37 mg cholesterol; 538 mg sodium; 36 g carbohydrate; 4 g fiber; 25 g protein

Skillet Beef Stew

MAKES 8 servings **PREP** 20 minutes **COOK** 55 minutes

- 2 tablespoons cooking oil
- 2 pounds beef stew meat, cut into 1-inch cubes
- 2 teaspoons dried thyme or oregano, crushed
- ¼ teaspoon salt
- ¼ teaspoon black pepper
- 6 medium carrots (1 pound), peeled and cut into quarters
- 4 stalks celery, trimmed and cut into 2-inch pieces
- 2 medium onions, peeled and cut into ½-inch slices
- 6 cups lower-sodium beef broth
- ⅓ cup all-purpose flour
- 8 medium Yukon gold potatoes, scrubbed (about 2¾ pounds)
- 1 cup milk or buttermilk
- ½ teaspoon salt
- ½ teaspoon black pepper
  Cracked black pepper

① In an extra-large skillet heat oil on medium-high heat. Add meat, half at a time, and sprinkle with thyme, the ¼ teaspoon salt, and the ¼ teaspoon pepper. Cook and stir until brown on all sides. Remove meat from skillet using a slotted spoon. Set aside.

② Add carrots, celery, and onions to skillet. Cook and stir on medium heat for 5 minutes. Return meat to pan. In a large bowl whisk together broth and flour. Stir broth mixture into meat mixture in skillet. Bring to boiling; reduce heat. Cover and simmer for 45 minutes. Uncover. Simmer for 10 to 15 minutes more or until meat and vegetables are tender.

③ Meanwhile, place 4 of the potatoes in a large microwave-safe bowl. Cover with vented lid or plastic wrap. Microwave potatoes on high for 8 minutes. Carefully remove bowl from oven. Set cooked potatoes aside. Repeat with the remaining 4 potatoes. Return all potatoes to the large bowl. Break up any larger potatoes with the back of a wooden spoon. Add milk, the ½ teaspoon salt, and the ½ teaspoon pepper. Using a potato masher, mash potato mixture until nearly smooth or desired consistency.

④ To serve, spoon mashed potatoes into each soup bowl, spreading to cover bottom of bowl. Spoon stew on top of potatoes. Sprinkle each serving with cracked black pepper.

PER SERVING 380 calories; 10 g total fat (3 g sat. fat); 64 mg cholesterol; 739 mg sodium; 40 g carbohydrate; 6 g fiber; 31 g protein

Three-Pepper Beef Stew

MAKES 6 servings **PREP** 35 minutes **COOK** 1½ hours

- 1 tablespoon canola oil
- 4 medium carrots, cut into 1-inch pieces
- 2 stalks celery, cut into 1-inch pieces
- 1 cup chopped onion (1 large)
- 6 cloves garlic, minced
- 2 pounds boneless beef chuck roast, trimmed of fat and cut into 1-inch cubes
- 1¾ cups dry red wine or one 14-ounce can lower-sodium beef broth
- 1 14-ounce can lower-sodium beef broth
- 2 tablespoons tomato paste
- 1 tablespoon Worcestershire sauce
- 2 to 3 teaspoons bottled hot pepper sauce
- ¼ to ½ teaspoon crushed red pepper
- 2 large potatoes, unpeeled, cut into 1-inch pieces
- 2 medium sweet red peppers, cut into 1-inch pieces
- 2 tablespoons cold water
- 1 tablespoon cornstarch
  Freshly ground black pepper (optional)

① In a 4- to 6-quart Dutch oven heat oil on medium heat. Add carrots, celery, onion, and garlic; cook about 5 minutes or until onion is tender, stirring occasionally. Add meat, half at a time, and cook about 15 minutes or until brown on all sides, stirring occasionally. Drain off fat.

② Stir in wine, broth, tomato paste, Worcestershire sauce, pepper sauce, and crushed red pepper. Bring to boiling; reduce heat. Cover and simmer for 1 hour, stirring occasionally.

③ Add potatoes and sweet peppers. Return to boiling; reduce heat. Cover and simmer for 15 to 20 minutes or until meat and potatoes are tender.

④ In a small bowl whisk together cold water and cornstarch; stir into meat mixture. Cook and stir until thickened and bubbly. Cook and stir for 2 minutes more. If desired, sprinkle with black pepper.

PER SERVING 401 calories; 10 g total fat (3 g sat. fat); 82 mg cholesterol; 358 mg sodium; 25 g carbohydrate; 4 g fiber; 36 g protein

Thai Shrimp Soup

Bowl O' Red Chili

MAKES 8 servings **PREP** 30 minutes **COOK** 1½ hours

3	pounds boneless lean beef chuck roast, cut into ½-inch cubes
½	teaspoon salt
½	teaspoon freshly ground black pepper
1	tablespoon canola oil
4	cups chopped onions (4 large)
3	tablespoons yellow cornmeal
3	tablespoons chili powder
6	cloves garlic, minced
1	tablespoon ground cumin
2	teaspoons dried oregano, crushed
¼	teaspoon cayenne pepper
1	14-ounce can lower-sodium beef broth
1¼	cups water
1	tablespoon packed brown sugar
	Chopped onion (optional)

① Sprinkle meat with ¼ teaspoon of the salt and ¼ teaspoon of the pepper. In a 4-quart Dutch oven brown meat, one-third at a time, in hot oil. (Add more oil during cooking if necessary.) Remove meat from Dutch oven; set aside.

② Add the 4 cups chopped onions to Dutch oven; cook on medium-high heat about 10 to 12 minutes or until tender. Stir in cornmeal, chili powder, garlic, cumin, oregano, and cayenne pepper; cook and stir for 1 minute.

③ Stir in browned meat, broth, the water, brown sugar, and the remaining ¼ teaspoon salt and ¼ teaspoon pepper. Bring to boiling; reduce heat. Cover and simmer about 1½ to 2 hours or until meat is tender. If desired, top each serving with additional chopped onion.

PER SERVING 333 calories; 12 g total fat (3 g sat. fat); 80 mg cholesterol; 376 mg sodium; 14 g carbohydrate; 3 g fiber; 40 g protein

Cornmeal may seem like an odd ingredient in Bowl O' Red Chili, but it acts as a thickener that adds a little texture.

Thai Shrimp Soup

MAKES 4 servings **START TO FINISH** 50 minutes

12	ounces fresh or frozen peeled and deveined shrimp (tails intact if desired)
1	14-ounce can reduced-sodium chicken broth
2¾	cups water
2	stalks lemongrass (white part only), cut into ½-inch-thick slices
2	medium fresh jalapeños, halved lengthwise and seeded*
1	cup stemmed and sliced fresh shiitake and/or button mushrooms or ½ of a 15-ounce can whole straw mushrooms, drained
1	cup chopped sweet red peppers
1	cup sliced carrots (2 medium)
2	tablespoons lime juice
2	tablespoons rice vinegar or white wine vinegar
2	teaspoons packed brown sugar
2	teaspoons fish sauce
¼	cup slivered or snipped fresh basil

① Thaw shrimp if frozen. Rinse shrimp; pat dry with paper towels. Cover and chill shrimp until needed.

② In a large saucepan combine broth and the water. Bring to boiling. Add lemongrass and jalapeños. Return to boiling; reduce heat. Cover and simmer for 10 minutes. Using a slotted spoon, remove lemongrass and jalapeños; discard.

③ Stir mushrooms, sweet peppers, carrots, lime juice, rice vinegar, brown sugar, and fish sauce into broth mixture in saucepan. Bring to boiling; reduce heat. Cover and simmer for 10 to 15 minutes or until vegetables are crisp-tender. Add shrimp. Cover and simmer for 2 to 4 minutes more or until shrimp are opaque. Sprinkle each serving with basil.

*Tip: Because hot chile peppers contain volatile oils that can burn your skin and eyes, avoid direct contact with chiles as much as possible. When working with chile peppers, wear plastic or rubber gloves. If your bare hands do touch the chile peppers, wash your hands and fingernails well with soap and warm water when you are done.

PER SERVING 146 calories; 2 g total fat (0 g sat. fat); 129 mg cholesterol; 623 mg sodium; 11 g carbohydrate; 2 g fiber; 20 g protein

Italian Fish Stew 🕒

MAKES 4 servings **START TO FINISH** 30 minutes

- 8 ounces fresh or frozen skinless cod fillets
- 6 ounces fresh or frozen peeled and deveined shrimp
- ½ cup chopped onion (1 medium)
- 1 cup sliced celery (2 stalks)
- 1 clove garlic, minced
- 2 teaspoons olive oil
- 1 cup reduced-sodium chicken broth
- ¼ cup dry white wine or reduced-sodium chicken broth
- 1 14.5-ounce can no-salt-added diced tomatoes, drained
- 1 8-ounce can no-salt-added tomato sauce
- 1 teaspoon dried oregano, crushed
- 1 tablespoon snipped fresh parsley

① Thaw fish and shrimp, if frozen. Rinse fish and shrimp; pat dry with paper towels. Cut fish into 1½-inch pieces. Cut shrimp in half lengthwise. Cover and chill fish and shrimp until needed.

② In a large saucepan cook onion, celery, and garlic in hot oil on medium heat until tender. Carefully stir in the broth and the wine. Bring to boiling; reduce heat. Simmer, uncovered, for 5 minutes. Stir in tomatoes, tomato sauce, oregano, ¼ teaspoon *salt*, and ⅛ teaspoon *pepper*. Return to boiling; reduce heat. Cover and simmer for 5 minutes.

③ Gently stir in fish and shrimp. Return just to boiling; reduce heat. Cover and simmer for 3 to 5 minutes more or until fish flakes easily with a fork and shrimp are opaque. Sprinkle with parsley.

PER SERVING 165 calories; 4 g total fat (1 g sat. fat); 87 mg cholesterol; 459 mg sodium; 12 g carbohydrate; 2 g fiber; 19 g protein

Italian Fish Stew

menu

Grapefruit and
Avocado Salad

Crispy Parmesan
Chips

Italian Shrimp Soup
[below]

Carrot-Pumpkin Bars

Italian Shrimp Soup 🕒

MAKES 2 (1-cup) servings **START TO FINISH** 30 minutes

- ½ cup chopped onion (1 medium)
- ½ cup chopped sweet green pepper (1 small)
- 1 clove garlic, minced
- 2 teaspoons olive oil
- 1 medium plum tomato, seeded and chopped
- 1 14-ounce can reduced-sodium chicken broth
- 1 tablespoon lemon juice
- ¼ teaspoon black pepper
- 8 ounces peeled and deveined fresh shrimp and/or fresh sea scallops
- 1 teaspoon snipped fresh basil or ¼ teaspoon dried basil, crushed
- 1 teaspoon snipped fresh thyme or ¼ teaspoon dried thyme, crushed
  Whole wheat bread (optional)

① In a medium saucepan cook onion, sweet pepper, and garlic in hot oil on medium heat until tender. Stir in tomato, broth, lemon juice, and black pepper. Bring to boiling.

② Stir in shrimp and/or scallops. Return to boiling; reduce heat. Cover and simmer for 2 to 3 minutes or until the shrimp and/or scallops are opaque. Stir in the basil and thyme. If desired, serve with whole wheat bread.

PER SERVING 200 calories; 7 g total fat (1 g sat. fat); 172 mg cholesterol; 316 mg sodium; 10 g carbohydrate; 2 g fiber; 25 g protein

Asian Shrimp and Vegetable Soup

Shrimp Chowder

MAKES 6 servings **START TO FINISH** 35 minutes

- 8 ounces fresh or frozen flounder fillets (about 2 medium fillets)
- 8 ounces fresh or frozen peeled and deveined medium shrimp
- 1 cup chopped onion (1 large)
- 2 cloves garlic, minced
- 1 tablespoon canola oil
- 1 14.5-ounce can diced tomatoes, undrained
- 1 14-ounce can vegetable or reduced-sodium chicken broth
- 1 cup water
- 1 cup cubed potatoes (2 medium)
- 1½ teaspoons Creole seasoning
- ⅛ to ¼ teaspoon crushed red pepper

  Dash bottled hot pepper sauce
- 3 ounces reduced-fat cream cheese (Neufchâtel), softened
- 1 cup fat-free milk
- 1½ cups fresh or frozen whole kernel corn

① Thaw fish and shrimp, if frozen. Rinse fish and shrimp; pat dry with paper towels. Cut fish into 1½-inch pieces. Cover and chill fish and shrimp until needed.

② In a 4- to 5-quart Dutch oven cook onion and garlic in hot oil on medium heat about 10 minutes or until onion is tender. Stir in tomatoes, broth, the water, potatoes, Creole seasoning, red pepper, and hot pepper sauce. Bring to boiling; reduce heat. Cover and simmer for 15 to 20 minutes or until potatoes are just tender.

③ Meanwhile, in a medium mixing bowl beat cream cheese with an electric mixer on medium to high until smooth. Gradually beat in milk on low until mixture is very smooth.

④ Add the cream cheese mixture, fish, shrimp, and corn to soup. Simmer, uncovered, about 5 minutes or until fish flakes easily with a fork and shrimp are opaque.

PER SERVING 256 calories; 7 g total fat (2 g sat. fat); 87 mg cholesterol; 599 mg sodium; 29 g carbohydrate; 4 g fiber; 21 g protein

Asian Shrimp and Vegetable Soup 🕥

MAKES 6 servings **START TO FINISH** 30 minutes

- 8 ounces fresh or frozen peeled and deveined large shrimp
- 4 green onions
- 2 teaspoons canola oil
- 1 cup thinly sliced carrots (2 medium)
- 8 ounces fresh shiitake or oyster mushrooms, stemmed and coarsely chopped
- 1 tablespoon grated fresh ginger or 1 teaspoon ground ginger
- 2 cloves garlic, minced
- 2 14-ounce cans reduced-sodium chicken broth
- 2 cups water
- 1 cup frozen shelled sweet soybeans (edamame)
- 1 tablespoon reduced-sodium soy sauce
- ¼ teaspoon crushed red pepper (optional)
- 1 cup trimmed sugar snap pea pods and/or coarsely shredded bok choy

  Slivered green onions (optional)

① Thaw shrimp, if frozen. Rinse shrimp; pat dry. Set aside. Diagonally slice the whole green onions into 1-inch-long pieces, keeping white parts separate from green tops. Set green tops aside.

② In a large nonstick saucepan heat oil on medium heat. Add white parts of the green onions, the carrots, and mushrooms; cook and stir for 5 minutes. Add ginger and garlic; cook and stir for 1 minute.

③ Add chicken broth, the water, soybeans, soy sauce, and crushed red pepper (if using) to mushroom mixture. Bring to boiling; reduce heat. Cover and simmer about 5 minutes or just until carrots are tender.

④ Add shrimp and pea pods. Return to boiling; reduce heat. Simmer, uncovered, about 2 minutes or until heated through. Stir in green onion tops just before serving. If desired, top each serving with slivered green onions.

PER SERVING 128 calories; 4 g total fat (0 g sat. fat); 74 mg cholesterol; 511 mg sodium; 9 g carbohydrate; 3 g fiber; 15 g protein

Green Garden Minestrone

MAKES 8 servings **START TO FINISH** 50 minutes

- 1 tablespoon olive oil
- 1 cup sliced celery (2 stalks)
- ⅔ cup finely chopped leeks (2 medium)
- 6 green onions, sliced
- 1 clove garlic, minced
- 4 cups reduced-sodium chicken broth
- 2 cups water
- 1½ cups sliced fresh green beans and/or fresh or frozen green peas
- ½ cup dried tiny shell pasta
- ¼ teaspoon black pepper
- 1 pound fresh asparagus, trimmed and thinly sliced, and/or 8 ounces baby zucchini, sliced
- 6 cups fresh baby spinach leaves, coarsely chopped, or 1½ cups finely shredded green cabbage
- ¼ cup snipped fresh basil
- 2 ounces thinly shaved Parmesan cheese (optional)

① In a 4-quart Dutch oven heat oil on medium heat. Add celery, leeks, green onions, and garlic; cook until vegetables are crisp-tender, stirring occasionally.

② Add broth, the water, green beans, pasta, and pepper. Bring to boiling; reduce heat. Simmer, uncovered, for 10 minutes. Stir in the asparagus and spinach. Simmer, uncovered, for 2 to 3 minutes more or until pasta and vegetables are tender. Stir in basil.

③ To serve, if desired, top each serving with Parmesan cheese.

PER SERVING 85 calories; 2 g total fat (0 g sat. fat); 0 mg cholesterol; 321 mg sodium; 13 g carbohydrate; 3 g fiber; 5 g protein

Red Bean Stew ③⓪

MAKES 4 servings **START TO FINISH** 25 minutes

- 2 teaspoons canola oil
- 1 cup chopped onion (1 large)
- 3 cloves garlic, minced
- 1 14-ounce can vegetable broth
- 2 tablespoons tomato paste
- 1 teaspoon snipped fresh oregano or ¼ teaspoon dried oregano, crushed
- 1 teaspoon adobo sauce from canned chipotle peppers in adobo sauce or ½ teaspoon adobo seasoning*
- 1 15- to 16-ounce can red kidney beans, rinsed and drained
- 1 tablespoon snipped fresh cilantro
- 2 cups hot cooked brown rice
  Lime wedges (optional)

① In a large saucepan heat oil on medium heat. Add onion and garlic; cook for 4 to 5 minutes or until onion is tender. Add broth, tomato paste, dried oregano (if using), and adobo sauce. Stir in kidney beans. Mash mixture slightly with a potato masher or with the back of a wooden spoon.

② Bring to boiling; reduce heat. Simmer, uncovered, for 5 minutes, stirring occasionally. Stir in cilantro and fresh oregano (if using). Serve with hot cooked rice and, if desired, lime wedges.

***Tip:** Look for adobo seasoning at a market that specializes in Hispanic foods.

PER SERVING 246 calories; 4 g total fat (0 g sat. fat); 0 mg cholesterol; 641 mg sodium; 48 g carbohydrate; 9 g fiber; 11 g protein

---

Eating all-vegetable soup makes you feel healthy and wise.

Green Garden Minestrone

Sweet Potato Soup with Toasted Pecans

Sweet Potato Soup with Toasted Pecans

MAKES 6 servings **START TO FINISH** 40 minutes

2	teaspoons canola oil
¾	cup thinly sliced carrots
½	cup finely chopped leek
⅓	cup chopped sweet orange or yellow pepper
⅓	cup finely chopped onion
1	clove garlic, minced
2	14-ounce cans reduced-sodium chicken broth
1	pound sweet potatoes peeled, halved lengthwise, and thinly sliced crosswise
1	small potato (4 ounces), peeled, halved lengthwise, and thinly sliced crosswise
⅓	cup dry white wine or reduced-sodium chicken broth
⅛	teaspoon black pepper
1	bay leaf
¼	cup chopped pecans, toasted

① In a large saucepan heat oil on medium-high heat. Add carrots, leek, sweet pepper, onion, and garlic; cook about 5 minutes or just until vegetables are tender, stirring occasionally.

② Add broth, sweet potatoes, potato, wine, black pepper, and bay leaf. Bring to boiling; reduce heat. Cover and simmer for 15 to 20 minutes or until the potatoes are tender. Discard the bay leaf. Remove from heat and let soup cool slightly.

③ Transfer half of the soup to a blender or food processor. Cover and blend or process until smooth. Repeat with remaining soup. Return all soup to saucepan. Heat through. Sprinkle each serving with toasted pecans.

PER SERVING 142 calories; 5 g total fat (0 g sat. fat); 0 mg cholesterol; 358 mg sodium; 20 g carbohydrate; 3 g fiber; 4 g protein

Sweet potatoes are one of the world's most nutrient-dense foods. Loaded with cancer-fighting beta-carotene, they also have antioxidant, anti-inflammatory, and blood sugar-regulating properties.

Yellow Pepper Soup with Yogurt and Cucumbers

MAKES 4 servings **STAND** 30 minutes **PREP** 25 minutes
COOK 20 minutes

1	cup plain low-fat yogurt (do not use fat-free)
1	teaspoon fennel seeds, crushed
5	cups coarsely chopped sweet yellow peppers (4 medium)
¼	cup chopped shallots (2 medium) or onion
¾	teaspoon ground cardamom
2	tablespoons olive oil
1	14-ounce can reduced-sodium chicken broth
1	cup water
2	tablespoons cider vinegar
¼	cup coarsely chopped cucumber
	Freshly ground black or white pepper

① In a small bowl combine the yogurt and fennel seeds. Cover and let stand at room temperature for 30 minutes.

② Meanwhile, in a large saucepan cook and stir the sweet peppers, shallots, and cardamom in the hot oil on medium heat about 15 minutes or just until peppers are beginning to soften. Add chicken broth, the water, and vinegar. Bring to boiling; reduce heat. Cover and simmer for 5 minutes more.

③ Remove from heat and let cool slightly. In a blender or food processor blend or process the sweet pepper mixture, half at a time, until smooth. Return all soup to saucepan. Cook and stir on medium heat until heated through.

④ To serve, ladle blended soup into individual bowls. Top with some of the yogurt mixture, cucumber, and black pepper. Serve warm or chilled.

PER SERVING 167 calories; 8 g total fat (2 g sat. fat); 4 mg cholesterol; 286 mg sodium; 19 g carbohydrate; 2 g fiber; 7 g protein

Zesty Gazpacho

MAKES 4 servings **PREP** 30 minutes **CHILL** 2 to 24 hours

- 1 19-ounce can cannellini beans (white kidney beans), rinsed and drained
- 1 14.5-ounce can Italian- or Mexican-style stewed tomatoes, undrained and cut up
- 2 cups tiny red pear-shape or cherry tomatoes, halved or quartered
- 1 11.5-ounce can low-sodium vegetable juice
- 1 cup water
- 1 cup coarsely chopped, seeded cucumber
- ½ cup coarsely chopped sweet yellow and/or red pepper (1 small)
- ¼ cup coarsely chopped red onion
- ¼ cup snipped fresh cilantro
- 3 tablespoons lime juice or lemon juice
- 2 cloves garlic, minced
- ¼ to ½ teaspoon bottled hot pepper sauce
   Lime wedges (optional)

① In a large bowl combine cannellini beans, stewed tomatoes, fresh tomatoes, vegetable juice, the water, cucumber, sweet pepper, red onion, cilantro, lime juice, garlic, and hot pepper sauce. Cover and chill for 2 to 24 hours. If desired, serve with lime wedges.

PER SERVING 152 calories; 1 g total fat (0 g sat. fat); 0 mg cholesterol; 605 mg sodium; 37 g carbohydrate; 10 g fiber; 10 g protein

Sage-White Bean Soup

Sage-White Bean Soup

MAKES 6 servings **START TO FINISH** 45 minutes

- 1 tablespoon olive oil
- ½ cup chopped onion (1 medium)
- 2 tablespoons minced garlic (12 cloves)
- 3 15-ounce cans Great Northern beans, rinsed and drained
- 2 14-ounce cans reduced-sodium chicken broth
- 2 tablespoons snipped fresh sage or 2 teaspoons dried leaf sage, crushed
- ¼ teaspoon black pepper
   Sage French Bread Toasts (optional)
   Fresh sage leaves (optional)

① In a 3- to 4-quart saucepan or Dutch oven heat oil on medium heat. Add onion and garlic; cook and stir over medium heat about 5 minutes or until onion is tender. Stir in beans, broth, dried sage (if using), and pepper. Bring to boiling; reduce heat. Cover and simmer for 20 minutes.

② Stir in snipped fresh sage (if using). Remove from heat. Mash bean mixture slightly with a potato masher or with the back of a wooden spoon. If desired, top individual servings with Sage French Bread Toasts and fresh sage leaves.

PER SERVING 286 calories; 3 g total fat (1 g sat. fat); 0 mg cholesterol; 325 mg sodium; 49 g carbohydrate; 11 g fiber; 18 g protein

Sage French Bread Toasts: Preheat oven to 425°F. Lightly coat both sides of eight ½-inch-thick slices whole grain baguette-style French bread with olive oil nonstick cooking spray. Sprinkle all sides of bread slices with 1 tablespoon snipped fresh sage or 1 teaspoon dried leaf sage, crushed. Arrange bread slices on an ungreased baking sheet. Bake for 5 to 7 minutes or until lightly browned and crisp, turning once.

It's perfectly fine to substitute cannellini or navy beans for the Great Northern beans in Sage-White Bean Soup. They're all white beans, after all!

Fiesta Corn Salad, page 255

Simply Sides

Summer Berries with Orange Cream Topping ✪

MAKES 12 servings **PREP** 20 minutes **CHILL** 1 to 3 hours

- 1   teaspoon finely shredded orange peel (set aside)
- 2   tablespoons orange juice
- 1   tablespoon orange liqueur or orange juice
- 1   tablespoon honey
- 1   teaspoon white or regular balsamic vinegar
- 6   cups assorted fresh berries, such as blueberries, blackberries, red and/or golden raspberries, and/or halved small strawberries
- ¾   cup frozen sugar-free or light whipped dessert topping, thawed
- ½   cup light sour cream
-     Kumquats, thinly sliced (optional)

① For dressing, in a screw-top jar combine orange juice, orange liqueur, honey, and balsamic vinegar. Cover and shake well to combine.

② Place berries in a large bowl. Drizzle dressing over berries; toss gently to coat. Cover and chill in the refrigerator for 1 to 3 hours, tossing occasionally.

③ For cream topping, in a small bowl fold together dessert topping, sour cream, and orange peel.

④ To serve, top berries with the cream topping. If desired, garnish with kumquats.

PER SERVING 64 calories; 2 g total fat (1 g sat. fat); 3 mg cholesterol; 7 mg sodium; 12 g carbohydrate; 2 g fiber; 1 g protein

Summer Berries with Orange Cream Topping

Strawberry-Radish Salad

MAKES 6 servings **PREP** 25 minutes **STAND** 10 minutes

- 2   cups fresh strawberries, hulled and halved or quartered
- 2   medium oranges, peeled and sectioned
- 6   radishes, very thinly sliced
- 3   green onions, thinly bias-sliced
- 4   teaspoons lemon juice
- 1   tablespoon sugar
- 1   5-ounce package mesclun mix or torn mixed salad greens
-     Lemon Vinaigrette

① In a medium bowl combine strawberries, orange sections, radishes, green onions, lemon juice, and sugar. Let stand at room temperature for 10 to 15 minutes to allow flavors to blend.

② In a large bowl toss the mesclun with the Lemon Vinaigrette. Arrange mesclun mixture on a serving platter. Spoon strawberry mixture on mesclun mixture.

Lemon Vinaigrette: In a small saucepan combine ⅓ cup finely chopped shallots, ¼ cup dry white wine, 2 tablespoons sugar, 1 tablespoon rice vinegar, and 3 cloves garlic, minced. Stir in 1 teaspoon cornstarch. Cook and stir until mixture is slightly thickened and bubbly. Cook and stir for 1 minute more; cool. Stir in 1 teaspoon finely shredded lemon peel, ¼ cup lemon juice, ¼ teaspoon salt, and ⅛ teaspoon black pepper. Cool completely before using.

PER SERVING 91 calories; 0 g total fat; 0 mg cholesterol; 111 mg sodium; 21 g carbohydrate; 3 g fiber; 2 g protein

To peel and section an orange, first cut a thin slice from both ends of the fruit using a paring knife. Place the flat end of the orange on a cutting board. Using the knife, cut away the peel and white part of the rind, working from the top to the bottom. Cut into the center of the peeled orange between one section and the membrane. Cut along the other side of the section next to the membrane, freeing each section. If you prefer, work over a bowl to catch the juices.

Strawberry-Radish Salad

Green Apple Slaw

Asian Coleslaw 🕐

MAKES 6 servings **START TO FINISH** 20 minutes

- 4 cups packaged shredded cabbage with carrot (coleslaw mix)
- 1 medium sweet yellow, orange, red, or green pepper, seeded and thinly sliced (1 cup)
- ¼ cup thinly sliced green onions (2)
- ¼ cup snipped fresh cilantro
- ½ cup bottled low-fat sesame ginger salad dressing

① In a large bowl combine coleslaw mix, sweet pepper, green onions, and cilantro. Drizzle ginger salad dressing over cabbage mixture; toss lightly to coat. Serve immediately. Or cover and chill up to 24 hours.

PER SERVING 68 calories; 3 g total fat (1 g sat. fat); 0 mg cholesterol; 207 mg sodium; 9 g carbohydrate; 1 g fiber; 1 g protein

Green Apple Slaw

MAKES 12 servings **PREP** 30 minutes **CHILL** 1 to 24 hours

- ½ cup light mayonnaise or salad dressing
- 2 teaspoons honey
- ½ teaspoon poppy seeds
- 4 Granny Smith apples, quartered and thinly sliced (4 cups)
- 1 tablespoon lemon juice
- 1½ cups chopped cabbage
- ¾ cup halved green seedless grapes
- ½ cup thinly sliced celery (1 stalk)

① For dressing, in a small bowl stir together mayonnaise, honey, and poppy seeds. Set aside.

② In a large salad bowl combine apples and lemon juice; toss gently to coat. Stir in cabbage, grapes, and celery. Spoon dressing over apple mixture; toss gently to coat. Cover and chill in the refrigerator for 1 to 24 hours before serving.

PER SERVING 67 calories; 3 g total fat (1 g sat. fat); 4 mg cholesterol; 73 mg sodium; 10 g carbohydrate; 1 g fiber; 0 g protein

Corn and Blueberry Salad ★

MAKES 6 to 8 servings **PREP** 25 minutes **CHILL** 2 to 24 hours

- 6 ears fresh sweet corn
- 1 cup fresh blueberries
- 1¼ cups sliced cucumber (1 small)
- ¼ cup finely chopped red onion
- ¼ cup snipped fresh cilantro
- 1 fresh jalapeño or serrano chile, seeded and finely chopped*
- 2 tablespoons lime juice
- 2 tablespoons olive oil
- 1 tablespoon honey
- ½ teaspoon salt
- ½ teaspoon ground cumin

① If husks have not been removed from corn, remove and discard. Use a vegetable brush to remove silks; rinse. In a covered large pot or Dutch oven cook corn in enough boiling, lightly salted water to cover about 5 minutes or until kernels are tender. Using tongs, remove corn from water and drain on a layer of paper towels. When cool enough to handle, cut corn from cobs.

② In a medium bowl combine corn, blueberries, cucumber, red onion, cilantro, and jalapeño.

③ For dressing, in screw-top jar combine lime juice, oil, honey, salt, and cumin. Cover and shake well to combine. Drizzle over corn mixture; toss gently to coat. Cover and chill for 2 to 24 hours.

***Tip:** Because hot chile peppers contain volatile oils that can burn your skin and eyes, avoid direct contact with chiles as much as possible. When working with chile peppers, wear plastic or rubber gloves. If your bare hands do touch the chile peppers, wash your hands and fingernails well with soap and water when you are done.

PER SERVING 152 calories; 6 g total fat (1 g sat. fat); 0 mg cholesterol; 211 mg sodium; 26 g carbohydrate; 3 g fiber; 4 g protein

Packaged shredded coleslaw mix is highly versatile for customizing slaw. Stir in additional vegetables or fruit, then toss with your favorite dressing. Ranch or blue cheese dressing makes delicious savory slaws.

Fresh Citrus and Cranberry Salad

MAKES 8 servings **PREP** 25 minutes **CHILL** 1 to 24 hours

- 2 cups fresh cranberries
- 4 oranges
- 1 cup thinly sliced celery (2 stalks)
- ⅓ cup finely chopped red onion (1 small)
- ¼ cup sugar
- 2 tablespoons fresh lemon juice
- 1 teaspoon grated fresh ginger
- 1 5-ounce package baby arugula salad
- ¼ cup snipped fresh mint
- 2 tablespoons walnut oil or olive oil

① In a food processor cover and pulse cranberries with on/off turns until coarsely chopped. (Or coarsely chop cranberries by hand.) Transfer cranberries to a medium bowl; set aside.

② Cut peel from oranges. Section oranges over a small bowl to catch the juice. Add orange sections and juice to cranberries. Stir in celery, onion, sugar, lemon juice, and ginger. Cover and chill in the refrigerator for 1 to 24 hours.

③ To serve, toss the arugula with mint and oil. Top with cranberry mixture.

PER SERVING 92 calories; 4 g total fat (0 g sat. fat); 0 mg cholesterol; 16 mg sodium; 15 g carbohydrate; 3 g fiber; 1 g protein

Fennel Apple Salad ㉚

MAKES 12 servings **START TO FINISH** 30 minutes

- 1 fennel bulb
- 2 Granny Smith apples, cored and thinly sliced
- 1 head radicchio, cored and thinly sliced
- 1 teaspoon finely shredded orange peel
- ½ cup orange juice
- ¼ cup olive oil
- 2 tablespoons lemon juice
- 1 large shallot, finely chopped
- 2 teaspoons Dijon mustard
- ¼ teaspoon salt
- ⅛ teaspoon freshly ground black pepper
- 1 ounce Parmesan cheese

① For fennel, cut off and discard fennel stalks. Reserve some of the fronds for garnish; finely chop or snip fronds. Set aside. Remove any wilted outer layers; cut a thin slice from base of bulb. Cut bulb in quarters lengthwise. Cut core out of each quarter. Thinly slice crosswise.

② In a very large bowl combine fennel, apple slices, and radicchio.

③ For dressing, in a screw-top jar combine orange peel, orange juice, olive oil, lemon juice, shallot, mustard, salt, and pepper. Cover and shake well to combine. Drizzle dressing over fennel mixture; toss gently to coat.

④ Using a vegetable peeler, shave Parmesan cheese into shards. Garnish salad with cheese shards and the reserved fronds.

PER SERVING 78 calories; 5 g total fat (1 g sat. fat); 2 mg cholesterol; 117 mg sodium; 7 g carbohydrate; 1 g fiber; 2 g protein

Crispy, crunchy salads are a refreshing foil for hearty roasted or grilled meats.

Mediterranean Chopped Salad

menu

Crispy Fish and
Peppers

Two-Cheese Garlic 'n'
Herb Biscuits

Mediterranean
Chopped Salad [below]

Whole Wheat Orzo Pilaf
with Mushrooms

Mediterranean Chopped Salad ㉚

MAKES 2 servings **START TO FINISH** 20 minutes

1   tablespoon basil pesto

2   teaspoons white balsamic vinegar or regular
    balsamic vinegar

⅓   cup chopped, seeded tomato

⅓   cup chopped zucchini

⅓   cup chopped sweet yellow or orange pepper

⅓   cup very small broccoli florets

2   cups torn mixed salad greens (optional)

2   tablespoons crumbled reduced-fat feta cheese

① In a small bowl combine pesto and vinegar. Stir in
tomato, zucchini, sweet pepper, and broccoli.

② If desired, divide salad greens between 2 serving
plates. Top with tomato mixture. Sprinkle with feta cheese.

PER SERVING 100 calories; 6 g total fat (1 g sat. fat); 4 mg cholesterol;
186 mg sodium; 7 g carbohydrate; 2 g fiber; 4 g protein

*Chopped salads are the most enjoyable to
eat—and look at—when all of the ingredients
are chopped as closely in size to one another
as possible.*

Layered Asian Salad

MAKES 8 servings **START TO FINISH** 40 minutes

4   cups fresh baby spinach

2   cups shredded napa cabbage

1   cup coarsely shredded carrots (2 medium)

1   cup fresh pea pods, trimmed, strings removed,
    and halved

1   large sweet red or yellow pepper, cut into
    thin strips

⅓   cup thinly sliced green onions

1   teaspoon finely shredded orange peel

⅓   cup orange juice

1   tablespoon rice vinegar or white wine vinegar

2   teaspoons reduced-sodium soy sauce

2   teaspoons honey

1   teaspoon toasted sesame oil

1   teaspoon sesame seeds, toasted

½   teaspoon grated fresh ginger or ⅛ teaspoon
    ground ginger

① Place the spinach in a 2½- to 3-quart clear glass salad
bowl. Top with cabbage, carrots, pea pods, sweet pepper,
and green onions.

② For dressing, in a screw-top jar combine orange peel
and juice, vinegar, soy sauce, honey, sesame oil, sesame
seeds, and ginger. Cover and shake well to combine.

③ Drizzle dressing over salad; toss gently to coat.

PER SERVING 42 calories; 1 g total fat (0 g sat. fat); 0 mg cholesterol;
70 mg sodium; 7 g carbohydrate; 2 g fiber; 2 g protein

Layered Asian Salad

Spinach Salad with Dijon Dressing 🕐30

MAKES 4 servings **START TO FINISH** 20 minutes

- 2 tablespoons lemon or lime juice
- 2 tablespoons water
- 1 small apple, cored and thinly sliced crosswise
- 4 cups fresh baby spinach and/or 4 cups fresh watercress (thick stems discarded)
- 2 packaged refrigerated cooked whole baby beets, thinly sliced
- ¼ cup bottled light honey-Dijon salad dressing
- 2 ounces soft goat cheese (chèvre), crumbled

① In a medium bowl combine lemon juice and the water. Add apple slices to juice mixture; turn slices to coat well. Set aside.

② Divide spinach and/or watercress among 4 serving plates. Drain the apple slices. Arrange apples and beets on top of the spinach. Drizzle with dressing and sprinkle with goat cheese.

PER SERVING 106 calories; 5 g total fat (2 g sat. fat); 7 mg cholesterol; 227 mg sodium; 12 g carbohydrate; 2 g fiber; 4 g protein

Grapefruit and Avocado Salad 🕐30

MAKES 6 servings **START TO FINISH** 25 minutes

- 4 cups fresh baby spinach
- 1 grapefruit, peeled and sectioned
- 1 small avocado, halved, seeded, peeled, and sliced
- 1 cup canned sliced beets
- 1 tablespoon sliced almonds, toasted
   Orange Vinaigrette

① Divide spinach among 6 salad plates. Arrange grapefruit, avocado, and beets on spinach. Sprinkle with almonds. Drizzle with Orange Vinaigrette.

Orange Vinaigrette: In a screw-top jar combine 1 teaspoon finely shredded orange peel, ⅓ cup orange juice, 2 teaspoons red wine vinegar, 2 teaspoons vegetable oil, ⅛ teaspoon salt, and dash black pepper. Cover and shake well to combine.

PER SERVING 106 calories; 7 g total fat (1 g sat. fat); 0 mg cholesterol; 122 mg sodium; 11 g carbohydrate; 4 g fiber; 2 g protein

Caesar-Style Salad with Crispy Parmesan Rounds 🕐30

MAKES 4 servings **PREP** 15 minutes **BAKE** 10 minutes
OVEN 300°F

- ½ cup finely shredded Parmesan cheese
- ⅛ teaspoon freshly ground black pepper
- ¾ cup 1-inch cubes whole grain baguette-style French bread
   Olive oil nonstick cooking spray
- 2 tablespoons light mayonnaise or salad dressing
- 1 tablespoon lemon juice
- ½ of a clove garlic, minced
- ⅛ teaspoon freshly ground black pepper
- 4 cups torn romaine lettuce
   Freshly ground black pepper (optional)

① Preheat oven to 300°F. Line a large baking sheet with parchment paper or foil. Draw four 4-inch circles on the paper or foil, spacing circles at least 1 inch apart. In a small bowl combine Parmesan cheese and the ⅛ teaspoon pepper. Divide cheese mixture among circles, spreading evenly to edges of circles.

② Bake for 10 to 15 minutes or until cheese is melted and just beginning to brown on the edges. Remove from oven; cool on baking sheet. Carefully remove cheese rounds from parchment paper or foil. Set aside.

③ Meanwhile, for croutons, place bread cubes in a small skillet; lightly coat with cooking spray. Turn cubes; lightly coat again with cooking spray. Cook on medium-high heat for 3 to 5 minutes or until bread is lightly toasted, tossing cubes occasionally.

④ For dressing, in a small bowl whisk together mayonnaise, lemon juice, garlic, and the ⅛ teaspoon pepper. Divide romaine among 4 salad plates. Drizzle each with dressing; top with croutons and a Parmesan round. If desired, sprinkle with additional pepper.

PER SERVING 96 calories; 6 g total fat (2 g sat. fat); 10 mg cholesterol; 256 mg sodium; 7 g carbohydrate; 2 g fiber; 5 g protein

Spinach Salad with Dijon Dressing

Fiesta Corn Salad

Cilantro-Bean Salad

MAKES 8 servings **PREP** 20 minutes **CHILL** 2 to 24 hours

- ⅓ cup rice vinegar or white wine vinegar
- 2 tablespoons olive oil
- 1 teaspoon packed brown sugar
- ⅛ teaspoon salt
- ⅛ teaspoon black pepper
- 1 15-ounce can navy beans or garbanzo beans (chickpeas), rinsed and drained
- 1 10-ounce package frozen baby lima beans
- 2 cups chopped carrots (2 medium)
- ¼ cup snipped fresh cilantro
- 1 fresh jalapeño or serrano chile, seeded and finely chopped*

① For dressing, in a large bowl whisk together vinegar, oil, brown sugar, salt, and black pepper.

② Stir navy beans, lima beans, carrots, cilantro, and jalapeño into dressing; toss gently to coat. Cover and chill for 2 to 24 hours, stirring occasionally.

*Tip: Because hot chile peppers contain volatile oils that can burn your skin and eyes, avoid direct contact with chiles as much as possible. When working with chile peppers, wear plastic or rubber gloves. If your bare hands do touch the chile peppers, wash your hands and fingernails well with soap and water when you are done.

PER SERVING 151 calories; 4 g total fat (1 g sat. fat); 0 mg cholesterol; 305 mg sodium; 22 g carbohydrate; 5 g fiber; 7 g protein

Cilantro-Bean Salad

Fiesta Corn Salad

MAKES 12 servings **START TO FINISH** 35 minutes

- 4 cups fresh or frozen whole kernel corn
- 1 cup frozen shelled sweet soybeans (edamame)
- ¼ cup chopped red onion
- ¼ cup snipped fresh cilantro
- 1 small fresh jalapeño, seeded and finely chopped*
- 2 tablespoons olive oil
- ½ teaspoon finely shredded lime peel
- 2 tablespoons lime juice
- 1½ teaspoons cumin seeds, toasted**
- 2 cloves garlic, minced
- ¼ teaspoon chili powder
- 2 medium tomatoes, seeded and chopped
  Snipped fresh cilantro (optional)

① In a covered large saucepan cook corn and soybeans in enough boiling, lightly salted water to cover for 2 minutes or until tender; drain. Rinse with cold water; drain again.

② In a large bowl stir together corn, soybeans, red onion, the ¼ cup snipped cilantro, and jalapeño.

③ For dressing, in a screw-top jar combine olive oil, lime peel and juice, cumin seeds, garlic, and chili powder. Cover and shake well to combine. Drizzle dressing over corn mixture. Add tomatoes; toss gently to coat.

④ If desired, garnish with additional cilantro. Serve immediately. (Or do not stir in tomatoes. Cover and chill in the refrigerator for 2 to 24 hours. Let stand for 30 minutes before serving; gently stir in tomatoes.)

**Tip: To toast cumin seeds, place seeds in a dry small skillet. Heat on medium heat about 2 minutes or until fragrant, shaking skillet often.

PER SERVING 96 calories; 4 g total fat (0 g sat. fat); 0 mg cholesterol; 6 mg sodium; 15 g carbohydrate; 2 g fiber; 4 g protein

Italian-Style Vegetables

MAKES 5 or 6 servings **PREP** 15 minutes **COOK** 5 minutes **CHILL** 4 to 24 hours

- 1 10-ounce package frozen lima beans
- 1 8-ounce package frozen sugar snap pea pods or one 9-ounce package frozen Italian green beans
- 1 6-ounce jar marinated artichoke hearts, undrained
- 1 tablespoon snipped fresh dill or 1 teaspoon dried dillweed
- ⅛ teaspoon crushed red pepper

  Romaine lettuce leaves
- 2 tablespoons thinly sliced green onion (1) (optional)

  Fresh dill (optional)

  Lemon wedges (optional)

① In a covered medium saucepan cook lima beans and snap peas in a small amount of boiling, lightly salted water for 5 to 8 minutes or until crisp-tender; drain. Rinse with cold water; drain again.

② In a medium bowl combine the lima bean mixture, artichoke hearts, the 1 tablespoon snipped fresh dill, and red pepper. Cover and chill in the refrigerator for 4 to 24 hours.

③ To serve, place the romaine leaves in a salad bowl. Spoon the lima bean mixture over romaine leaves. If desired, sprinkle with green onion and additional fresh dill, and serve with lemon wedges.

PER SERVING 114 calories; 4 g total fat (1 g sat. fat); 0 mg cholesterol; 48 mg sodium; 17 g carbohydrate; 6 g fiber; 5 g protein

Italian-Style Vegetables

Squash, Corn, and Barley Succotash

MAKES 12 servings **PREP** 15 minutes **COOK** 40 minutes

- 4 cups water
- ½ cup regular barley
- ¾ teaspoon salt
- 1 tablespoon olive oil
- 1 cup finely chopped onion
- 1 2-pound butternut squash, peeled, seeded, and cut into ½-inch cubes (about 4 cups)
- ¾ cup reduced-sodium chicken broth
- ¼ teaspoon black pepper
- ⅛ teaspoon dried thyme, crushed
- 3 cups frozen whole kernel corn
- ¼ cup snipped fresh parsley

① In a medium saucepan bring the water to boiling. Add barley and ½ teaspoon of the salt. Return to boiling; reduce heat. Cover and simmer about 40 minutes or until barley is tender, stirring occasionally. Drain; set aside.

② Meanwhile, in large skillet heat oil on medium-high heat. Add onion; cook and stir about 5 minutes or until tender. Stir in the remaining ¼ teaspoon salt, squash, broth, pepper, and thyme. Bring to boiling; reduce heat. Cover and simmer about 10 minutes or until squash is tender. Stir in corn; cover and cook for 5 minutes more. Stir in barley and parsley; heat through.

PER SERVING 109 calories; 2 g total fat (0 g sat. fat); 0 mg cholesterol; 187 mg sodium; 23 g carbohydrate; 4 g fiber; 3 g protein

Attempting to peel a butternut squash with a knife can be dangerous—it's easy to slip and cut yourself. The best way is to use a vegetable peeler. You may have to go over the same area two or three times or more until all of the peel is gone—but it's much safer.

Squash, Corn, and Barley Succotash

Tomato and Sweet Pepper Salad

Tomato and Sweet Pepper Salad ㉚

MAKES 8 servings **START TO FINISH** 25 minutes

- 3 large sweet yellow peppers, seeded and thinly sliced into rings (about 3 cups)
- 4 cups fresh watercress (thick stems discarded) or fresh baby spinach
- 3 or 4 medium tomatoes (about 1 pound), cut into wedges
  Herb-Dijon Vinaigrette
- ¼ cup crumbled Gorgonzola or blue cheese (1 ounce)

① In a covered large saucepan cook sweet pepper rings in a large amount of boiling, lightly salted water for 1 to 2 minutes or just until crisp-tender; drain in a colander. Rinse with cold water; drain well.

② Arrange watercress on a serving platter. Top with sweet pepper rings and tomato wedges. Shake dressing; drizzle over salad. Sprinkle with cheese.

Herb-Dijon Vinaigrette: In a screw-top jar combine 2 tablespoons olive oil, 2 tablespoons white wine vinegar or balsamic vinegar, 1 tablespoon snipped fresh chives, 2 teaspoons snipped fresh basil, ½ teaspoon sugar, ½ teaspoon Dijon mustard, and ⅛ teaspoon black pepper. Cover and shake well to combine.

PER SERVING 85 calories; 5 g total fat (1 g sat. fat); 3 mg cholesterol; 78 mg sodium; 9 g carbohydrate; 2 g fiber; 3 g protein

Tomato and Red Onion Salad

MAKES 6 to 8 servings **PREP** 25 minutes **STAND** 25 minutes

- 4 cups ice water
- 2 teaspoons salt
- 1 medium red onion, cut into ¼-inch-thick slices and separated into rings
- ½ cup cider vinegar
- ¼ cup sugar
- ¾ teaspoon salt
- ¾ teaspoon freshly ground black pepper
- 8 cups whole red grape tomatoes, yellow pear tomatoes, cherry tomatoes, and/or small yellow tomatoes, (halved, if desired)

① In medium bowl combine the ice cold water and the 2 teaspoons salt; stir to dissolve salt. Add onion slices. Let stand 20 minutes; drain.

② Meanwhile, for dressing, in small bowl whisk together vinegar, sugar, the ¾ teaspoon salt, and pepper. In an extra-large bowl combine tomatoes and the drained onions. Drizzle with dressing; toss gently to coat. Let stand 5 minutes before serving.

PER SERVING 88 calories; 1 g total fat (0 g sat. fat); 0 mg cholesterol; 401 mg sodium; 20 g carbohydrate; 3 g fiber; 2 g protein

Tomato and Red Onion Salad

Greek Vegetable Salad ③⓪

MAKES 4 servings **START TO FINISH** 30 minutes

- 1 cup coarsely chopped tomatoes (2 medium)
- ½ cup coarsely chopped cucumber
- ¼ cup chopped sweet yellow, red, or green pepper
- 2 tablespoons finely chopped red onion
- ¾ teaspoon snipped fresh thyme or ¼ teaspoon dried thyme, crushed
- ½ teaspoon snipped fresh oregano or ⅛ teaspoon dried oregano, crushed
- 1 tablespoon white balsamic vinegar or regular balsamic vinegar
- 1 tablespoon olive oil
  Leaf lettuce (optional)
- ¼ cup crumbled reduced-fat feta cheese (1 ounce)

① In a medium bowl combine tomatoes, cucumber, sweet pepper, red onion, thyme, and oregano.

② For dressing, in a small bowl whisk together balsamic vinegar and olive oil. Drizzle dressing over tomato mixture; toss gently to coat.

③ If desired, line a serving bowl with lettuce; spoon in tomato mixture. Sprinkle with feta cheese.

PER SERVING 65 calories; 5 g total fat (1 g sat. fat); 3 mg cholesterol; 120 mg sodium; 4 g carbohydrate; 1 g fiber; 2 g protein

Southwest Pasta Salad ③⓪

MAKES 6 to 8 servings **START TO FINISH** 30 minutes

- 4 ounces dried multigrain penne pasta (1¼ cups)
- ½ cup thin bite-size strips jicama
- ½ cup thin bite-size strips zucchini
- ½ cup chopped sweet green or red pepper
- ¼ cup frozen whole kernel corn, thawed and drained
- ¼ cup sliced radishes
  Creamy Spinach Pesto

① Cook pasta in boiling, lightly salted water according to package directions; drain in colander. Rinse with cold water; drain again. Transfer to a large bowl.

② Add jicama, zucchini, sweet pepper, corn, and radishes to pasta. Drizzle with Creamy Spinach Pesto; toss gently to coat.

③ Serve immediately. Or cover and chill for up to 24 hours. If chilled, stir before serving.

Creamy Spinach Pesto: In a blender or food processor combine 1¼ cups lightly packed fresh spinach; ½ cup lightly packed fresh cilantro; 2 tablespoons sliced almonds, toasted; 2 tablespoons water; 1 tablespoon olive oil; ½ teaspoon salt; ⅛ to ¼ teaspoon crushed red pepper; and ⅛ teaspoon black pepper. Cover and blend or process until smooth. Add ¼ cup light sour cream. Cover and blend or process just until combined.

PER SERVING 130 calories; 5 g total fat (1 g sat. fat); 3 mg cholesterol; 219 mg sodium; 18 g carbohydrate; 3 g fiber; 5 g protein

With the addition of a chicken breast or piece of salmon, a side salad becomes a main dish.

Greek Garden Pasta Salad

Greek Garden Pasta Salad

MAKES 12 servings **PREP** 35 minutes **CHILL** 3 to 6 hours

6	ounces dried whole grain or multigrain bow tie or rotini pasta (2⅔ cups)
1	6-ounce carton regular plain fat-free yogurt or Greek-style plain fat-free yogurt (⅔ cup)
⅓	cup light mayonnaise or salad dressing
2	tablespoons snipped fresh parsley
2	tablespoons snipped fresh dill or 1½ teaspoons dried dill
2	tablespoons fat-free milk
1	teaspoon finely shredded lemon peel
1	tablespoon lemon juice
½	teaspoon freshly ground black pepper
1½	cups chopped English cucumber (1 medium)
1½	cups halved grape tomatoes
¾	cup chopped sweet green pepper (1 medium)
⅓	cup sliced green onions
⅓	cup quartered pitted kalamata olives

① Cook pasta in boiling, lightly salted water according to package directions; drain in colander. Rinse with cold water; drain again. Transfer to a large bowl.

② For dressing, in a medium bowl stir together yogurt, mayonnaise, parsley, dill, milk, lemon peel and juice, and pepper.

③ Stir cucumber, tomatoes, sweet pepper, and green onions into pasta. Drizzle with the dressing; toss gently to coat. Cover and chill in the refrigerator for 3 to 6 hours before serving.

④ To serve, fold in the kalamata olives.

PER SERVING 98 calories; 3 g total fat (0 g sat. fat); 3 mg cholesterol; 100 mg sodium; 15 g carbohydrate; 2 g fiber; 3 g protein

To hard-cook eggs and not get any unattractive (though harmless) green tinge and sulfury taste in the yolks, use this method: Place the eggs in a saucepan and cover with about an inch of water. Bring the water to a boil, then cover the pan and turn off the heat. Let the pan sit for 12 minutes. Run the eggs under cold running water to stop the cooking process, then peel.

New Potato Salad

MAKES 16 servings **PREP** 40 minutes **CHILL** 6 to 24 hours

2	pounds tiny new potatoes
1	cup low-fat mayonnaise or light salad dressing
1	cup chopped celery
1	cup chopped onion
⅓	cup chopped sweet or dill pickles
½	teaspoon salt
¼	teaspoon coarsely ground black pepper
2	hard-cooked eggs, chopped
1	to 2 tablespoons fat-free milk
	Coarsely ground black pepper

① In a covered large saucepan cook potatoes in enough boiling, lightly salted water to cover for 15 to 20 minutes or just until tender; drain. Cool potatoes. Cut potatoes into quarters.

② In a large bowl combine mayonnaise, celery, onion, pickles, salt, and the ¼ teaspoon pepper. Add the potatoes and eggs; toss gently to coat. Cover and chill in the refrigerator for 6 to 24 hours.

③ To serve, stir enough of the milk into salad to reach desired consistency. Season to taste with additional pepper.

PER SERVING 86 calories; 3 g total fat (1 g sat. fat); 27 mg cholesterol; 254 mg sodium; 14 g carbohydrate; 1 g fiber; 2 g protein

New Potato Salad

Roasted Vegetable Couscous

MAKES 6 to 8 servings **PREP** 20 minutes **ROAST** 45 minutes
STAND 20 minutes **OVEN** 375°F

    Nonstick cooking spray
1 Japanese eggplant or 1 small eggplant, halved lengthwise
1 small sweet onion (such as Vidalia, Walla Walla, or Maui), halved
1 carrot, halved lengthwise, or 4 ounces packaged peeled fresh baby carrots
1 sweet yellow or red pepper, halved lengthwise and seeded
1 or 2 yellow banana peppers, halved lengthwise and seeded
1 cup water
¾ cup couscous
    Balsamic-Mustard Dressing
    Butterhead lettuce leaves (optional)

1. Preheat oven to 375°F. Lightly coat a shallow baking pan with cooking spray. Place vegetables, cut sides down, in prepared baking pan. Roast for 45 to 60 minutes or until tender.

2. Wrap eggplant and peppers in foil; let stand for 20 minutes. Set remaining vegetables aside. Peel eggplant and peppers. Cut all vegetables into bite-size pieces.

3. In a medium saucepan bring the water to boiling. Stir in couscous. Remove from heat; cover and let stand for 5 minutes. Using a fork, fluff couscous mixture.

4. In a large bowl combine vegetables, couscous, and Balsamic-Mustard Dressing; toss gently to combine. If desired, line a shallow serving bowl with lettuce leaves. Spoon in couscous mixture. Serve at room temperature or chilled.

Balsamic-Mustard Dressing: In a screw-top jar combine ¼ cup white or regular balsamic vinegar, 1 tablespoon canola oil, 1½ teaspoons Dijon mustard, ¼ teaspoon seasoned salt, and ¼ teaspoon garlic powder. Cover and shake well to combine.

PER SERVING 141 calories; 3 g total fat (0 g sat. fat); 0 mg cholesterol; 105 mg sodium; 25 g carbohydrate; 3 g fiber; 4 g protein

Blood Orange and Toasted Almond Couscous 30

MAKES 8 servings **START TO FINISH** 15 minutes

2 cups orange juice
1 tablespoon butter or margarine
½ teaspoon salt
½ teaspoon ground cardamom
1 10-ounce package couscous
½ cup dried cherries or dried cranberries
2 large blood oranges or Cara Cara oranges, peeled, halved or quartered, and sliced
½ cup slivered almonds, toasted
1 teaspoon finely shredded lime peel

1. In a large saucepan combine orange juice, butter, salt, and cardamom. Bring to boiling. Stir in couscous and cherries. Remove from heat; cover and let stand for 5 minutes.

2. Using a fork, fluff couscous mixture. Transfer to a large bowl; stir in oranges, almonds, and lime peel. Serve warm.

PER SERVING 402 calories; 5 g total fat (1 g sat. fat); 4 mg cholesterol; 167 mg sodium; 77 g carbohydrate; 6 g fiber; 11 g protein

Eggplant-Zucchini Parmesan

MAKES 8 servings **PREP** 20 minutes
SLOW COOKER 4 to 5 hours (low) or 2 to 2½ hours (high)

1 medium eggplant, peeled and cut into 1-inch cubes
1 medium zucchini, cut into 1-inch cubes
1 medium onion, cut into thin wedges
1½ cups light spaghetti sauce
⅓ cup shredded Parmesan cheese
    Shredded Parmesan cheese (optional)

1. In a 3½- or 4-quart slow cooker combine eggplant, zucchini, onion, spaghetti sauce, and the ⅓ cup Parmesan cheese.

2. Cover and cook on low-heat setting for 4 to 5 hours or on high-heat setting for 2 to 2½ hours. If desired, sprinkle each serving with the additional Parmesan cheese.

PER SERVING 55 calories; 1 g total fat (1 g sat. fat); 2 mg cholesterol; 210 mg sodium; 9 g carbohydrate; 3 g fiber; 3 g protein

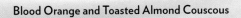

Curried Wild Rice Salad

Curried Wild Rice Salad

MAKES 10 servings **PREP** 20 minutes **COOK** 40 minutes
COOL 25 minutes **CHILL** 4 to 24 hours **STAND** 30 minutes

3	cups water
⅔	cup uncooked wild rice, rinsed and drained
⅔	cup uncooked brown rice
1	cup frozen peas, thawed
1	medium sweet red or yellow pepper, seeded and chopped
¼	cup thinly sliced green onions (2)
¼	cup dried currants or raisins
3	tablespoons canola oil
3	tablespoons orange juice
1	tablespoon honey
1	teaspoon curry powder
¼	teaspoon salt
¼	cup chopped peanuts (optional)

① In a medium saucepan combine the water, wild rice, and brown rice. Bring to boiling; reduce heat. Cover and simmer about 40 minutes or until rice is tender; drain if necessary.

② Transfer cooked rice to a large bowl; let cool about 25 minutes or until rice is room temperature. Stir peas, sweet pepper, green onions, and currants into rice mixture.

③ For dressing, in a screw-top jar combine oil, orange juice, honey, curry powder, and salt. Cover and shake well to combine.

④ Drizzle dressing over rice mixture in bowl; toss gently to combine. Cover and chill in the refrigerator for 4 to 24 hours. Let salad stand at room temperature for 30 minutes before serving. If desired, sprinkle with chopped peanuts just before serving.

PER SERVING 155 calories; 5 g total fat (0 g sat. fat); 0 mg cholesterol; 80 mg sodium; 25 g carbohydrate; 2 g fiber; 4 g protein

Wild rice isn't rice at all, but rather the seed of an aquatic grass that grows profusely in shallow streams in cool climates. It's harvested, then toasted in large kettles over open fires. Always rinse it well in cool water before cooking it.

Whole Wheat Orzo Pilaf with Mushrooms 🕒

MAKES 6 servings **PREP** 15 minutes **COOK** 15 minutes

2	teaspoons olive oil
8	ounces fresh button, shiitake, portobello, and/or cremini mushrooms, sliced
½	cup chopped onion (1 medium)
1	14-ounce can reduced-sodium chicken broth
1	cup dried whole wheat orzo
2	pine nuts, toasted
2	tablespoons snipped fresh parsley

① In large saucepan heat oil on medium heat. Add mushrooms and onion; cook about 10 minutes or until vegetables are tender, stirring occasionally.

② Add broth to mushroom mixture; bring to boiling. Stir in orzo; reduce heat. Cover and simmer about 15 minutes or until orzo is tender and most of the liquid is absorbed, stirring occasionally. Remove from heat. Stir in pine nuts and parsley. Serve warm.

PER SERVING 148 calories; 4 g total fat (0 g sat. fat); 0 mg cholesterol; 160 mg sodium; 23 g carbohydrate; 5 g fiber; 6 g protein

Sesame Asparagus

MAKES 4 servings **PREP** 15 minutes **CHILL** 1 to 4 hours

1	pound fresh asparagus, trimmed
4	teaspoons reduced-sodium soy sauce
¼	teaspoon toasted sesame oil
	Sesame seeds, toasted

① In a covered large saucepan cook asparagus in a small amount of boiling, lightly salted water for 1 minute. Using tongs, transfer asparagus to a large bowl of ice water. Let stand for 2 minutes. Drain well; pat dry with paper towels. Place asparagus in a large resealable plastic bag.

② For dressing, in a small bowl whisk together soy sauce and sesame oil. Pour dressing over asparagus. Seal bag. Chill in the refrigerator for 1 to 4 hours. Drain, discarding dressing.

③ To serve, sprinkle asparagus with sesame seeds.

PER SERVING 28 calories; 1 g total fat (0 g sat. fat); 0 mg cholesterol; 178 mg sodium; 4 g carbohydrate; 2 g fiber; 3 g protein

Spring Risotto

MAKES 6 servings **PREP** 25 minutes **COOK** 20 minutes

- 1 tablespoon olive oil
- 1 medium fennel bulb, trimmed and chopped, or ½ cup chopped onion (1 medium)
- 2 cloves garlic, minced
- 1 cup uncooked arborio rice
- 1 14-ounce can vegetable broth
- 1¾ cups water
- 12 ounces fresh asparagus and/or green beans, trimmed and cut into 1-inch pieces
- 2 cups coarsely chopped fresh arugula or baby spinach leaves
- ½ cup chopped radishes
- ¼ cup snipped fresh parsley
- ¼ cup snipped fresh mint or basil

① In a large saucepan heat oil on medium heat. Add fennel and garlic; cook about 5 minutes or until fennel is tender, stirring occasionally. Add rice; cook about 5 minutes or until rice is golden brown. Remove from heat.

② Meanwhile, in a medium saucepan bring broth and the water to boiling. Add green beans, if using. Cover and cook for 5 minutes. Add asparagus, if using. Cover and cook for 2 to 3 minutes more or just until vegetables are crisp-tender. Using a slotted spoon, transfer vegetables to a bowl, reserving broth mixture in saucepan. Set vegetables aside. Reduce heat and simmer.

③ Slowly add 1 cup of the broth mixture into the rice mixture, stirring constantly. Continue to cook and stir on medium heat until liquid is absorbed. Add another 1 cup of the broth mixture to the rice mixture, stirring constantly. Continue to cook and stir until the liquid is absorbed. Add another 1 cup of the broth mixture, ½ cup at a time, stirring frequently until the broth has been absorbed. (This should take about 20 minutes.)

④ Stir in the remaining broth mixture. Cook and stir until rice is tender yet slightly firm in center and creamy. Remove from heat. Stir in cooked asparagus and/or beans, the arugula, radishes, parsley, and mint. Serve immediately.

PER SERVING 125 calories; 2 g total fat (0 g sat. fat); 0 mg cholesterol; 227 mg sodium; 24 g carbohydrate; 2 g fiber; 3 g protein

Heartland Baked Beans ✪

MAKES 12 servings **STAND** 1 hour **PREP** 25 minutes
COOK 1 hour **BAKE** 2¼ hours **OVEN** 300°F

- 1 pound dry navy beans or Great Northern beans (2⅓ cups)
- 4 ounces turkey bacon, chopped
- ¾ cup chopped onion
- ½ cup chopped celery (1 stalk)
- 2 cloves garlic, minced
- 1 teaspoon grated fresh ginger or ½ teaspoon ground ginger
- 3 tablespoons packed brown sugar
- ½ cup ketchup
- 2 tablespoons cider vinegar
- 1 teaspoon dry mustard
- ¼ teaspoon black pepper

① Rinse beans. In a 4- to 5-quart oven-going Dutch oven combine beans and 8 cups water. Bring to boiling; reduce heat. Simmer, uncovered, for 2 minutes. Remove from heat. Cover and let stand for 1 hour. (Or place beans and 8 cups water in Dutch oven. Cover and let soak in a cool place overnight.) Drain and rinse beans.

② Return beans to Dutch oven. Stir in 8 cups fresh water. Bring to boiling; reduce heat. Cover and simmer for 1 to 1¼ hours or until beans are tender, stirring occasionally. Drain beans in a colander, reserving bean liquid.

③ Preheat oven to 300°F. In the same Dutch oven combine turkey bacon, onion, celery, garlic, and ginger; cook on medium heat until onion is tender, stirring occasionally. Add brown sugar; cook and stir until sugar is dissolved. Stir in ketchup, vinegar, dry mustard, and pepper. Stir in drained beans and 1 cup of the reserved bean liquid.

④ Bake, covered, about 2¼ hours or until desired consistency, stirring occasionally. If necessary, stir in additional reserved bean liquid.

PER SERVING 181 calories; 3 g total fat (1 g sat. fat); 9 mg cholesterol; 233 mg sodium; 30 g carbohydrate; 10 g fiber; 10 g protein

Grilled Vegetables with Vinaigrette

Grilled Vegetables with Vinaigrette

MAKES 8 servings **PREP** 20 minutes
MARINATE 1 to 4 hours **GRILL** 8 minutes

- 1 pound fresh asparagus, trimmed
- 1 pound green and/or yellow pattypan squash, halved, or 1 pound zucchini and/or yellow summer squash, cut into 1-inch pieces
- 2 medium sweet red and/or yellow peppers, seeded and cut into ½-inch strips
- 2 cups red and/or yellow cherry tomatoes
- ¾ cup bottled light balsamic vinaigrette salad dressing

  Black pepper

① In a very large bowl combine asparagus, squash, sweet peppers and tomatoes. Add balsamic vinaigrette; toss to coat. Cover and marinate in the refrigerator for 1 to 4 hours. Remove vegetables from vinaigrette, reserving vinaigrette.

② For a charcoal grill, place vegetables in a lightly greased grill wok on the rack of an uncovered grill directly over medium-hot coals. Grill for 8 to 10 minutes or until crisp-tender, stirring occasionally. If the vegetables appear dry while cooking, brush with some of the reserved vinaigrette. (For a gas grill, preheat grill. Reduce heat to medium-high. Place vegetables in a lightly greased grill wok on a grill rack directly over heat. Cover and grill as above.)

③ To serve, arrange vegetables on a serving platter. Sprinkle with black pepper. Drizzle with the reserved vinaigrette.

PER SERVING 53 calories; 1 g total fat (0 g sat. fat); 0 mg cholesterol; 223 mg sodium; 10 g carbohydrate; 3 g fiber; 2 g protein

To remove the woody stem end of asparagus, starting at the base of each spear, bend the spear several times, working toward the tip, until you find a place where it breaks easily. Break off the woody base and discard it.

Asian Stir-Fry Vegetables 30

MAKES 4 servings **START TO FINISH** 30 minutes

- ½ cup cold water
- 1 tablespoon reduced-sodium soy sauce
- 1 teaspoon cornstarch
- ½ teaspoon ground ginger
- 1 tablespoon cooking oil
- 2 cups broccoli and/or cauliflower florets*
- ¾ cup thinly bias-sliced carrot*
- ¼ cup chopped onion*
- 1 clove garlic, minced
- 1 large sweet red or green pepper, seeded and cut into strips, or 1 cup fresh sugar snap peas, tips and strings removed*
- ½ of a 14-ounce can whole baby corn, drained and halved crosswise

① For sauce, in a small bowl stir together the water, soy sauce, cornstarch, and ginger; set aside.

② In a wok or large skillet heat oil on medium-high heat. Add broccoli, carrot, onion, and garlic; cook and stir for 6 to 8 minutes or just until vegetables are tender. Add sweet pepper and baby corn; cook and stir for 2 minutes. Push vegetables from center of wok.

③ Stir sauce; add to center of wok. Stir to combine vegetables and sauce. Cook and stir until thickened and bubbly. Cook and stir for 2 minutes more.

***Tip:** If desired, substitute one 16-ounce package frozen broccoli stir-fry vegetable blend for the broccoli, carrot, onion, and sweet pepper. Prepare as directed above in Step 1. In a wok or large skillet heat oil on medium-high heat. Add broccoli stir-fry vegetable blend and garlic; cook and stir for 4 to 5 minutes or until almost tender. Add baby corn; cook and stir for 2 minutes more. Continue as directed above in Step 3.

PER SERVING 78 calories; 4 g total fat (0 g sat. fat); 0 mg cholesterol; 163 mg sodium; 10 g carbohydrate; 3 g fiber; 3 g protein

Green Bean Salad

MAKES 4 to 6 servings **PREP** 10 minutes **STAND** 30 minutes

- 12 ounces fresh green beans
- 2 tablespoons water
- ⅓ cup snipped fresh parsley
- 4 green onions, sliced (green tops only)
- 2 stalks celery, cut into ½-inch slices
- 2 tablespoons olive oil
- 2 tablespoons lime juice
  Smoked sea salt, sea salt, or kosher salt
  Lime wedges (optional)

① Wash beans; remove ends and strings. In a 1½- or 2-quart microwave-safe casserole combine green beans and the water. Microwave, covered, on high for 5 to 7 minutes or just until crisp-tender, stirring once after 3 minutes. Drain in a colander. Rinse with cold water; drain again.

② Transfer beans to a serving dish. Add parsley, green onion tops, celery, oil, and lime juice; toss gently to coat. Cover and let stand for 30 minutes.

③ Sprinkle with sea salt just before serving. If desired, squeeze lime wedges over each serving.

PER SERVING 96 calories; 7 g total fat (1 g sat. fat); 0 mg cholesterol; 134 mg sodium; 8 g carbohydrate; 4 fiber; 2 g protein

Green Bean Salad

Broccoli with Lemon and Dill 30

MAKES 6 to 8 servings **START TO FINISH** 25 minutes

- ½ cup chopped onion (1 medium) or leek, white part only (1 large)
- 1 clove garlic, minced
- 1 tablespoon olive oil
- ½ cup reduced-sodium chicken broth
- 1½ pounds broccoli, cut into spears
- 1 tablespoon lemon juice
- 1 teaspoon all-purpose flour
- 2 tablespoons snipped fresh dill or 1 teaspoon dried dill, crushed
  Salt
  Black pepper
  Lemon slices (optional)

① In a large saucepan cook and stir onion and garlic in hot oil about 3 minutes or until tender. Carefully add broth; bring to boiling. Add broccoli. Return to boiling; reduce heat. Cover and simmer for 8 to 10 minutes or until tender.

② Using a slotted spoon, transfer broccoli to a serving platter, reserving the broth mixture in saucepan (add additional broth, if necessary, to measure ½ cup).

③ For sauce, in a small bowl combine lemon juice and flour; add to broth mixture in saucepan. Cook and stir until thickened and bubbly. Cook and stir for 1 minute more. Add dill; season to taste with salt and pepper. Spoon sauce over broccoli; toss gently to coat. If desired, garnish with lemon slices.

PER SERVING 49 calories; 3 g total fat (0 g sat. fat); 0 mg cholesterol; 119 mg sodium; 6 g carbohydrate; 2 fiber; 3 g protein

Leeks can contain lots of grit and dirt between their many layers. To clean them, slice thinly, then swirl in cool water. If you have a salad spinner, dry them in the salad spinner. If not, blot them dry between layers of clean paper towels.

Skillet-Roasted Vegetables

Broccoli and Cauliflower Saute (30)

MAKES 4 servings **START TO FINISH** 20 minutes

- **2 teaspoons olive oil**
- **1 cup broccoli florets**
- **1 cup cauliflower florets**
- **1 clove garlic, thinly sliced**
- **¼ cup dry white wine or reduced-sodium chicken broth**
- **3 tablespoons water**
- **⅛ teaspoon salt**
- **⅛ teaspoon black pepper**

① In a large skillet heat oil on medium-high heat. Add broccoli, cauliflower, and garlic; cook for 2 minutes, stirring occasionally. Carefully add wine, the water, salt, and pepper; reduce heat to low. Cover and cook for 2 minutes. Uncover and raise heat to medium. Cook about 2 minutes more or until vegetables are tender.

PER SERVING 47 calories; 2 g total fat (0 g sat. fat); 0 mg cholesterol; 88 mg sodium; 4 g carbohydrate; 1 g fiber; 1 g protein

Loaded Mashed Sweet Potatoes (30)

MAKES 6 servings **START TO FINISH** 20 minutes

- **2 teaspoons canola oil**
- **1½ cups sliced fresh mushrooms**
- **1 medium sweet onion (such as Vidalia, Walla Walla, or Maui), quartered and thinly sliced**
- **¼ teaspoon ground cumin**
- **⅛ teaspoon ground coriander**
- **1 24-ounce package refrigerated mashed sweet potatoes**

① In a large nonstick skillet heat oil on medium-high heat. Add mushrooms and onion to skillet; cook about 8 minutes or until tender and lightly browned, stirring occasionally.

② Add cumin and coriander to mushroom mixture. Stir in sweet potatoes. Cook and stir until heated through.

PER SERVING 100 calories; 2 g total fat (1 g sat. fat); 1 mg cholesterol; 87 mg sodium; 18 g carbohydrate; 3 g fiber; 2 g protein

Skillet-Roasted Vegetables

MAKES 6 servings **PREP** 20 minutes **COOK** 22 minutes

- **8 ounces baby beets (assorted colors) with tops or small beets**
- **8 ounces tiny new potatoes or small fingerling potatoes, quartered**
- **1 small sweet potato, peeled and cut in narrow wedges**
- **2 to 3 tablespoons peanut oil**
- **1 cup fresh sugar snap or snow pea pods, trimmed and strings removed**
- **¼ teaspoon salt**
- **⅛ teaspoon freshly ground black pepper**
- **¼ cup snipped fresh cilantro or parsley**
- **2 tablespoons lemon juice**
- **Lemon wedges**

① Cut tops off beats; reserve ½ cup of the green tops. Wash green tops; drain. Set aside. Use kitchen shears to trim root ends. Halve baby beets or quarter small beets.

② In a covered large skillet cook beets and potatoes in hot oil on medium heat for 10 minutes, turning occasionally. Uncover and cook for 10 to 15 minutes more or until tender and brown on all sides, turning occasionally. Add pea pods to beet mixture; sprinkle with salt and pepper. Cover and cook for 2 to 3 minutes or until pea pods are crisp-tender.

③ Add reserved green tops, cilantro, and lemon juice to skillet; toss gently to coat. Serve with lemon wedges.

PER SERVING 116 calories; 5 g total fat (1 g sat. fat); 0 mg cholesterol; 146 mg sodium; 17 g carbohydrate; 3 g fiber; 2 g protein

Peanut oil has a relatively high smoke point, which means it reaches a high temperature without breaking down. This makes it very good for frying. Frying in peanut oil crisps, caramelizes, and sweetens the beets, potatoes, and sugar snap peas in Skillet-Roasted Vegetables.

menu

Mediterranean
Stuffed Chicken

Broccoli with Lemon
and Dill

Cheesy Potatoes
[below]

Fresh Citrus and
Cranberry Salad

Cheesy Potatoes ✪

MAKES 12 servings **PREP** 15 minutes **BAKE** 65 minutes
STAND 10 minutes **OVEN** 350°F

- 1   10.75-ounce can reduced-fat and reduced-sodium condensed cream of chicken soup
- 1   cup shredded reduced-fat sharp cheddar cheese (4 ounces)
- ½   cup fat-free milk
- ½   cup light sour cream
- ⅓   cup finely chopped onion or 2 tablespoons dried minced onion
- ½   teaspoon black pepper
- 1   30- or 32-ounce package frozen shredded or diced hash brown potatoes, thawed
- ½   cup crushed cornflakes or wheat cereal flakes

① Preheat oven to 350°F. Lightly grease a 2-quart rectangular baking dish; set aside. In a very large bowl combine soup, cheese, milk, sour cream, onion, and pepper. Stir in potatoes. Spread mixture evenly in prepared baking dish.

② Cover and bake for 45 minutes; stir potatoes. Sprinkle with cornflakes. Uncover. Bake for 20 to 25 minutes more or until heated through and bubbly. Let stand for 10 minutes before serving.

PER SERVING 129 calories; 3 g total fat (2 g sat. fat); 11 mg cholesterol; 236 mg sodium; 20 g carbohydrate; 1 g fiber; 5 g protein

Garden Veggie Corn Bread

MAKES 9 servings **PREP** 20 minutes **BAKE** 25 minutes
OVEN 400°F

-     Nonstick cooking spray
- 1   cup cornmeal
- ¾   cup white whole wheat flour or whole wheat flour
- 2   tablespoons snipped fresh chives
- 2½   teaspoons baking powder
- ¾   teaspoon salt
- 2   eggs, lightly beaten
- 1   cup fat-free milk
- 2   tablespoons honey
- ¾   cup coarsely shredded carrots (2 to 3 small)
- ½   cup finely chopped sweet red pepper

① Preheat oven to 400°F. Lightly coat a 2-quart square baking dish with cooking spray; set aside. In a large bowl stir together cornmeal, flour, chives, baking powder, and salt; set aside.

② In a medium bowl whisk together eggs, milk, and honey. Add milk mixture all at once to cornmeal mixture; stir just until moistened. Fold in carrots and sweet pepper. Pour batter into prepared baking dish.

③ Bake for 25 to 30 minutes or until a toothpick inserted near center comes out clean and edges are golden brown. Cool slightly; serve warm.

PER SERVING 139 calories; 1 g total fat (0 g sat. fat); 48 mg cholesterol; 328 mg sodium; 31 g carbohydrate; 2 g fiber; 5 g protein

Garden Veggie Corn Bread

Cheesy Potatoes

Tomato-Artichoke Focaccia

Two-Cheese Garlic 'n' Herb Biscuits ⭐ ③⓪

MAKES 9 biscuits **PREP** 20 minutes **BAKE** 10 minutes **OVEN** 450°F

- 1 cup all-purpose flour
- ½ cup white whole wheat flour or whole wheat flour
- 1 tablespoon snipped fresh basil or 1 teaspoon dried basil, crushed
- 2 teaspoons baking powder
- 2 cloves garlic, minced
- ¼ teaspoon cream of tartar
- ⅛ teaspoon salt
- 2 ounces soft goat cheese (chèvre) or reduced-fat cream cheese (Neufchâtel)
- 2 tablespoons butter
- ¼ cup finely shredded Parmesan cheese (1 ounce)
- ½ cup fat-free milk

① Preheat oven to 450°F. In a medium bowl stir together all-purpose flour, whole wheat flour, basil, baking powder, garlic, cream of tartar, and salt. Using a pastry blender, cut in goat cheese and butter until mixture resembles coarse crumbs. Stir in 3 tablespoons of the Parmesan cheese. Make a well in the center of the flour mixture. Add milk all at once; stir just until dough clings together.

② Turn out dough on a lightly floured surface. Knead by folding and gently pressing dough for 4 to 6 strokes or until nearly smooth. Pat or lightly roll dough into an 8 x 6-inch rectangle.

③ Cut dough into 9 rectangles. Sprinkle tops with the remaining 1 tablespoon Parmesan cheese. Place rectangles 1 inch apart on an ungreased baking sheet.

④ Bake for 10 to 12 minutes or until golden brown. Serve warm.

PER BISCUIT 127 calories; 5 g total fat (3 g sat. fat); 12 mg cholesterol; 171 mg sodium; 17 g carbohydrate; 1 g fiber; 5 g protein

Make Tomato-Artichoke Focaccia at the peak of tomato season, when tomatoes are at their sweetest and ripest. Use a mix of colors for the most eye-catching flatbread.

Tomato-Artichoke Focaccia

MAKES 12 servings **PREP** 30 minutes **RISE** 1¼ hours **STAND** 15 minutes **BAKE** 25 minutes **OVEN** 450°F

- 3½ to 4 cups all-purpose flour
- 1 package active dry yeast
- 1 teaspoon salt
- 1¼ cups warm water (120°F to 130°F)
- 2 tablespoons olive oil
- ¼ cup cornmeal
  Nonstick cooking spray
- 1¼ pounds plum tomatoes and/or green or yellow tomatoes, thinly sliced
- 1 14-ounce can artichoke hearts, drained and quartered
- 1 tablespoon olive oil
- 1 tablespoon snipped fresh rosemary or 1 teaspoon dried rosemary, crushed
- 1 small red onion, very thinly sliced and separated into rings
- 4 cloves garlic, cut into thin slivers or slices

① In a large mixing bowl combine 1½ cups of the flour, yeast, and salt. Add warm water and 2 tablespoons olive oil. Beat with an electric mixer on low to medium for 30 seconds. Beat on high for 3 minutes. Using a wooden spoon, stir in cornmeal and as much of the remaining flour as you can.

② Turn dough onto a lightly floured surface. Knead in remaining flour to make a moderately soft dough that is smooth and elastic (3 to 5 minutes). Shape into a ball. Place dough in a lightly greased bowl, turning once.

③ Cover and let dough rise in a warm place until double in size (45 to 60 minutes). Punch down dough; let rest 10 minutes. Grease a 15 x 10 x 1-inch baking pan. Place dough in prepared baking pan; shape into a 15 x 8-inch rectangle. Lightly coat dough with cooking spray. Cover loosely with plastic wrap; let rise in a warm place until nearly double in size (about 30 minutes).

④ Preheat oven to 450°F. Arrange tomato slices and artichoke quarters on a double thickness of paper towels. Let stand 15 minutes. Using fingers, press deep indentations in dough 2 inches apart. Brush with 1 tablespoon olive oil. Sprinkle with rosemary. Arrange tomato slices, artichoke quarters, onion rings, and garlic slivers on top of dough.

⑤ Bake 25 minutes or until golden brown. Transfer to a wire rack; cool. Cut into rectangles.

PER SERVING 197 calories; 4 g total fat (1 g sat. fat); 0 mg cholesterol; 310 mg sodium; 35 g carbohydrate; 3 g fiber; 5 g protein

Sweet Somethings

Chocolate Chunk-Cherry Cookies ✪

MAKES about 28 cookies **PREP** 30 minutes
BAKE 8 minutes per batch **COOL** 1 minute **OVEN** 350°F

- ¼ cup tub-style 60% to 70% vegetable oil spread
- ⅓ cup granulated sugar
- ⅓ cup packed brown sugar
- ½ teaspoon baking soda
- ⅛ teaspoon salt
- ¼ cup refrigerated or frozen egg product, thawed, or 1 egg
- 2 tablespoons unsweetened cocoa powder
- 1 teaspoon vanilla
- ⅔ cup all-purpose flour
- ⅔ cup rolled oats
- ¼ cup flaxseed meal
- 4 ounces dark chocolate, chopped
- 2 ounces white baking chocolate, chopped
- ½ cup dried tart cherries, coarsely chopped

① Preheat oven to 350°F. In a large mixing bowl beat vegetable oil spread with an electric mixer on medium to high for 30 seconds. Add granulated sugar, brown sugar, baking soda, and salt. Beat until well mixed, scraping sides of bowl occasionally. Beat in egg, cocoa powder, and vanilla until combined. Beat in flour. Using a wooden spoon, stir in oats and flaxseed meal. Stir in 3 ounces of the dark chocolate, 2 tablespoons of the white chocolate, and ⅓ cup of the cherries.

② Drop dough by rounded teaspoons 2 inches apart onto an ungreased cookie sheet. Top with remaining dark chocolate, white chocolate, and cherries.

③ Bake for 8 to 10 minutes or until edges are set. Cool on cookie sheet for 1 minute. Transfer cookies to wire rack; cool.

PER COOKIE 84 calories; 4 g total fat (2 g sat. fat); 0 mg cholesterol; 53 mg sodium; 14 g carbohydrate; 1 g fiber; 1 g protein

Hint-of-Herb Butter Cookies

MAKES about 48 cookies **PREP** 20 minutes **FREEZE** 4 hours
BAKE 12 minutes per batch **OVEN** 325°F

- ½ cup butter
- 1 cup sugar
- 1 egg
- 1½ cups all-purpose flour
- 1 teaspoon baking powder
- ¼ teaspoon salt
- Snipped fresh lavender, tarragon, lemon verbena, mint, thyme, and/or seeds (such as anise, fennel, sesame, or poppy)

① In a medium mixing bowl beat butter with an electric mixer on medium to high for 30 seconds. Add sugar; beat until combined. Add egg; beat until combined. Beat in flour, baking powder, and salt. Divide dough in half. Shape each half into a 12-inch-long rope. Wrap in plastic wrap; place in a freezer bag. Freeze about 4 hours or until firm.

② Preheat oven to 325°F. Unwrap dough; carefully slice the frozen dough into ½-inch slices. Place slices on an ungreased cookie sheet. Top with desired herbs and/or seeds. If necessary, press in gently.

③ Bake for 12 to 15 minutes or until edges are golden. Transfer cookies to wire rack; cool.

PER COOKIE 48 calories; 2 g total fat (1 g sat. fat); 10 mg cholesterol; 33 mg sodium; 7 g carbohydrate; 0 g fiber; 1 g protein

When a cookie has just a smattering of ingredients, it's important that the ingredients are high quality because the flavor of each is going to come through in each bite. Hint-of-Herb Butter Cookies, for example, depend on the quality of the butter that's used to make them. Buy the best you can afford—and don't substitute margarine.

Chocolate Chunk-Cherry Cookies

Loaded Oatmeal Cookies

Lemon-Cherry Oat Cookies ✪

MAKES about 30 cookies **PREP** 25 minutes
BAKE 8 minutes per batch **COOL** 1 minute **OVEN** 375°F

- ½ cup tub-style 60% to 70% vegetable oil spread
- ¾ cup packed brown sugar
- 2 teaspoons baking powder
- ¼ teaspoon salt
- 2 egg whites, lightly beaten
- 1 teaspoon vanilla
- 1 cup all-purpose flour
- 1¼ cups quick-cooking oats
- ¾ cup dried tart cherries, coarsely chopped
- 1 teaspoon finely shredded lemon peel

① Preheat oven to 375°F. In a large mixing bowl beat vegetable oil spread with an electric mixer on medium to high for 30 seconds. Add brown sugar, baking powder, and salt. Beat until fluffy. Add egg whites and vanilla. Beat until combined. Beat in as much of the flour mixture as you can with the mixer. Using a wooden spoon, stir in any remaining flour, oats, cherries, and lemon peel.

② Drop dough by rounded teaspoonfuls onto an ungreased cookie sheet. Bake for 8 to 9 minutes or until edges are lightly browned. Cool on cookie sheet for 1 minute. Transfer cookies to wire rack; cool.

Tip: To store cookies, place between sheets of waxed paper in an airtight container. Store at room temperature for 3 days or freeze for up to 3 months.

PER COOKIE 84 calories; 3 g total fat (0 g sat. fat); 0 mg cholesterol; 80 mg sodium; 15 g carbohydrate; 1 g fiber; 1 g protein

Loaded Oatmeal Cookies ✪

MAKES about 30 cookies **PREP** 30 minutes
BAKE 9 minutes per batch **COOL** 1 minute **OVEN** 350°F

- ¼ cup butter, softened
- ½ cup packed brown sugar
- ⅓ cup granulated sugar
- 1 teaspoon ground cinnamon
- ½ teaspoon baking soda
- ⅛ teaspoon salt
- 1 egg
- 1 teaspoon vanilla
- ¾ cup all-purpose flour
- ¾ cup rolled oats
- ¼ cup flaxseed meal
- ¼ cup wheat germ
- 2 ounces dark chocolate, finely chopped
- ¼ cup dried cranberries
- ¼ cup chopped walnuts, toasted

① Preheat oven to 350°F. In a large mixing bowl beat butter with an electric mixer on medium to high for 30 seconds. Add brown sugar, granulated sugar, cinnamon, baking soda, and salt. Beat until combined, scraping sides of bowl occasionally. Beat in egg and vanilla until combined. Beat in flour. Using a wooden spoon, stir in oats, flaxseed meal, wheat germ, chocolate, cranberries, and walnuts (dough will be crumbly).

② Drop dough by rounded teaspoons 2 inches apart onto an ungreased cookie sheet. Bake for 9 to 11 minutes or until tops are lightly browned. Let cookies cool on cookie sheet for 1 minute. Transfer cookies to wire rack; cool.

PER COOKIE 79 calories; 4 g total fat (2 g sat. fat); 11 mg cholesterol; 45 mg sodium; 12 g carbohydrate; 1 g fiber; 2 g protein

With the addition of whole grains and dried fruit, a cookie can be a healthful treat.

Must-Have Chocolate Chip Cookies ●

MAKES about 40 cookies **PREP** 20 minutes
BAKE 10 minutes per batch **OVEN** 350°F

1	cup raisins
½	cup boiling water
½	cup peanut butter
¼	cup butter, softened
½	cup sugar
½	cup refrigerated or frozen egg product, thawed, or 2 eggs, lightly beaten
1	teaspoon ground cinnamon
1	teaspoon vanilla
½	teaspoon baking soda
½	cup all-purpose flour
1¼	cups regular rolled oats
1	cup semisweet chocolate pieces or chunks

① Preheat oven to 350°F. In a small bowl combine raisins and the boiling water; set aside.

② In a large mixing bowl combine peanut butter and butter. Beat with an electric mixer on medium for 30 seconds. Add sugar, egg, cinnamon, vanilla, and baking soda. Beat until combined. Add the flour; beat until smooth. Using a wooden spoon, stir in oats.

③ Drain raisins; stir raisins and chocolate pieces into oat mixture.

④ Drop dough by rounded teaspoons onto an ungreased cookie sheet. Bake about 10 minutes or until lightly browned. Transfer to a wire rack; cool.

PER COOKIE 87 calories; 4 g total fat (2 g sat. fat); 3 mg cholesterol; 47 mg sodium; 12 g carbohydrate; 1 g fiber; 2 g protein

Turbinado sugar is raw and less processed than white granulated sugar. Its light brown crystals—larger than those of granulated sugar—have a delicate molasses flavor similar to brown sugar. Find it in the baking aisle of most supermarkets.

Smart Chocolate Chip Cookies ✪

MAKES about 48 cookies **PREP** 30 minutes
BAKE 9 minutes per batch **COOL** 1 minute **OVEN** 375°F

1½	cups turbinado sugar
1	cup tub-style 60% to 70% vegetable oil spread
1	teaspoon baking soda
¼	teaspoon salt
1	egg
1	teaspoon vanilla
½	cup finely shredded zucchini
¼	cup flaxseed meal
2	cups whole wheat flour
¾	cup all-purpose flour
1	cup semisweet chocolate pieces

① Preheat oven to 375°F. In a large mixing bowl beat sugar, vegetable oil spread, baking soda, and salt with an electric mixer on medium until well mixed, scraping sides of bowl as needed. Beat in egg and vanilla. Beat in zucchini and flaxseed meal. Beat in as much of the whole wheat flour and all-purpose flour as you can with the mixer. Stir in any remaining flour and chocolate pieces.

② Drop dough by rounded teaspoons 2 inches apart on an ungreased cookie sheet. Bake for 9 to 11 minutes or until cookies are set and tops are lightly browned. Cool on cookie sheets for 1 minute. Transfer cookies to wire rack; cool.

Tip: To store, layer cookies between sheets of waxed paper in an airtight freezer container. Seal, label, and freeze for up to 3 months.

PER COOKIE 95 calories; 4 g total fat (2 g sat. fat); 4 mg cholesterol; 71 mg sodium; 14 g carbohydrate; 1 g fiber; 1 g protein

Rosemary-Kissed
Thumbprint Coo

Rosemary-Kissed Orange Thumbprint Cookies Tuscano

MAKES 24 cookies **PREP** 30 minutes **CHILL** 1 hour
BAKE 14 minutes **COOL** 1 minute **OVEN** 325°F

1	cup all-purpose flour
½	cup cornstarch
1	teaspoon snipped fresh rosemary
¼	teaspoon salt
¾	cup butter, softened
⅓	cup powdered sugar
	Few drops almond extract
¼	cup orange marmalade
	Powdered sugar (optional)

① In small bowl stir together the flour, cornstarch, rosemary, and salt; set aside. In a medium mixing bowl beat butter with an electric mixer on medium to high for 30 seconds. Add the ⅓ cup powdered sugar and almond extract; beat until combined. Beat in flour mixture until combined. Wrap and chill dough about 1 hour or until easy to handle.

② Preheat oven to 325°F. Line 2 cookie sheets with parchment paper; set aside. Shape dough into twenty-four 1¼-inch balls. Place balls 2 inches apart on prepared cookie sheets. Use thumb to make an indentation into each ball. Spoon about ½ teaspoon of the marmalade into the center of each ball.

③ Bake about 14 minutes or until edges are light golden. Cool on cookie sheets for 1 minute. Transfer to wire rack; cool. If desired, sprinkle with additional powdered sugar.

PER COOKIE 105 calories; 6 g total fat (4 g sat. fat); 15 mg cholesterol; 67 mg sodium; 13 g carbohydrate; 0 g fiber; 1 g protein

Whole Wheat Carrot-Raisin Cookies

MAKES about 36 cookies **PREP** 30 minutes
BAKE 8 minutes per batch **OVEN** 375°F

½	cup butter, softened
1	cup packed brown sugar
2	teaspoons baking soda
1	teaspoon ground cinnamon
1	teaspoon ground ginger
¼	teaspoon salt
1	egg
¼	cup applesauce
1	teaspoon vanilla
2	cups whole wheat flour
1	cup finely shredded carrots (2 medium)
¾	cup raisins
¾	cup finely chopped walnuts

① Preheat oven to 375°F. In a large mixing bowl beat butter with an electric mixer on medium for 30 seconds. Beat in brown sugar, baking soda, cinnamon, ginger, and salt until combined. Beat in egg, applesauce, and vanilla. Beat in as much of the flour as you can with the mixer. Using a wooden spoon, stir in any remaining flour, carrots, raisins, and walnuts just until combined.

② Drop by slightly rounded teaspoons 2 inches apart onto an ungreased cookie sheet. Bake for 8 to 9 minutes or until edges are firm. Transfer cookies to wire rack; cool.

PER COOKIE 98 calories; 4 g total fat (2 g sat. fat); 13 mg cholesterol; 111 mg sodium; 14 g carbohydrate; 1 g fiber; 2 g protein

Surprising ingredients—such as fresh herbs and carrots—make these cookies interesting.

Raspberry Meringues

MAKES about 20 meringue cookies **PREP** 30 minutes **STAND** 1 hour **OVEN** 300°F

- 2   egg whites
- 1   tablespoon low-sugar seedless red raspberry jam (at room temperature)
- 6   drops red food coloring
- ⅓   cup superfine sugar or granulated sugar
- ⅓   cup sifted powdered sugar
- ⅛   teaspoon cream of tartar

① Let egg whites stand, covered, in a large stainless-steel or glass mixing bowl at room temperature for 30 minutes. Meanwhile cover 2 large baking sheets with parchment paper.

② Preheat oven to 300°F. In a small mixing bowl stir together seedless raspberry jam (at room temperature) and red food coloring. Set aside.

③ In a small bowl, combine the superfine sugar and powdered sugar; set aside. Uncover eggs and add cream of tartar. Beat with an electric mixer on medium until soft peaks form (tips curl). Add sugar mixture, 1 tablespoon at a time, beating for 5 to 7 minutes on medium or until stiff glossy peaks form (tips stand straight) and sugar is dissolved.

④ Use a spatula to gently fold ½ cup of the meringue mixture into the jam; then gently fold jam mixture into the remaining meringue.

⑤ Using a pastry bag fitted with a large star tip, pipe the meringue in 2-inch freeform hearts or Xs and Os onto the parchment paper.

⑥ Place baking sheets in preheated oven. Turn off oven. Let meringues dry in oven, with door closed, for 1 hour or until dry and crisp but still light in color. Let cool on parchment paper. Gently remove meringues.

PER MERINGUE 22 calories; 0 g total fat; 0 mg cholesterol; 6 mg sodium; 5 g carbohydrate; 0 g fiber; 0 g protein

Almond Sandwich Cookies

MAKES about 30 filled cookies **PREP** 30 minutes **BAKE** 10 minutes per batch **OVEN** 325°F

-     Nonstick cooking spray
- 1   cup rolled oats
- ¾   cup sugar
- 2   tablespoons all-purpose flour
- 1   teaspoon ground cardamom
- ¼   teaspoon salt
- ¼   teaspoon baking powder
- ¼   cup refrigerated or frozen egg product, thawed, or 1 egg, lightly beaten
- ½   cup butter, melted
- 1   teaspoon vanilla
- 1   cup slivered almonds
-     Vanilla Cream

① Preheat oven to 325°F. Line a cookie sheet with foil and lightly coat foil with nonstick cooking spray; set aside.

② In a large mixing bowl combine oats, sugar, flour, cardamom, salt, and baking powder. In a medium bowl whisk together the egg, butter, and vanilla until well combined. Add egg mixture to flour mixture; stir until well combined. Add the almonds and stir until evenly distributed.

③ Drop level teaspoons of dough 3 inches apart on prepared cookie sheet. Bake for 10 to 12 minutes or until edges are brown. Let cookies cool completely, then peel from foil. Repeat with remaining dough.

④ For each sandwich cookie, spread bottom side of a cookie with a rounded teaspoon of Vanilla Cream. Place another cookie, top side up, on filling.

Vanilla Cream: In a large mixing bowl beat together ¼ cup butter, softened, with 1 cup powdered sugar until smooth. Beat in 1 teaspoon vanilla. Gradually beat in an additional ½ cup powdered sugar until mixture is smooth.

PER COOKIE 118 calories; 7 g total fat (3 g sat. fat); 12 mg cholesterol; 58 mg sodium; 14 g carbohydrate; 1 g fiber; 1 g protein

Two-Tone Biscotti

Chocolate Honey-Graham Cookies

MAKES about 48 cookies **PREP** 30 minutes
BAKE 8 minutes per batch **STAND** 30 minutes **OVEN** 375°F

- ½ cup butter, softened
- ¼ cup packed brown sugar
- 1 teaspoon baking powder
- ¼ teaspoon baking soda
- ¼ teaspoon salt
- ¼ teaspoon ground cinnamon
- 2 eggs, lightly beaten
- ¼ cup honey
- ½ teaspoon vanilla
- 1¼ cups all-purpose flour
- 1 cup white whole wheat flour or whole wheat flour
- ½ cup miniature semisweet chocolate pieces
- 3 ounces bittersweet chocolate or ½ cup miniature semisweet chocolate pieces
- ½ teaspoon shortening

① Preheat oven to 375°F. In a large mixing bowl beat butter with an electric mixer on medium to high for 30 seconds. Add brown sugar, baking powder, baking soda, salt, and cinnamon. Beat until light and fluffy, scraping sides of bowl occasionally.

② Beat in eggs, honey, and vanilla until combined. Beat in as much of the all-purpose flour and the whole wheat flour as you can with the mixer. Using a wooden spoon, stir in any remaining flour. Stir in ½ cup semisweet chocolate pieces.

③ Shape dough into 1-inch balls. Place balls 1 inch apart on an ungreased cookie sheet. Flatten slightly. Bake for 8 to 9 minutes or until bottoms are lightly browned. Transfer cookies to a wire rack; cool.

④ In a small saucepan combine bittersweet chocolate and shortening; heat over low heat until melted and smooth, stirring often. Cool slightly. Transfer melted chocolate mixture to a small resealable plastic bag; seal bag. Snip a small hole in one corner of the bag; pipe chocolate on tops of cookies. Let stand about 30 minutes or until set.

PER COOKIE 68 calories; 3 g total fat (2 g sat. fat); 14 mg cholesterol; 41 mg sodium; 9 g carbohydrate; 1 g fiber; 1 g protein

Chocolate Chocolate-Dipped Graham Cookies: Prepare as above, except add ¼ cup unsweetened cocoa powder with the all-purpose flour.

PER COOKIE 70 calories; 3 g total fat (2 g sat. fat), 14 mg cholesterol; 41 mg sodium, 9 g carbohydrate; 1 g fiber; 1 g protein

Two-Tone Biscotti

MAKES about 70 cookies **PREP** 20 minutes
BAKE 25 minutes + 20 minutes **COOL** 1 hour
OVEN 375°F/325°F

- ⅔ cup butter, softened
- 1⅓ cups sugar
- 1 tablespoon baking powder
- ¼ teaspoon salt
- 4 eggs
- 1 teaspoon vanilla
- 4 cups all-purpose flour
- 1½ cups semisweet chocolate pieces, melted and cooled
- 1 cup finely chopped hazelnuts (filberts)
- 1 tablespoon finely shredded orange peel

① Preheat oven to 375°F. In a large mixing bowl beat butter with an electric mixer on medium to high for 30 seconds. Add sugar, baking powder, and salt; beat until combined, scraping sides of bowl occasionally. Beat in eggs and vanilla until combined. Beat in as much of the flour as you can with the mixer. Using a wooden spoon, stir in any remaining flour.

② Divide dough in half; place each half in a bowl. Into half of the dough, stir the melted chocolate and ½ cup of the nuts. Into the other half of the dough stir the orange peel and the remaining ½ cup nuts.

③ Divide each half of the dough into 3 portions. With lightly floured hands, shape each dough portion into a rope about 14 inches long. Place a rope of each color side by side on an ungreased cookie sheet. Twist ropes together several times. Flatten slightly to a 2-inch width. Repeat with the other ropes to make 3 twists total, placing twists about 4 inches apart on a cookie sheet.

④ Bake about 25 minutes or until lightly browned. Cool on cookie sheet on wire rack about 1 hour or until completely cool.

⑤ Reduce oven to 325°F. Transfer baked twists to a cutting board. Cut into ½-inch slices. Place slices on the same cookie sheet. Bake for 10 minutes. Turn slices over; bake for 10 to 15 minutes more or until dry and crisp. Transfer cookies to wire rack; cool.

PER COOKIE 91 calories; 4 g total fat (1 g sat. fat); 17 mg cholesterol; 12 g carbohydrate; 1 g fiber; 2 g protein

Pumpkin Blondies

MAKES 24 bars **PREP** 15 minutes **BAKE** 20 minutes
OVEN 350°F

Nonstick cooking spray
- ⅓ cup canola oil
- 3 tablespoons butter, melted
- 1 tablespoon molasses
- 1⅓ cups packed dark brown sugar
- ½ cup canned pumpkin
- 1 egg
- 1 egg white
- 1 teaspoon vanilla
- 1 cup white whole wheat flour
- ½ cup unbleached all-purpose flour
- 1 tablespoon flaxseed meal
- 1½ teaspoons baking powder
- ½ teaspoon salt
- ½ teaspoon ground cinnamon
- ¼ teaspoon baking soda
- ¼ teaspoon ground nutmeg
- ⅛ teaspoon ground allspice
- ½ cup coarsely chopped walnuts

① Preheat oven to 350°F. Coat a 13 x 9 x 2-inch baking pan with cooking spray and line with parchment paper; set aside.

② In a large mixing bowl beat oil, butter, and molasses with an electric mixer on medium until combined. Add brown sugar and beat until smooth. Add pumpkin, beating until combined. Beat in egg, egg white, and vanilla until combined. In a medium bowl combine whole wheat flour, all-purpose flour, flaxseed meal, baking powder, salt, cinnamon, baking soda, nutmeg, and allspice. Add to sugar mixture, beating just until flour mixture is moistened.

③ Spread batter into prepared pan. Sprinkle with walnuts. Bake for 20 to 22 minutes or until a wooden toothpick inserted near the center comes out clean. Cool completely in pan on a wire rack. Cut into squares.

PER BAR 137 calories; 6 g total fat (1 g sat. fat); 13 mg cholesterol; 104 mg sodium; 19 g carbohydrate; 1 g fiber; 2 g protein

Carrot-Pumpkin Bars ✿

MAKES 16 triangles or bars **PREP** 25 minutes **BAKE** 25 minutes
OVEN 350°F

Nonstick cooking spray
- 1¼ cups all-purpose flour
- 1 teaspoon baking powder
- ½ teaspoon ground allspice
- ¼ teaspoon baking soda
- ¼ teaspoon salt
- 1 teaspoon finely shredded lime peel
- ½ cup refrigerated or frozen egg product, thawed, or 2 eggs, lightly beaten
- ½ cup sugar
- ¾ cup canned pumpkin
- ⅓ cup vegetable oil
- 2 tablespoons lime juice
- ½ cup finely shredded carrot (1 medium)
- ⅓ cup chopped macadamia nuts or almonds
  Powdered sugar (optional)

① Preheat oven to 350°F. Coat a 9 x 9 x 2-inch baking pan with cooking spray; set aside.

② In a large bowl stir together flour, baking powder, allspice, baking soda, and salt. Stir in lime peel; set aside.

③ In a medium bowl combine eggs and sugar. Stir in pumpkin, oil, and lime juice. Stir in carrot and nuts. Add pumpkin mixture all at once to flour mixture, stirring just until combined. Spread batter evenly into prepared pan.

④ Bake for 25 to 30 minutes or until a wooden toothpick inserted near the center comes out clean. Cool completely in pan on wire rack.

⑤ To serve, cut into triangles or bars. If desired, sift powdered sugar over triangles or bars.

PER BAR 128 calories; 7 g total fat (1 g sat. fat); 0 mg cholesterol; 89 mg sodium; 15 g carbohydrate; 1 g fiber; 2 g protein

White whole wheat flour is relatively new to the market. It has all the fiber and nutrition of whole wheat flour yet bakes as light in texture as all-purpose flour. Use it in place of all-purpose flour, in most recipes.

Pumpkin Blondies

Cherry-Ginger Upside-Down Cake

Cherry-Ginger Upside-Down Cake

MAKES 10 servings **PREP** 25 minutes **BAKE** 30 minutes
COOL 5 minutes **OVEN** 350°F

1½	cups frozen unsweetened pitted dark sweet cherries, thawed and drained
1¼	cups all-purpose flour
⅔	cup white whole wheat flour or all-purpose flour
2	to 3 teaspoons finely snipped crystallized ginger
1½	teaspoons baking powder
½	teaspoon ground ginger
¼	teaspoon salt
¾	cup fat-free milk
½	cup refrigerated or frozen egg product, thawed, or 2 eggs, lightly beaten
½	cup packed brown sugar
¼	cup canola oil
	Powdered sugar (optional)
	Snipped crystallized ginger (optional)
	Fresh mint leaves (optional)

① Preheat oven to 350°F. Lightly grease a 9 x 1½-inch round cake pan. Line bottom of pan with parchment paper and lightly grease the paper. Arrange cherries in bottom of the cake pan; set side. In a large bowl stir together all-purpose flour, whole wheat flour, the 2 teaspoons crystallized ginger, baking powder, ground ginger, and salt. Set aside.

② In a medium bowl whisk together milk, eggs, brown sugar, and oil. Add egg mixture all at once to flour mixture; stir just until combined. Spoon batter into prepared pan over cherries, spreading evenly.

③ Bake for 30 to 35 minutes or until a wooden toothpick inserted near the center comes out clean. Cool in pan on a wire rack for 5 minutes. Run a small knife around the edge of the pan to loosen sides of cake. Invert cake onto a serving plate. Remove parchment paper.

④ Serve cake warm. If desired, sprinkle with powdered sugar and/or additional crystallized ginger. If desired, garnish with mint leaves.

PER SERVING 201 calories; 6 g total fat (0 g sat. fat); 0 mg cholesterol; 128 mg sodium; 34 g carbohydrate; 2 g fiber; 5 g protein

Zucchini-Banana Snack Cake ✪

MAKES 24 servings **PREP** 20 minutes **BAKE** 20 minutes
OVEN 350°F

	Nonstick cooking spray
1	cup all-purpose flour
1	cup whole wheat flour
¼	cup flaxseed meal or wheat germ
¼	cup unsweetened cocoa powder
2	teaspoons baking powder
½	teaspoon salt
½	cup refrigerated or frozen egg product, thawed, or 2 eggs, slightly beaten
¾	cup sugar
½	cup canola oil
⅓	cup fat-free milk
1	cup peeled (if desired) and shredded zucchini
1	medium-size ripe banana, mashed (½ cup)
½	cup miniature semisweet chocolate pieces (optional)

① Preheat oven to 350°F. Lightly coat a 13 x 9 x 2-inch baking pan with nonstick cooking spray; set aside. In a large bowl combine all-purpose flour, whole wheat flour, flaxseed meal, cocoa powder, baking powder, and salt. Make a well in center of flour mixture; set aside.

② In a medium bowl whisk together egg, sugar, canola oil, and milk until well mixed. Stir in zucchini and banana. Add zucchini mixture all at once to flour mixture. Stir just until moistened. Fold in chocolate pieces. Pour batter into prepared pan, spreading evenly.

③ Bake 20 to 25 minutes or until top springs back when lightly touched. Cool completely on a wire rack. Cut into rectangles.

PER SERVING 118 calories; 5 g total fat (0 g sat. fat); 0 mg cholesterol; 80 mg sodium; 16 g carbohydrate; 1 g fiber; 2 g protein

Citrus Angel Tea Cakes

MAKES 6 servings **PREP** 35 minutes **STAND** 30 minutes
BAKE 10 minutes **COOL** 45 minutes **OVEN** 350°F

⅓ **cup egg whites (2 to 3 large)**

¼ **cup sifted cake flour or sifted all-purpose flour**

2 **tablespoons powdered sugar**

¼ **teaspoon cream of tartar**

⅛ **teaspoon vanilla**

3 **tablespoons granulated sugar**

1 **teaspoon finely shredded lemon peel**

Lemon Cream Topping or Raspberry Cream Topping

Small fresh raspberries, chopped or quartered fresh strawberries, shredded lemon peel, and/ or small sliced lemon pieces (optional)

Powdered sugar (optional)

① In a medium mixing bowl allow egg whites to stand at room temperature for 30 minutes. Meanwhile, sift flour and the 2 tablespoons powdered sugar together 3 times; set aside.

② Preheat oven to 350°F. Add cream of tartar and vanilla to egg whites. Beat with an electric mixer on medium until soft peaks form (tips curl). Gradually add granulated sugar, about 1 tablespoon at a time, beating until stiff peaks form (tips stand straight).

③ Sift about one-third of the flour mixture over beaten egg whites. Sprinkle with the 1 teaspoon lemon peel; fold in gently. Sift half of the remaining flour mixture over egg white mixture; fold in gently. Repeat with remaining flour mixture. Spoon batter into 18 ungreased 1¾-inch muffin cups, filling each to the top.

④ Bake about 10 minutes or until tops are lightly browned and spring back when lightly touched. Immediately invert muffin pan onto a wire rack; let stand until completely cool. Loosen cakes from sides of muffin cups with a thin metal spatula; remove cakes.

⑤ To serve, use a serrated knife to split cakes in half horizontally. Place cake bottoms on a serving platter; spoon or pipe half of the Lemon Cream Topping onto the cake bottoms; add cake tops. Spoon or pipe on the remaining topping. (Or leave cakes whole and spoon or pipe topping over cakes.)

⑥ If desired, top with raspberries, strawberries, additional lemon peel, and/or lemon pieces. If desired, sprinkle lightly with additional powdered sugar.

Lemon Cream Topping: In a small bowl whisk together ½ cup light sour cream, 4 teaspoons purchased lemon curd, and ½ teaspoon finely shredded lemon peel until well mixed. Fold in ⅔ cup frozen light whipped dessert topping, thawed. (Note: If leaving the mini tea cakes whole, halve this recipe.) Makes about 1 cup.

Raspberry Cream Topping: In a small bowl whisk together ⅔ cup light sour cream and 2 tablespoons low-sugar raspberry or strawberry preserves (snipping any large pieces of fruit if necessary). Fold in ¼ cup frozen light whipped dessert topping, thawed. (Note: If leaving the mini tea cakes whole, halve this recipe.) Makes about 1 cup.

PER SERVING (3 cakes) 89 calories; 2 g total fat (1 g sat. fat); 5 mg cholesterol; 30 mg sodium; 17 g carbohydrate; 0 g fiber; 2 g protein

Pretty as a picture and light as a feather, these tiny cakes are perfect for a girls' tea party.

Upside-Down Pecan-Apple Cake

Upside-Down Pecan-Apple Cake

MAKES 16 servings **PREP** 30 minutes **BAKE** 45 minutes
COOL 45 minutes **OVEN** 350°F

Nonstick spray for baking
2 tablespoons coarsely chopped pecans or almonds
2 tablespoons packed brown sugar
2 tablespoons finely chopped crystallized ginger
2 cups all-purpose flour
½ cup white whole wheat flour or whole wheat flour
½ cup flaxseed meal
2 teaspoons baking powder
1 teaspoon ground ginger
½ teaspoon baking soda
¼ teaspoon salt
¾ cup packed brown sugar
¾ cup unsweetened applesauce
¾ cup refrigerated or frozen egg product, thawed, or 3 eggs, lightly beaten
½ cup canola oil
2 small red cooking apples (such as Jonathan, Rome, or Braeburn)
2½ cups chopped, cored red cooking apples (such as Jonathan, Rome, or Braeburn)

① Preheat oven to 350°F. Coat a 10-inch tube pan with nonstick spray for baking; set on a foil-lined baking pan. In a small bowl combine pecans, the 2 tablespoons brown sugar, and the crystallized ginger. Sprinkle evenly in bottom of prepared pan. Set aside.

② In a large bowl stir together all-purpose flour, whole wheat flour, flaxseed meal, baking powder, the ground ginger, baking soda, and salt; make a well in center of flour mixture. In a medium bowl combine the ¾ cup brown sugar, applesauce, eggs, and oil. Set aside.

③ Slice small apples crosswise into ⅛-inch slices. Remove any seeds from slices. Arrange apple slices over pecan mixture in tube pan, overlapping the slices as needed.

④ Add the brown sugar mixture all at once to the flour mixture; stir just until combined. Fold in chopped apples. Spoon batter over apple slices in pan, spreading evenly.

⑤ Bake for 45 to 55 minutes or until a wooden skewer inserted near the center comes out clean. Cool in pan on wire rack for 15 minutes. Invert cake onto wire rack; remove pan. Replace any nuts that stick in the pan. Cool for 30 minutes more. Serve warm or cool completely.

PER SERVING 228 calories; 9 g total fat (1 g sat. fat); 0 mg cholesterol; 133 mg sodium; 35 g carbohydrate; 3 g fiber; 4 g protein

Berry Pudding Cake

MAKES 6 servings **PREP** 20 minutes **BAKE** 20 minutes
OVEN 400°F

Nonstick cooking spray
2 eggs, lightly beaten
¼ cup granulated sugar
1 teaspoon vanilla
Dash salt
1 cup fat-free milk
½ cup all-purpose flour
½ teaspoon baking powder
3 cups fresh berries (such as raspberries, blueberries, and/or quartered strawberries)
2 teaspoons powdered sugar (optional)

① Preheat oven to 400°F. Lightly coat six 6-ounce individual quiche dishes with cooking spray. Arrange in a 15 x 10 x 1-inch baking pan; set aside. In a medium bowl whisk together eggs, granulated sugar, vanilla, and salt until light and frothy. Whisk in milk until combined. Whisk in flour and baking powder until smooth.

② Divide berries among prepared quiche dishes. Pour batter over berries. (Batter will not cover berries completely.) Bake about 20 minutes or until puffed and golden. Serve warm. If desired, sift powdered sugar over each serving.

PER SERVING 141 calories; 2 g total fat (1 g sat. fat); 71 mg cholesterol; 86 mg sodium; 26 g carbohydrate; 3 g fiber; 5 g protein

Berry Pudding Cake

Raspberry-Lemonade Shortcakes

MAKES 12 servings **PREP** 35 minutes **STAND** 30 minutes
BAKE 20 minutes **OVEN** 350°F

- 2 eggs
- 1 cup all-purpose flour
- 1 teaspoon baking powder
- 1 teaspoon finely shredded lemon peel
- ¾ cup sugar
- ½ cup fat-free milk
- 2 tablespoons tub-style 60% to 70% vegetable oil spread
-    Raspberry-Lemonade Sauce

① Allow eggs to stand at room temperature for 30 minutes. Meanwhile, grease a 9 x 9 x 2-inch baking pan. Line pan with waxed paper. Grease and flour waxed paper; set pan aside. In a small bowl stir together flour, baking powder, and lemon peel; set aside.

② Preheat oven to 350°F. In a medium mixing bowl beat eggs with an electric mixer on high about 4 minutes or until thick. Gradually add sugar, beating on medium for 4 to 5 minutes or until light and fluffy. Add flour mixture; beat on low to medium just until combined.

③ In a small saucepan heat and stir milk and vegetable oil spread until spread melts; add to batter, beating until combined. Pour batter into prepared pan.

④ Bake for 20 to 25 minutes or until a toothpick inserted near center comes out clean. Cool cake in pan on wire rack for 10 minutes. Invert cake onto wire rack lined with waxed paper; carefully peel off top waxed paper and cool completely.

⑤ Cut cake into 12 pieces. Split each cake piece in half horizontally. Place cake bottoms on individual dessert plates. Spoon half of the Raspberry-Lemonade Sauce on cake bottoms. Top with cake tops. Spoon remaining sauce onto cakes.

Raspberry-Lemonade Sauce: Place 3 cups fresh or frozen raspberries in a medium bowl. (Thaw frozen raspberries, if using; in the bowl, do not drain.) Mash berries with a potato masher. In a small saucepan combine ⅓ cup sugar, ¾ teaspoon cornstarch, and ½ teaspoon finely shredded lemon peel. Add mashed raspberries. Cook and stir until thickened and bubbly; cook and stir for 2 minutes more. Remove from heat. Cool about 10 minutes. Stir in 4 cups fresh or frozen (thawed and drained) raspberries. Makes about 3½ cups.

PER SERVING 175 calories; 3 g total fat (1 g sat. fat); 35 mg cholesterol; 49 mg sodium; 35 g carbohydrate; 5 g fiber; 3 g protein

Apple Cake ✪

MAKES 8 servings **PREP** 12 minutes **BAKE** 25 minutes
COOL 5 minutes **OVEN** 350°F

-    Nonstick cooking spray
- 1 cup all-purpose flour
- 1 teaspoon baking powder
- ½ teaspoon baking soda
- ½ teaspoon salt
- ½ teaspoon ground cinnamon
- 2 large eggs
- ⅔ cup sugar
- ½ cup unsweetened applesauce
- 2 tablespoons vegetable oil
- 1 teaspoon vanilla
- 1 medium Granny Smith apple, peeled, cored, and thinly sliced
-    Fat-free caramel ice cream topping and/or low-fat nondairy whipped topping (optional)
-    Apple slices (optional)

① Preheat oven to 350°F. Coat a 9 x 1½-inch round cake pan with cooking spray.

② In a small bowl combine flour, baking powder, baking soda, salt, and cinnamon. In a large bowl whisk together eggs, sugar, applesauce, oil, and vanilla. Stir in the medium sliced apple. Stir flour mixture into apple mixture until combined. Spread evenly into prepared pan.

③ Bake about 25 minutes or until a toothpick inserted into center comes out clean. Cool in pan on wire rack for 5 minutes. Remove cake from pan; cool on rack.

④ If desired, serve cake with caramel topping and/or whipped topping. If desired, garnish with additional apple slices.

PER SERVING 190 calories; 5 g total fat (1 g sat. fat); 55 mg cholesterol; 289 mg sodium; 34 g carbohydrate; 1 g fiber; 3 g protein

A grating of fresh nutmeg adds an aromatic and tasty touch to a wedge of Apple Cake. Buy whole nutmeg in the spice aisle and simply grate on a Microplane. Store whole nutmeg in a tightly sealed container in a cool, dry place. It will last indefinitely.

Country Apple Tart

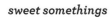

Country Apple Tart ☆

MAKES 10 servings **PREP** 35 minutes **BAKE** 55 minutes
COOL 30 minutes **OVEN** 375°F

Oat Pastry

- 1 tablespoon all-purpose flour
- ½ teaspoon ground cinnamon*
- ¼ teaspoon ground ginger*
- ⅛ teaspoon ground nutmeg*
  Dash ground cloves*
- 3 large red-skin cooking apples (such as Braeburn, Jonathan, or Rome), cored and sliced
- ¼ cup pure maple syrup
- 2 tablespoons coarsely chopped pecans
- 1 tablespoon regular rolled oats
  Fat-free milk

① Preheat oven to 375°F. Line a baking sheet with foil; sprinkle lightly with flour. Place Oat Pastry on foil. Using your hands, slightly flatten dough ball. Using a rolling pin, roll dough from center to edges into a circle 12 inches in diameter. Set aside.

② In a large bowl stir together the 1 tablespoon flour, the cinnamon, ginger, nutmeg, and cloves. Add apple slices and maple syrup. Toss gently to coat. Mound apple mixture in center of pastry circle, leaving a 2-inch border around the edges. Fold border up over apples, pleating dough as needed. Sprinkle apples with pecans and oats. Brush pastry lightly with milk.

③ Bake for 55 to 60 minutes or until apples are tender. If necessary to prevent overbrowning, cover tart with foil for the last 10 to 15 minutes of baking. Cool for 30 minutes and serve warm. (Or cool completely.)

Oat Pastry: In a medium bowl stir together ¾ cup all-purpose flour, ½ cup oat flour or whole wheat flour, 2 tablespoons flaxseed meal, and ¼ teaspoon salt. Using a pastry blender, cut in ⅓ cup chilled tub-style 60% to 70% vegetable oil spread until pieces are pea size. Sprinkle 1 tablespoon ice water over part of the flour mixture; gently toss with a fork. Push moistened pastry to the side of the bowl. Repeat moistening flour mixture, using 1 tablespoon ice water at a time, until all flour mixture is moistened (3 to 4 tablespoons cold water total). Gather flour mixture into a ball, kneading gently until it holds together.

***Tip:** If desired, substitute 1 teaspoon apple pie spice for the cinnamon, ginger, nutmeg, and cloves.

PER SERVING 158 calories; 7 g total fat (2 g sat. fat); 0 mg cholesterol; 108 mg sodium; 23 g carbohydrate; 2 g fiber; 2 g protein

Fresh Fruit Tart

MAKES 12 servings **PREP** 30 minutes **BAKE** 10 minutes
OVEN 450°F

Single-Crust Pastry

- 1 8-ounce carton fat-free or light sour cream
- 2 tablespoons sugar
- ⅓ cup shredded coconut, toasted
- 2 to 3 cups assorted fresh fruit (such as sliced peaches, sliced strawberries, blueberries, raspberries, pitted dark sweet cherries, sliced bananas, and/or sliced mango)

① Preheat oven to 450°F. Prepare Single-Crust Pastry. On a lightly floured surface, flatten the ball of dough with your hands. Roll dough from center to edges into a circle about 11 inches in diameter. To transfer pastry, wrap it around the rolling pin. Unroll pastry into a 9-inch tart pan with a removable bottom. Ease pastry into tart pan, being careful not to stretch pastry. Press pastry into fluted side of tart pan. Trim pastry to the edge of the tart pan. Prick the bottom and side of pastry generously with the tines of a fork.

② Bake for 10 to 12 minutes or until pastry is golden. Cool in pan on a wire rack.

③ In a small bowl stir together sour cream and sugar; spread over cooled crust. Cover and chill for up to 2 hours. To serve, sprinkle tart with half of the coconut; arrange fruit on top. Sprinkle with remaining coconut.

Single-Crust Pastry: In a large bowl stir together 1¼ cups all-purpose flour and ¼ teaspoon salt. Using a pastry blender, cut in ⅓ cup shortening until pieces are pea size. Sprinkle 1 tablespoon cold water over part of the mixture; gently toss with a fork. Push moistened dough to the side of the bowl. Repeat moistening dough, using 1 tablespoon cold water at a time, until all the dough is moistened (4 to 5 tablespoons cold water total). Form dough into a ball.

PER SERVING 138 calories; 7 g total fat (3 g sat. fat); 2 mg cholesterol; 86 mg sodium; 17 g carbohydrate; 1 g fiber; 2 g protein

Key Lime Phyllo Tarts

MAKES 24 tarts **PREP** 20 minutes **CHILL** 2 hours

- 1 14-ounce can fat-free sweetened condensed milk
- ½ teaspoon finely shredded lime peel
- ½ cup Key lime juice or regular lime juice*
- 1 drop green and 1 drop yellow food coloring (optional)
- 24 baked miniature phyllo dough shells
  Frozen fat-free whipped dessert topping (optional)
  Thin lime slices, cut into quarters (optional)

① For filling, in a small bowl gradually whisk together sweetened condensed milk, lime peel, lime juice, and, if desired, food coloring. Cover and chill about 2 hours or until mixture mounds slightly.

② Spoon about 1 tablespoon chilled filling into each phyllo dough shell. If desired, top tarts with dessert topping and lime wedges.

*Tip: To get ½ cup lime juice, squeeze 10 to 12 Key limes or 4 to 6 Persian limes. Or use bottled Key lime juice.

Make-Ahead Directions: Prepare as directed, except do not top with dessert topping or lime wedges. Cover and chill filled tarts for up to 8 hours. If desired, top tarts with dessert topping and lime wedges.

PER TART 70 calories; 1 g total fat (0 g sat. fat); 0 mg cholesterol; 10 mg sodium; 13 g carbohydrate; 0 g fiber; 2 g protein

Mango-Blueberry Tart

Mango-Blueberry Tart

MAKES 10 servings **PREP** 30 minutes **CHILL** 2 to 4 hours

- 8 ounces firm light silken-style tofu (fresh bean curd) (about 1 cup)
- 1 6-ounce carton plain fat-free or low-fat yogurt
- ¼ cup lemon curd
- ½ teaspoon finely shredded lemon peel
- ½ teaspoon vanilla
  Baked Oil Pastry
- 1¼ cups fresh blueberries
- 1¼ cups pitted, peeled, and chopped fresh mango
- 2 kiwifruits, peeled and chopped

① For filling, in a food processor combine tofu, yogurt, lemon curd, lemon peel, and vanilla. Cover and process until smooth, scraping sides as necessary.

② Spread filling into Baked Oil Pastry. Top with blueberries, mango, and kiwifruits. Cover loosely and chill for 2 to 4 hours.

Baked Oil Pastry: Preheat oven to 450°F. In a medium bowl stir together 1⅓ cups all-purpose flour and ¼ teaspoon salt. Add ⅓ cup vegetable oil and 3 tablespoons fat-free milk all at once. Stir gently with a fork. Form into a ball. On a well-floured surface, use your hands to lightly flatten dough. Using a rolling pin, roll from center to edges into a circle 11 inches in diameter. To transfer, wrap pastry circle around a rolling pin. Unroll into a 9-inch tart pan with a removable bottom. Ease pastry into pan without stretching. Press pastry into fluted sides of tart pan, trimming pastry as needed. Line pastry with a double thickness of foil. Bake for 8 minutes. Remove foil. Bake about 5 minutes more or until golden brown. Cool on wire rack.

PER SERVING 204 calories; 8 g total fat (1 g sat. fat); 7 mg cholesterol; 99 mg sodium; 29 g carbohydrate; 3 g fiber; 5 g protein

Old-Fashioned Peach Cobbler

Old-Fashioned Peach Cobbler ✪

MAKES 12 servings **PREP** 30 minutes **BAKE** 25 minutes
COOL 30 minutes **OVEN** 400°F

⅓ **cup sugar**

2 **tablespoons cornstarch**

½ **teaspoon ground cinnamon**

10 **cups sliced fresh peaches (3½ to 4 pounds) or 10 cups frozen unsweetened peach slices, thawed**

½ **cup water**

1¼ **cups whole wheat flour**

2 **tablespoons sugar**

¾ **teaspoon baking powder**

¼ **teaspoon baking soda**

¼ **teaspoon salt**

¼ **cup butter**

½ **cup buttermilk or sour milk***

4 **cups vanilla frozen yogurt (optional)**

① Preheat oven to 400°F. For filling, in a very large bowl stir together the ⅓ cup sugar, cornstarch, and cinnamon; add peaches and toss gently to mix. Gently stir in the water. Spread fruit mixture evenly in a 3-quart rectangular baking dish. Set aside.

② For topping, in a medium bowl stir together whole wheat flour, the 2 tablespoons sugar, baking powder, baking soda, and salt. Using a pastry blender, cut in butter until mixture resembles coarse crumbs. Make a well in the center of the flour mixture. Add buttermilk all at once. Using a fork, stir just until moistened. Knead mixture gently to shape into a ball.

③ On a lightly floured surface, roll dough to ½-inch thickness. Using a 2- to 2½-inch star cookie cutter, cut out 12 stars, rerolling scraps as needed. Arrange dough stars on top of fruit mixture.

④ Bake for 25 to 30 minutes or until stars are lightly browned and fruit mixture is bubbly in the center. Cool on wire rack for 30 minutes. Serve warm. If desired, serve with frozen yogurt.

***Tip:** To make ½ cup sour milk, place 1½ teaspoons lemon juice or vinegar into a glass measuring cup. Add enough milk to equal ½ cup total; stir. Let stand 5 minutes before using.

PER SERVING 175 calories; 4 g total fat (3 g sat. fat); 11 mg cholesterol; 129 mg sodium; 34 g carbohydrate; 4 g fiber; 3 g protein

Apple Crumble with Oat Crust ✪

MAKES 6 servings **PREP** 20 minutes **BAKE** 40 minutes
OVEN 350°F

½ **cup regular rolled oats**

2 **tablespoons whole wheat pastry flour**

3 **tablespoons packed brown sugar**

½ **teaspoon ground cinnamon**

1 **tablespoon cold butter, cut into small pieces**

3 **medium Golden Delicious apples, cored and cut into thin wedges**

2 **tablespoons water**

1 **tablespoon lemon juice**

Frozen yogurt or low-fat vanilla yogurt (optional)

① Preheat oven to 350°F. In a medium bowl combine oats, flour, 2 tablespoons of the brown sugar, and the cinnamon. Add butter; with a pastry blender, a fork, or your fingers, work in butter until the mixture begins to form clumps.

② In a large bowl toss apples with the water, lemon juice, and the remaining 1 tablespoon brown sugar. Transfer apple mixture to a 9-inch pie plate. Sprinkle the oat mixture evenly over apple mixture.

③ Bake for 40 to 45 minutes or until the topping is golden and the apples are tender. Serve warm. If desired, top with yogurt.

PER SERVING 137 calories; 3 g total fat (1 g sat. fat); 5 mg cholesterol; 17 mg sodium; 27 g carbohydrate; 3 g fiber; 3 g protein

Individual Apple Crumbles: Preheat oven to 350°F. Prepare as above, except divide the apple mixture among six 6- to 8-ounce custard cups or ramekins. Sprinkle with oat mixture. Bake about 35 minutes or until apples are tender.

Apple Crumble with Oat Crust

Ginger-Chocolate Crunch-Topped Pumpkin ✪

MAKES 8 servings **PREP** 25 minutes **BAKE** 45 minutes
COOL 1 hour **CHILL** 2 to 24 hours **OVEN** 350°F

- 1   15-ounce can pumpkin
- ⅓   cup sugar
- 2   tablespoons honey or pure maple syrup
- 1½   teaspoons pumpkin pie spice
- ½   cup refrigerated or frozen egg product, thawed, or 2 eggs, lightly beaten
- 1   teaspoon vanilla
- ¾   cup evaporated fat-free milk

    Ginger-Chocolate Crunch, Cranberry-Orange Almond Crunch, or Maple-Apple Pecan Crunch

① Preheat oven to 350°F. Lightly grease a 1½-quart soufflé dish, 8-inch springform pan, or eight 4-ounce ramekins; set aside. For filling, in a medium bowl combine pumpkin, sugar, honey, and pumpkin pie spice. Add eggs and vanilla. Beat lightly with a fork just until combined. Gradually stir in evaporated milk. Pour into the prepared soufflé dish, springform pan,* or ramekins.*

② Bake for 45 to 50 minutes for soufflé dish or springform pan, 30 to 35 minutes for ramekins, or until center(s) appear set when gently shaken. Cool on a wire rack for 1 hour. Cover and chill for 2 to 24 hours before serving.

③ To serve, top with Ginger-Chocolate Crunch, Cranberry-Orange Almond Crunch, or Maple-Apple Pecan Crunch.

④ If using a springform pan, loosen pumpkin mixture from side of pan by running a thin metal spatula around the edge of pan. Remove side of pan. Cut into wedges to serve. If using a soufflé dish, spoon pumpkin mixture onto dessert plates.

Ginger-Chocolate Crunch: Preheat oven to 350°F. Top chilled pumpkin mixture with 8 gingersnaps, broken. Then top evenly with 2 ounces dark or bittersweet chocolate (60% to 70% cacao), chopped, and 2 teaspoons finely chopped crystallized ginger. Bake, uncovered, for 4 to 6 minutes or just until chocolate is softened slightly. Serve warm.

*Tip: If using a springform pan, place on a foil-lined baking sheet. If using ramekins, place in a 15 x 10 x 1-inch baking pan.

PER SERVING 140 calories; 4 g total fat (2 g sat. fat); 1 mg cholesterol; 105 mg sodium; 30 g carbohydrate; 2 g fiber; 5 g protein

Cranberry-Orange Almond Crunch: In a small bowl combine ½ cup lightly sweetened toasted oat bran cereal flakes with oat clusters, such as Smart Start; ⅓ cup coarsely chopped almonds, toasted; ¼ cup dried cranberries; and ½ teaspoon finely shredded orange peel. Spoon on top of chilled pumpkin mixture.

PER SERVING: 141 calories; 2 g total fat (0 g sat. fat); 1 mg cholesterol; 76 mg sodium; 27 g carbohydrate; 3 g fiber; 5 g protein

Maple-Apple Pecan Crunch: Core, quarter, and thinly slice 2 medium Gala or Jonathan apples or 2 ripe pears. In a large skillet cook apples or pears, covered, in ¼ cup water on medium heat for 5 minutes or just until softened and pliable but not mushy. Drain off liquid. Arrange apple or pear slices on top of chilled pumpkin mixture. Sprinkle with ¼ cup coarsely chopped pecans or walnuts, toasted, and drizzle with 1 tablespoon pure maple syrup.

PER SERVING 143 calories; 3 g total fat (0 g sat. fat), 1 mg cholesterol; 60 mg sodium; 27 g carbohydrate; 3 g fiber; 4 g protein

Crown this creamy, nicely spiced pumpkin custard with the topping of your choice.

Raspberry Strudel Croissants

Raspberry Strudel Croissants ✪

MAKES 8 croissants **PREP** 20 minutes **BAKE** 12 minutes
OVEN 375°F

¼   cup frozen red raspberries, thawed and drained, or fresh red raspberries

2   tablespoons low-sugar red raspberry preserves

¼   teaspoon finely shredded lemon peel

6   sheets frozen phyllo dough (14 x 9-inch rectangles), thawed

Butter-flavor nonstick cooking spray

Powdered sugar and/or finely shredded lemon peel (optional)

Fresh raspberries (optional)

① In a small bowl combine the ¼ cup raspberries, preserves, and the ¼ teaspoon lemon peel. Using a potato masher or the back of a large spoon, mash berry mixture.

② Preheat oven to 375°F. Line a baking sheet with parchment paper; set aside. Unfold phyllo dough; place 1 sheet of the dough on a clean flat surface. (Cover the remaining phyllo dough with plastic wrap to prevent it from drying out.) Lightly coat phyllo sheet with cooking spray. Place another sheet of the phyllo dough on top of the first sheet; coat with cooking spray. Repeat layering with 2 more sheets, coating each with cooking spray. (You should have a stack of 4 sheets.) Using a pastry wheel or pizza cutter, cut out a circle from dough 8½ inches in diameter, discarding scraps.

③ Cut circle into 8 wedges. Spread the raspberry mixture over wedges, leaving a ¼-inch border. Starting at the wide end of each wedge, loosely roll toward the point. Place rolls, point sides down, 2 to 3 inches apart on the prepared baking sheet. Lightly coat filled croissants with cooking spray.

④ Bake for 12 to 14 minutes or until pastry is golden. Transfer to wire rack; cool. If desired, sprinkle croissants with powdered sugar and/or additional lemon peel. If desired, garnish with additional fresh raspberries.

PER CROISSANT 35 calories; 0 g total fat; 0 mg cholesterol; 30 mg sodium; 8 g carbohydrate; 0 g fiber; 1 g protein

Black Forest Parfaits

MAKES 2 (¾-cup) servings **PREP** 10 minutes **BAKE** 5 minutes
COOL 5 minutes **OVEN** 350°F

½   cup cubed ladyfingers (two ½-ounce ladyfingers)

½   cup frozen unsweetened pitted tart red or dark sweet cherries, thawed and drained

1   3.75-ounce container sugar-free chocolate ready-to-eat pudding

2   tablespoons sliced almonds, toasted

① Preheat oven to 350°F. Place ladyfinger cubes on a baking sheet. Bake for 5 minutes or until toasted. Set aside to cool.

② Divide the ladyfinger cubes between two 6-ounce dishes. Top with cherries, pudding, and almonds. Serve immediately.

PER SERVING 107 calories; 4 g total fat (1 g sat. fat); 16 mg cholesterol; 96 mg sodium; 16 g carbohydrate; 2 g fiber; 3 g protein

There are two types of ladyfingers. The more common spongecake type is soft and tender. The Savoiardi type is lighter and less sweet—more pastrylike—and have a crisper, harder texture. If you use the Savoiardi type in Black Forest Parfaits, skip the toasting step.

Blueberry Pudding

MAKES 6 servings **PREP** 25 minutes **BAKE** 40 minutes
COOL 20 minutes **OVEN** 300°F

Nonstick cooking spray

3 cups reduced-fat milk

⅓ cup packed brown sugar

½ teaspoon ground cinnamon

¼ teaspoon ground ginger

½ cup white cornmeal

1½ cups fresh blueberries

① Preheat oven to 300°F. Lightly coat six 6-ounce ramekins or custard cups with cooking spray. Set ramekins in a shallow baking pan. Set aside.

② In a large saucepan heat and stir milk, brown sugar, cinnamon, and ginger on medium heat until sugar is dissolved. Slowly stir in cornmeal. Cook and stir until bubbly. Reduce heat to medium-low; cook and stir for 3 minutes more. Mixture will thicken.

③ Spoon half of the cornmeal mixture evenly into prepared ramekins. Top with blueberries. Spoon remaining cornmeal mixture over blueberries.

④ Bake for 40 to 50 minutes or until edges are bubbly. Cool on a wire rack for 20 to 30 minutes. Serve warm.

PER SERVING 165 calories; 3 g total fat (2 g sat. fat); 10 mg cholesterol; 58 mg sodium; 31 g carbohydrate; 2 g fiber; 5 g protein

Blueberry Pudding

Cardamom-Cranberry Rice Pudding

MAKES 6 servings **START TO FINISH** 45 minutes

1½ cups water

¾ cup long grain rice

Dash salt

½ of a 12-ounce can (¾ cup) evaporated fat-free milk

2 teaspoons honey

¼ teaspoon ground cardamom

½ cup dried cranberries*

¼ cup chopped pecans, toasted (optional)

Ground cardamom (optional)

⅓ cup vanilla fat-free yogurt (optional)

① In a medium saucepan stir together the water, uncooked rice, and salt. Bring to boiling; reduce heat. Simmer, covered, for 15 to 20 minutes or until rice is tender and most of the liquid is absorbed.

② Stir evaporated milk, honey, and the ¼ teaspoon cardamom into cooked rice. Bring just to boiling; reduce heat to medium-low. Cook, uncovered, about 5 minutes or until mixture is thick and creamy, stirring frequently.

③ Serve warm. Just before serving, stir in cranberries and, if desired, pecans. If desired, sprinkle with additional cardamom and serve with yogurt.

*Tip: For softer cranberries, place them in a small bowl; cover with boiling water. Let stand for 5 minutes. Drain well before stirring into rice pudding.

PER SERVING 151 calories; 0 g total fat; 1 mg cholesterol; 67 mg sodium; 33 g carbohydrate; 1 g fiber; 4 g protein

To toast nuts, spread them in a single layer on a baking sheet. Toast them in a 350°F oven for 6 to 8 minutes, stirring once, until nuts are golden brown and fragrant.

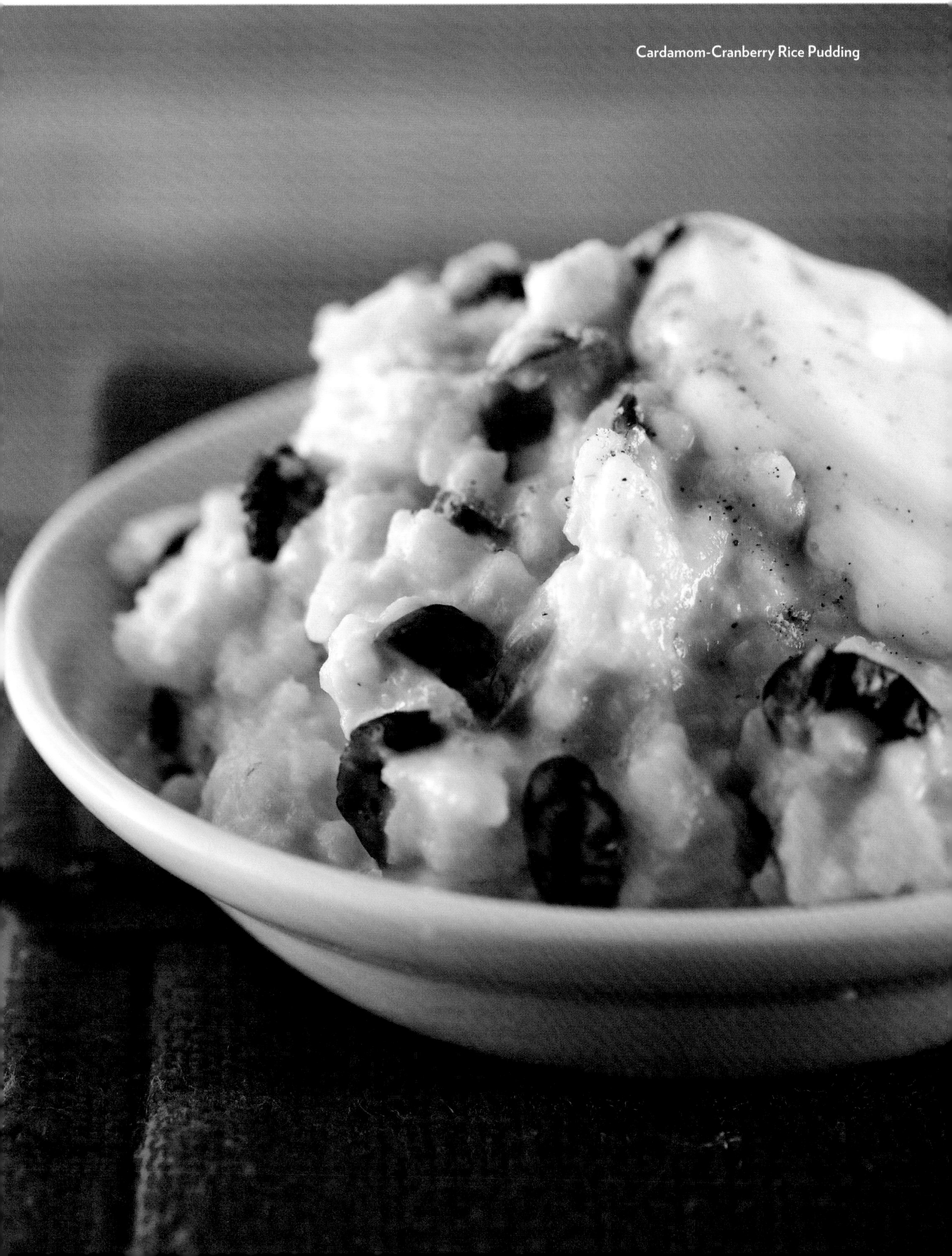
Cardamom-Cranberry Rice Pudding

Tri-Color Sherbet

Tri-Color Sherbet

MAKES 18 servings **PREP** 40 minutes **FREEZE** 7 to 8 hours **STAND** 20 minutes

- 1 cup sugar
- 1 envelope unflavored gelatin
- 1 12-ounce can evaporated fat-free milk
- ¾ cup fresh or frozen sliced unsweetened rhubarb*
- ¾ cup fresh raspberries
- 1½ cups fresh blackberries
- 1 16-ounce carton light sour cream
- 6 ounces white chocolate (with cocoa butter), chopped
- 1 8-ounce package reduced-fat cream cheese (Neufchâtel), cubed
- 1 cup fat-free milk

① In a medium saucepan combine sugar and unflavored gelatin. Stir in evaporated milk. Cook and stir until sugar and gelatin are dissolved. Remove from heat.

② Place rhubarb and raspberries in a large bowl. Place blackberries in another large bowl. Divide hot sugar mixture between the two bowls. Let stand for 5 minutes. Using a potato masher, mash fruit in each bowl. Spoon half the sour cream into each bowl; stir until well mixed. Pour fruit mixtures into two separate 2-quart square baking dishes or 2-quart shallow freezer containers. Cover and freeze about 5 hours or until mixtures are firm but not totally frozen, stirring occasionally so mixtures freeze evenly.

③ Meanwhile, in the same medium saucepan heat white chocolate on low heat until melted and smooth, stirring frequently. Gradually add cream cheese, stirring until well mixed. Gradually stir in milk until smooth. Pour mixture into another 2-quart square baking dish. Cover and freeze for 3 to 4 hours or until firm but not totally frozen, stirring occasionally so mixture freezes evenly.

④ For each frozen mixture, break up mixture and transfer to a large food processor or large chilled mixing bowl. Cover and process until smooth but not melted. Or if using the large bowl, beat with an electric mixer on medium until smooth and fluffy but not melted. Spread mixtures into the 2-quart baking dishes, keeping them separate. Cover and freeze for 2 to 3 hours or until frozen. Let stand at room temperature for 20 minutes before serving.

*Tip: If using frozen rhubarb, measure while frozen. Thaw; do not drain.

PER SERVING 198 calories; 9 g total fat (6 g sat. fat); 21 mg cholesterol; 109 mg sodium; 24 g carbohydrate; 1 g fiber; 6 g protein

Grown-Up S'mores

MAKES 6 servings **START TO FINISH** 15 minutes

- 6 graham cracker squares
- 1 1.45-ounce bar dark chocolate, divided into 6 portions
- 1 teaspoon finely shredded orange peel
- 1 teaspoon snipped fresh rosemary
  Nonstick cooking spray
- 6 large marshmallows
- 6 fresh raspberries

① Place graham crackers in a single layer on a platter. Top each with a portion of chocolate; set aside. In a small bowl combine orange peel and rosemary; set aside. Lightly coat a long metal skewer with cooking spray. Thread marshmallows onto the skewer, leaving ½ inch between marshmallows.

② For a charcoal grill, using an oven mitt, hold skewer with marshmallows just above grill rack directly over medium coals for about 2 minutes or until marshmallows are soft and lightly toasted, turning occasionally. (For a gas grill, preheat grill. Reduce heat to medium. Using an oven mitt, hold skewer with marshmallows just above grill rack over heat. Grill as above, leaving grill uncovered.)

③ Working quickly, use a fork to push 1 marshmallow onto each chocolate-topped graham cracker. Sprinkle with orange peel mixture and top each with a raspberry.

PER SERVING 91 calories; 3 g total fat (1 g sat. fat); 0 mg cholesterol; 57 mg sodium; 16 g carbohydrate; 1 g fiber; 1 g protein

The higher the percentage of cacao in a chocolate bar, the harder and firmer it is—which means it melts less easily. To ensure that these s'mores have some degree of meltability, buy a dark chocolate bar that is no more than 60% cacao. Most bars simply labeled "dark chocolate" work just fine.

Banana Split Ice Cream Pie ✪

MAKES 10 servings   **PREP** 20 minutes   **BAKE** 5 minutes
FREEZE 4 hours to 1 week   **OVEN** 375°F

1	reduced-fat graham cracker crumb pie shell
1	egg white, lightly beaten
1½	cups low-fat or light chocolate ice cream, softened
1½	cups low-fat or light vanilla ice cream, softened
1	large banana, sliced
1	cup sliced fresh strawberries
2	tablespoons light chocolate-flavor syrup
⅔	cup frozen light whipped dessert topping, thawed (optional)

① Preheat oven to 375°F. Brush pie shell with egg white. Bake for 5 minutes. Cool on a wire rack. Spread chocolate ice cream in the bottom of the cooled pie shell. Spread vanilla ice cream evenly over chocolate ice cream. Cover and freeze for at least 4 hours or up to 1 week.

② To serve, arrange banana and strawberry slices over ice cream layers. Drizzle with chocolate syrup. If desired, top each serving with whipped topping.

PER SERVING 167 calories; 5 g total fat (2 g sat. fat); 6 mg cholesterol; 115 mg sodium; 27 g carbohydrate; 1 g fiber; 3 g protein

Banana Split Ice Cream Pie

Milk Chocolate-Berry Ice Cream ✪

MAKES 10 servings   **PREP** 40 minutes   **CHILL** 8 to 24 hours
FREEZE per manufacturer's directions   **RIPEN** 4 hours

6	ounces milk chocolate, chopped
2½	cups reduced-fat milk
½	cup sugar
2	eggs, lightly beaten
1	teaspoon vanilla
1	cup chopped fresh strawberries

① Reserve ¼ cup of the chopped chocolate; cover and set aside. In a medium saucepan stir together the remaining chopped chocolate, the milk, and sugar. Cook on medium heat just until boiling, whisking constantly. Whisk about ½ cup of the milk mixture into the eggs. Return egg mixture to the remaining milk mixture in saucepan. Cook and stir for 1 minute (do not boil). Remove from heat and place saucepan in a large bowl of ice water; stir constantly for 2 minutes. Strain through a fine-mesh sieve into a bowl; stir in vanilla. Cover and chill for 8 to 24 hours.

② Pour chilled mixture into a 1½-quart ice cream freezer. Freeze according to the manufacturer's directions. Stir in the reserved ¼ cup chopped chocolate and the strawberries. Transfer mixture to a 2-quart freezer container. Cover and freeze for 4 hours before serving.

PER SERVING 181 calories; 7 g total fat (5 g sat. fat); 51 mg cholesterol; 55 mg sodium; 24 g carbohydrate; 1 g fiber; 5 g protein

When making homemade ice cream, add stir-ins such as the chopped chocolate and berries in Milk Chocolate-Berry Ice Cream toward the end of the freezing process, when they can still easily be incorporated. Stir-ins can interfere with the freezing process if they are added too soon.

Vanilla Bean Panna Cotta with Strawberries

Vanilla Bean Panna Cotta with Strawberries

MAKES 2 servings **PREP** 15 minutes **STAND** 30 minutes
CHILL 8 hours

- 1   teaspoon unflavored gelatin
- 2   tablespoons cold water
- ¼   of a vanilla bean or ½ teaspoon vanilla*
- 1   cup fat-free half-and-half
- 2   teaspoons sugar
- 1   tablespoon champagne vinegar or white balsamic vinegar
- 1   teaspoon sugar
- 1   cup fresh strawberries, halved
     Whole strawberries (optional)

① For panna cotta, in a heatproof 2-cup glass measuring cup sprinkle gelatin over the cold water. Let stand for 3 minutes to soften. Scrape vanilla beans from the pod into the measuring cup; add the pod. Place in a saucepan of simmering water. Cook and stir on medium heat until gelatin is dissolved. Remove from heat. Stir in half-and-half and the 2 teaspoons sugar; stir until sugar is dissolved. Let stand at room temperature for 30 minutes.

② Remove vanilla bean pod and stir mixture. Pour into two 6-ounce martini or champagne glasses or 6-ounce custard cups. Cover and chill for at least 8 hours or until firm.

③ About 1 hour before serving, in a small bowl combine vinegar and the 1 teaspoon sugar. Add halved strawberries, tossing to coat. Cover and chill, tossing strawberries occasionally. Drain strawberries before serving.

④ To serve, spoon strawberries over panna cotta in glasses. If desired, top each dessert with a whole strawberry.

*Tip: If using vanilla, add it with the half-and-half and omit the standing time.

PER SERVING 127 calories; 2 g total fat (1 g sat. fat); 6 mg cholesterol; 177 mg sodium; 23 g carbohydrate; 1 g fiber; 5 g protein

Watermelon-Berry Granita

MAKES 10 servings **PREP** 30 minutes **FREEZE** 3½ hours

- ¾   cup water
- ⅓   cup sugar
- 3   cups seeded watermelon cubes
- 2   cups fresh blueberries and/or strawberries, halved

① In a small saucepan combine the water and sugar; bring to boiling, stirring until sugar is dissolved. Boil gently, uncovered, for 2 minutes. Remove from heat; cool slightly.

② Meanwhile, in a blender or large food processor combine watermelon and berries. Cover and blend or process until nearly smooth. Add the sugar mixture; blend or process until smooth. Transfer to a 3-quart rectangular baking dish. Cover and freeze about 2½ hours or until almost solid.

③ Using a fork, break up the frozen mixture until almost smooth but not melted. Cover and freeze for 1 hour more.*

④ To serve, break up the frozen mixture with a fork and serve in paper cups or shallow bowls.

*Tip: If mixture is frozen longer than the final hour, let it stand at room temperature about 20 minutes before breaking up mixture with a fork and serving.

PER SERVING 56 calories; 0 g total fat; 0 mg cholesterol; 1 mg sodium; 14 g carbohydrate; 1 g fiber; 0 g protein

If you have an extra vanilla bean—or even part of a bean—here's a neat trick to use it up: Split the bean open, then tuck it into a container of 2 cups of granulated sugar. Seal the container and let it sit for two weeks in a cool, dry place, shaking it once or twice to distribute the vanilla oil and seeds into the sugar. Sprinkle the vanilla sugar on fresh fruit, stir it into hot coffee, or use it in baked goods.

Index

Note: Page references in **bold** type indicate photographs.

In-a-Pinch Substitutions

It can happen to the best of us: Halfway through a recipe,
you find you're completely out of a key ingredient. Here's what to do:

Recipe Calls For:	You May Substitute:
1 square unsweetened chocolate	3 Tbsp. unsweetened cocoa powder + 1 Tbsp. butter/margarine
1 cup cake flour	1 cup less 2 Tbsp. all-purpose flour
2 Tbsp. flour (for thickening)	1 Tbsp. cornstarch
1 tsp. baking powder	¼ tsp. baking soda + ½ tsp. cream of tartar + ¼ tsp. cornstarch
1 cup corn syrup	1 cup sugar + ¼ cup additional liquid used in recipe
1 cup milk	½ cup evaporated milk + ½ cup water
1 cup buttermilk or sour milk	1 Tbsp. vinegar or lemon juice + enough milk to make 1 cup
1 cup sour cream (for baking)	1 cup plain yogurt
1 cup firmly packed brown sugar	1 cup sugar + 2 Tbsp. molasses
1 tsp. lemon juice	¼ tsp. vinegar (not balsamic)
¼ cup chopped onion	1 Tbsp. instant minced
1 clove garlic	¼ tsp. garlic powder
2 cups tomato sauce	¾ cup tomato paste + 1 cup water
1 Tbsp. prepared mustard	1 tsp dry mustard + 1 Tbsp. water

How to Figure What You Need

Making a shopping list based on a recipe can be tricky if you don't know
how many tomatoes yields 3 cups chopped. Our handy translations:

When the Recipe Calls For:	You Need:
4 cups shredded cabbage	1 small cabbage
1 cup grated raw carrot	1 large carrot
2½ cups sliced carrots	1 lb. raw carrots
4 cups cooked cut fresh green beans	1 lb. beans
1 cup chopped onion	1 large onion
4 cups sliced raw potatoes	4 medium-size potatoes
1 cup chopped sweet pepper	1 large pepper
1 cup chopped tomato	1 large tomato
2 cups canned tomatoes	16-oz. can
4 cups sliced apples	4 medium-size apples
1 cup mashed banana	3 medium-size bananas
1 tsp. grated lemon rind	1 medium-size lemon
2 Tbsp. lemon juice	1 medium-size lemon
4 tsp. grated orange rind	1 medium-size orange
1 cup orange juice	3 medium-size oranges
4 cups sliced peaches	8 medium-size peaches
2 cups sliced strawberries	1 pint
1 cup soft bread crumbs	2 slices fresh bread
1 cup bread cubes	2 slices fresh bread
2 cups shredded Swiss or cheddar cheese	8 oz cheese
1 cup egg whites	6 or 7 large eggs
1 egg white	2 tsp. egg white powder + 2 Tbsp. water
4 cups chopped walnuts or pecans	1 lb. shelled